The Cambridge Companion to the Piano

The Cambridge Companion to the Piano is an informative and
practical guide to one of the world's most popular instruments. This
collection of specially commissioned essays offers an accessible
introduction to the history of the piano, performance styles and its
vast repertory. Part 1 reviews the evolution of the piano, from its
earliest forms up to the most recent developments, including the
acoustics of the instrument, and the history of its performance. Part
2 explores the varied repertory in its social and stylistic contexts, up
to the present, with a final chapter on jazz, blues and ragtime. The
Companion also contains a glossary of important terms and will be a
valuable source for the piano performer, student and enthusiast.

Cambridge Companions to Music

The Cambridge Companion to Brass Instruments
Edited by Trevor Herbert and John Wallace
0 521 56243 7 (hardback)
0 521 56522 7 (paperback)

The Cambridge Companion to the Clarinet
Edited by Colin Lawson
0 521 47066 8 (hardback)
0 521 47668 2 (paperback)

The Cambridge Companion to the Recorder
Edited by John Mansfield Thomson
0 521 35269 X (hardback)
0 521 35816 7 (paperback)

The Cambridge Companion to the Violin
Edited by Robin Stowell
0 521 39923 8 (paperback)

The Cambridge Companion to the Organ
Edited by Nicholas Thistlethwaite and Geoffrey Webber
0 521 57309 2(hardback)
0 521 57584 2 (paperback)

The Cambridge Companion to the Saxophone
Edited by Richard Ingham
0 521 59348 4 (hardback)
0 521 59666 1 (paperback)

The Cambridge Companion to Bach
Edited by John Butt
0 521 45350 X (hardback)
0 521 58780 8 (paperback)

The Cambridge Companion to Berg
Edited by Anthony Pople
0 521 56374 7 (hardback)
0 521 56489 1 (paperback)

The Cambridge Companion to Chopin
Edited by Jim Samson
0 521 47752 2 (paperback)

The Cambridge Companion to Handel
Edited by Donald Burrows
0 521 45425 5 (hardback)
0 521 45613 4 (paperback)

The Cambridge Companion to Schubert
Edited by Christopher Gibbs
0 521 48229 1 (hardback)
0 521 48424 3 (paperback)

The Cambridge Companion to the

PIANO

EDITED BY
David Rowland

CAMBRIDGE
UNIVERSITY PRESS

PUBLISHED BY THE PRESS SYNDICATE OF THE UNIVERSITY OF CAMBRIDGE
The Pitt Building, Trumpington Street, Cambridge CB2 1RP, United Kingdom

CAMBRIDGE UNIVERSITY PRESS
The Edinburgh Building, Cambridge CB2 2RU, United Kingdom http://www.cup.cam.ac.uk
40 West 20th Street, New York, NY 10011–4211, USA http://www.cup.org
10 Stamford Road, Oakleigh, Melbourne 3166, Australia

First published 1998

Printed in the United Kingdom at the University Press, Cambridge

Typeset in Adobe Minion 10.75/14 pt, in QuarkXpress™ [se]

A catalogue record for this book is available from the British Library

Library of Congress cataloguing in publication data
The Cambridge companion to the piano / edited by David Rowland.
    p.   cm. – (Cambridge companions to music)
Includes bibliographical references and index.
ISBN 0 521 47470 1 (hardback) ISBN 0 521 47986 X (paperback)
1. Piano.   I. Rowland, David, Dr. II. Series.
ML650.C3   1998

786.2–dc21   97–41860   CIP   MN

ISBN 0 521 47470 1 hardback
ISBN 0 521 47986 X paperback

Contents

Figures

Music examples

Notes on the contributors

Mervyn Cooke was for six years a Research Fellow and Director of Music at Fitzwilliam College, Cambridge, before being appointed Lecturer in Music at the University of Nottingham. His publications include Cambridge University Press handbooks on Britten's *Billy Budd* and *War Requiem*, a monograph *Britten and the Far East* and two volumes devoted to jazz (Thames and Hudson); he is currently involved in the preparation of an edition of Britten's letters and editing the *Cambridge companion to Britten*. He is also active as a pianist and composer, his compositions having been broadcast on BBC Radio 3 and Radio France, and performed at London's South Bank and St John's Smith Square.

Cyril Ehrlich is Emeritus Professor of Social and Economic History at the Queen's University Belfast and has also been Visiting Professor in Music at Royal Holloway and Bedford New College. He has written extensively on musical matters in his books *First Philharmonic: a history of the Royal Philharmonic Society*; *Harmonious alliance: a history of the Performing Right Society* and *The music profession in Britain since the eighteenth century*. His book *The piano: a history* has become essential reading for piano historians.

Kenneth Hamilton is well known as a concert pianist and writer on music. He has performed extensively both in Britain and abroad, specialising mainly in the Romantic repertory, and has broadcast on radio and television. His book on Liszt's Sonata in B minor is published by Cambridge University Press, and he is currently working on a large-scale study of Liszt and nineteenth-century pianism. He has premiered many unpublished virtuoso works by Liszt and others (some in his own completion), and is at present a member of the music department of Birmingham University.

Barrie Jones is a Lecturer in Music at the Open University. His main interests lie in the nineteenth century, particularly keyboard music. He has made extensive contributions to several Open University courses, has translated and edited Fauré's letters, *Gabriel Fauré: a life in letters* (Batsford, 1989) and published a number of articles on Schumann, Liszt, Granados and Parry. He continues to perform regularly on the piano.

Robert Philip is a producer at the BBC's Open University Production Centre, and a Visiting Research Fellow at the Qpen University. He has written and presented many programmes for BBC Radio 3, often on the subject of early recordings. His book *Early recordings and musical style* (Cambridge, 1992) was the first large-scale survey of performance practice in the early twentieth century. He has also contributed chapters to *Performance practice*, ed. Howard Mayer Brown and Stanley Sadie (London, 1989) and *Performing Beethoven*, ed. Robin Stowell (Cambridge, 1994). He is currently writing *A century of performance*, a survey of trends in twentieth-century performance.

Brian Priestley is a performer, writer and broadcaster who taught jazz piano for many years at University of London, Goldsmith's College. Now an Associate Lecturer at the University of Surrey, he is a contributor to the *International directory of black composers* and to the *New Grove* dictionaries of American music and of jazz, and has written several widely praised biographies. For the best part of twenty-five years, he has presented a weekly radio programme, currently on Jazz FM.

Bernard Richardson is currently a Lecturer in the Department of Physics and Astronomy at the University of Wales at Cardiff. For the past twenty years he has undertaken scientific research into the acoustics of stringed musical instruments. These research activities stem from a long-standing passion for making and playing musical instruments. He lectures world-wide on the subject and has contributed to *The Cambridge companion to the violin*, *The encyclopedia of acoustics* and many journals.

David Rowland is a lecturer in music and Sub-Dean in the Faculty of Arts at the Open University and Director of Music at Christ's College, Cambridge. His book, *A history of pianoforte pedalling*, was published in 1993 and he has contributed chapters and articles on aspects of piano performance and repertory history to *The Cambridge companion to Chopin*, *Chopin studies 2*, *Performing Beethoven* and a number of journals. Since winning the St Albans International Organ Competition in 1981 he has continued to perform and record extensively on the organ, harpsichord and early piano.

Dorothy de Val completed a doctoral dissertation at King's College London on the development of the English piano and has since taught music history at the Royal Academy of Music. She is a contributor to the *Haydn Companion*, published by Oxford University Press. Her interests include nineteenth-century London concert life, women pianists and the beginnings of the early music and folk-song revival in Britain in the late nineteenth century. She now resides and lectures in Oxford.

Acknowledgements

A wide-ranging volume such as this could not have been written without substantial help from a number of individuals and institutions. I would therefore like to thank Vicki Cooper, Commissioning Editor for the volume, for her ideas and help throughout the project. I would also like to thank Richard Maunder for many interesting hours discussing piano matters, for reading the drafts of my chapters and for his assistance with diagrams and illustrations. David Hunt has been of invaluable assistance in technical piano matters and has never hesitated to spend time on the telephone or in his workshop answering my questions. Cyril Ehrlich has also provided advice on piano history and read some of my drafts. All of the chapter authors have been most patient and co-operative in discussing details of their material with me and with each other and making changes as necessary. Rosemary Kingdon of the Open University deserves thankful recognition for the many hours spent preparing the typescript of this volume.

A number of individuals and collections have kindly provided illustrative material. Details of the sources accompany the list of figures, but I would especially like to thank the following for their help in locating suitable photographs: Richard Burnett and William Dow at Finchcocks, Alec Cobbe of The Cobbe Foundation, Stewart Pollens of The Metropolitan Museum of Art, the Master and Fellows of Emmanuel College, Cambridge, the Faculty of Music, Cambridge University, the staff of the Russell Collection, Edinburgh.

I am grateful to a number of libraries for allowing me to use music in their possession, especially the Pendlebury Library and University Library in Cambridge and New York Public Library.

Finally, I would like to thank my wife, Ruth, and daughters, Kate, Hannah and Eleanor, for the many hours they have spent waiting for me to return home from the office.

Bibliographical abbreviations

The following abbreviations have been used:

AMZ   *Allgemeine musikalische Zeitung*
EM   *Early Music*
ML   *Music & Letters*
MQ   *The Musical Quarterly*
MT   *The Musical Times*
New Grove   Stanley Sadie (ed.), *The New Grove Dictionary of Music and Musicians* (London, 1980)

Pitch notation   When referring to keyboard compasses the following notation has been used, which is similar to, or identical with, that most commonly found in the literature on the keyboard:

Introduction

DAVID ROWLAND

The Cambridge companion to the piano brings together in a single volume a collection of essays which covers the history of the instrument, the history of its performance and a study of its repertory. Each chapter is written by a specialist with access to the most recent research on his or her topic, but all the authors have written accessibly, with the student of the instrument, or an enthusiastic amateur, in mind.

Chapters 1–3 bring together as much up-to-date piano history as is possible in the space available. In recent years, some extremely important work has been published on the early history of the piano. Stewart Pollens's *The early pianoforte* and Michael Cole's *The pianoforte in the Classical era* between them provide a comprehensive survey of the technical developments which took place in the eighteenth century. These developments are summarised in chapters 1 and 2 along with information about the specific kinds of instrument played by the early pianists. Necessary technical terms are explained in the glossary at the end of the volume. The equivalent history of the piano in the first half of the nineteenth century is much less well documented and a new, detailed history of the piano in the nineteenth century is urgently needed. It is remarkable that Rosamond Harding's book *The piano-forte*, first published as long ago as 1933, remains the standard text for this period. Nevertheless, new work is emerging in this field by scholars, curators and restorers and it has been possible to draw on much of this material for the brief history of the piano found in the remainder of chapter 2 and in chapter 3. Cyril Ehrlich's *The piano: a history* continues to be a major source of information for the piano industry in the later nineteenth and twentieth centuries

Many issues in the early performance history of the piano are intimately associated with the nature of the instruments themselves. It is not possible, for example, to assess whether Mozart composed some of his earlier music for the piano, or for the harpsichord or clavichord, without a knowledge of the general availability of pianos in Europe in the second half of the eighteenth century. Likewise, an understanding of the differences between English and 'Viennese' pianos is crucial to an understanding of some of the performance issues associated with the music of Beethoven and his contemporaries. For reasons such as these, the study of piano performance to *c.*1825 will be found alongside the history of the instrument in chapters 1 and 2. The way in which later pianists played is investigated in two chapters. Chapter 4 assesses those pianists whose playing styles can be studied only through written sources – concert reviews, memoirs, letters and so on. Chapter 5 studies those pianists who belong to the recording era.

Part 1 of this volume, which deals only with instruments and performers, concludes with an examination of the precise way in which sound is generated in a modern grand piano, and how that sound is transmitted to an audience.

Part 2 concerns the repertory of the piano. Rather than devote single chapters to studies of the sonata, the concerto and so on, authors have written about the music in the wider context of its performance setting and stylistic development. The discussion begins in chapter 7 with an examination of the emergence of a 'standard' repertory in the nineteenth century (which continues to form the basis of the repertory for most modern pianists). Even by the early years of the century, an enormous volume of music had been written for the piano; yet only a small proportion of what was written came to be played by subsequent generations, and an even smaller proportion of it has come to be considered 'canonic' or 'exemplary'. Chapter 7 explores how and why this was so.

Chapters 8–10 examine the piano music of the eighteenth and nineteenth centuries in some detail. The way in which composers wrote for the instrument at the time was shaped by a variety of factors. For early pianists such as Mozart the sonata was the most common vehicle for solo expression; yet within a generation, sonatas were no longer in widespread fashion and composers were beginning to concentrate their energies on shorter, 'character' or dance pieces. At least part of the reason for this change lay in the rapidly increasing public demand for shorter works, many of which were written for the burgeoning amateur market catered for by a growing publishing industry. At the same time, a distinctive piano style emerged which displaced a keyboard style capable of realisation on the harpsichord and clavichord as well as on the piano. Virtuosos of the piano emerged who achieved celebrity status in their public performances. These pianists wrote difficult concert études and concertos for themselves to play in public; but they also wrote more intimately for the salons in which they performed and for the amateur, domestic market (chapter 9). Within the concert and salon repertory towards the middle of the nineteenth century there was a strong interest in musical elements of eastern Europe (such as the Polish ingredients in Chopin's music, or those from Hungary in Liszt's). These and other nationalistic elements from, for example, Russia and Scandinavia, are reviewed in chapter 10. The twentieth century has seen many new developments in piano writing.

Many novel techniques emerged during the first half of the century (chapter 11) and there has been an increasing appreciation of the 'popular' styles of ragtime, blues and jazz (chapter 12). Many classically trained pianists now play music in these styles and the cross-over of 'art' music and 'popular' music styles can be seen in integrated works by composers such as Gershwin.

This volume, in common with all of the others in the *Cambridge companion* series, cannot claim to be comprehensive. Nevertheless, it will give the reader a breadth of information on the subject rarely found elsewhere, written by specialists who have made their own thorough studies.

PART ONE

Pianos and pianists

1 The piano to *c*.1770

DAVID ROWLAND

Italy and the Iberian peninsula

Bartolomeo Cristofori (1655–1732) is generally credited with the invention of the piano in Florence at the end of the seventeenth century. Although some earlier accounts of keyboard actions survive, it is only from Cristofori that a continuous line of development can be drawn.[1]

Cristofori entered the service of Prince Ferdinando de' Medici in 1688 as curator and instrument maker. In this capacity he maintained harpsichords, spinets and organs and made a variety of keyboard (and possibly stringed) instruments.[2] His work on the piano may have begun as early as 1698, certainly by 1700,[3] and in 1709 or 1710 Scipione Maffei noted that Cristofori had 'made three so far, two sold in Florence, one to Cardinal Ottoboni'.[4] In 1711 Maffei published a detailed description of Cristofori's pianos, including a diagram of the action (Fig. 1.1).[5]

The action in Maffei's diagram works in the following way: as the key (C) is depressed one end of the intermediate lever (E) – which pivots around the pin (F) – is raised. This causes the escapement (G) to push the hammer (O) towards the string (A). The escapement then 'escapes' from contact with the hammer and allows it to fall back to its resting position, on a silk thread (P). When the key is released, the escapement, which is hinged and attached to a spring (L), slides back into its resting position and the damper (R) – which had been lowered when the key was depressed – comes back into contact with the string in order to damp the sound.

Many aspects of piano design evidently continued to occupy Cristofori, since the three surviving pianos by him, dated 1720, 1722 and 1726, as well as a keyboard and action of *c*.1725, differ from each other and from Maffei's description in certain aspects of their mechanism and construction. Nevertheless, all of the existing instruments share certain characteristics: they are lightly constructed, compared with later pianos, and have small hammers (in two of the pianos, made only of rolled and glued parchment covered with leather). The instruments produce a gentle sound and their keyboard compass is just four octaves (1722, *c*.1725 and 1726) or four and a half octaves (1720) – considerably smaller than the five octaves or so of the biggest harpsichords of the time.

Cristofori's work was continued by his pupils, the most important of

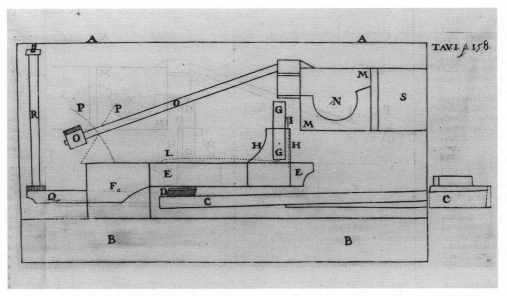

Figure 1.1 Maffei's diagram of Cristofori's piano action from the *Giornale de'letterati d'Italia*, 5 (1711).

whom was probably Giovanni Ferrini (*fl.*1699(?)–1758) who, like his teacher, made harpsichords as well as pianos in Florence.[6] Indeed, his only surviving instrument with piano action is a combination harpsichord/piano, with an upper and lower manual operating the piano and harpsichord respectively. Such combination instruments continued to be popular throughout the period during which the relative merits of the two types of keyboard instrument were debated – until at least the 1780s. In the meantime, the fame of the Florentine makers spread to the Iberian peninsula, where other makers began to construct instruments based on Cristofori's design.[7]

Who used these early pianos, and for what purpose? Very little evidence has survived but it is likely that a number of well-known musicians encountered pianos in southern Europe during the early decades of the century. George Frederic Handel (1685–1759) may have seen Cristofori's instruments in Florence and Rome. Domenico Scarlatti (1685–1757) almost certainly played a number of Florentine pianos: he stayed in Florence for several months in 1702 and he taught Don Antonio of Portugal, the dedicatee of the first music known to be published for the piano – twelve sonatas by Lodovico Giustini (1685–1743), which appeared in Florence in 1732. He was also employed at the court of Maria Barbara of Spain, who owned five Florentine pianos, according to an inventory made in the year following Scarlatti's death.[8] Farinelli, the

Figure 1.2 Piano by Cristofori, 1720.

famous castrato and Scarlatti's colleague in Spain for twenty-two years, also owned a piano dated 1730, according to Burney.[9]

From the start, the piano seems to have been regarded as a solo instrument. Maffei wrote that 'its principal intention' was 'to be heard alone, like the lute, the harp, the six-stringed viol, and other most sweet instruments'.[10] Giustini's sonatas were written for solo piano, and Farinelli played solos on his piano when Burney visited him in 1770. It has also been suggested that a significant proportion of Scarlatti's sonatas were written for the piano, though the evidence cannot be regarded as conclusive.[11] Nevertheless, early pianos had certain shortcomings as solo instruments and Maffei was the first to voice a common complaint of the eighteenth century: 'this instrument does not have a powerful tone, and is not quite so loud' as the harpsichord.[12] Perhaps it was this problem that caused Maria Barbara to convert two of her Florentine pianos into harpsichords.[13] Whatever the extent of the piano's use for solo performances, it also had some success in accompanying one or more other instruments in chamber music: Maffei and several other eighteenth-century writers recommended its use in this way.

Germany and Austria

The history of the piano in German-speaking lands is complex. Christoph Gottlieb Schröter (1699–1782) claimed to have invented a keyboard action in 1717 for an instrument in which the strings were struck by hammers.[14] The inspiration for Schröter's invention was Pantaleon Hebenstreit's (1669–1750) performance on the 'pantalon'. Hebenstreit's pantalon was an enlarged dulcimer measuring about nine feet in length which had one set of metal strings and one of gut. It was played with wooden beaters held in the hands, and had no dampers. The pantalon was reputed to be extremely difficult to play and expensive to maintain, but its sound was much admired and a small, elite group of performers toured Europe throughout much of the eighteenth century.[15] By designing a hammer action operated from a keyboard Schröter no doubt wished to capture the sound of the pantalon while avoiding the strenuous efforts required of a performer. He presented his solution in the form of two hammer-action models – one striking the strings from below, the other from above – to the Elector of Saxony in Dresden in 1721. However, no complete instrument ever seems to have been made, and Schröter's contribution to the development of the hammer-action instruments with keyboard was probably confined to some articles in eighteenth-century German journals. The idea of the keyed pantalon lived on, however. A number of instruments survive with bare wooden hammers which are called 'pantalon' in the literature of the time. The term *pantalonzug* ('pantalon stop') is also commonly found to describe the stop or lever which removed the dampers from the strings (equivalent to the right pedal on a modern piano), in imitation of the undamped sound of the pantalon.[16]

Early piano making in Germany seems to have been concentrated in the area just south of Leipzig. Gottfried Silbermann (1683–1753) worked in Freiberg and Christian Ernst Friederici (1709–80), reputedly Silbermann's pupil, worked about sixty miles to the west, in Gera. Silbermann was making pianos in the early 1730s.[17] No details of these instruments survive, but it is possible that they followed Cristofori's design, published by Maffei in 1711 and subsequently in German translation in Mattheson's *Critica musica* (Hamburg, 1725). One of Silbermann's early instruments evidently failed to satisfy Johann Sebastian Bach (1685–1750) who, according to his pupil Johann Friedrich Agricola, had 'praised, indeed admired, its tone; but he had complained that it was too weak in the high register, and was too hard to play'. Agricola goes on to describe how Silbermann was angered at Bach's reaction, but decided nevertheless

> not to deliver any more of these instruments, but instead to think all the harder about how to eliminate the faults Mr. J. S. Bach had observed. He worked for many years on this. And that this was the real cause of the postponement I have the less doubt since I myself heard it frankly acknowledged by Mr. Silbermann. Finally, when Mr. Silbermann had really achieved many improvements, notably in respect to the action, he sold one again to the Court of the prince of Rudolstadt. Shortly thereafter His Majesty the King of Prussia had one of these instruments ordered, and, when it met with His Majesty's Most Gracious approval, he had several more ordered from Mr. Silbermann.[18]

In fact, according to Forkel,[19] the King ordered a total of fifteen pianos from Silbermann, and prior to the second world war three of these instruments still existed. Now only two of the King's pianos survive, one of them dated 1746. In addition, however, there is another grand piano by Silbermann dated 1749 in the Germanisches Nationalmuseum in Nürnberg.[20]

The actions of the surviving Silbermann pianos resemble the extant Cristofori instruments extremely closely and suggest that Silbermann copied one of Cristofori's later pianos. The instruments by the two makers differ in some respects, however. Not surprisingly, the appearance of the case of Silbermann's pianos resembles that of contemporary German harpsichords, as does the range of the instruments – just under five octaves with FF as the lowest note. The devices to modify the sound of the instrument are also different. Cristofori included just one on his instruments – a pair of stop knobs to shift the keyboard laterally, thereby causing the hammer to hit only one string, the precursor of the modern *una corda* and probably a legacy from Italian harpsichords which often had two registers operated by means of stops. Silbermann included two tone-modifying devices, neither of which was the *una corda*. One was a stop knob which operated a mechanism to introduce small pieces of ivory between the hammers and the strings, producing a harpsichord-like sound. The other was a stop which was used to raise the dampers from the strings – the precursor of the modern damper or sustaining pedal.

According to Agricola, Silbermann's later pianos were approved by J. S. Bach, whose visit to Frederick the Great's court in 1747 was also reported in a contemporary newspaper. The King evidently

> went at Bach's entrance to the so-called forte and piano, condescending also to play, in person and without any preparation, a theme to be executed by

Capellmeister Bach in a fugue. This was done so happily by the
aforementioned Capellmeister that not only His Majesty was pleased to
show his satisfaction thereat, but also all those present were seized with
astonishment.[21]

Further evidence of Bach's approval is his signature on a voucher for the
sale of one of Silbermann's pianos to Count Branitzky of Poland dated 9
May 1749.[22] Despite Bach's fascination with the piano, however, the
instrument cannot have been of any significance for his keyboard music
written before the 1740s – Silbermann's improved pianos were not made
before then.

By the middle of the eighteenth century German pianos were being
made in forms other than the conventional grand. The upright grand came
to be associated with northern European makers, especially Christian Ernst
Friederici, although a similar instrument by the southern European maker
Domenico del Mela (1683–c.1760?), of 1739, survives. In 1745 Friederici
published an engraving of one of his upright grands and at least one, possibly more, of his is still in existence.[23] Friederici is also credited with the
invention of the square piano, which was being made in Germany around
the middle of the eighteenth century.[24] Square pianos were much smaller
and cheaper than either the conventional or upright grand, and were ultimately to become extremely popular in the home, but in mid-eighteenth-
century Germany they had a formidable rival in the clavichord, which
keyboard players continued to use until at least the end of the century.

Much of what happened to the development of the piano in German-
speaking lands in the third quarter of the eighteenth century is shrouded
in uncertainty. One of the most important makers during this time was
evidently Johann Heinrich Silbermann (1727–99; Gottfried's nephew) in
Strasbourg, some of whose pianos from the 1770s survive.[25] His instruments share many features of those made by his uncle, Gottfried
Silbermann: pianos by both makers have transposing devices which are
operated by moving the keyboard laterally and the actions of both makers
are similar, even to the extent of having hammers made from rolled
parchment covered with leather (rather than wood and leather), as on two
of Cristofori's pianos. But apart from these instruments, the absence of
other grands as well as the lack of detail in contemporary literature, make
it impossible to describe how, when and indeed if any developments took
place. One thing at least is clear, however, the piano did not immediately
take the place of either the clavichord or the harpsichord in the affections
of keyboard players. On the contrary, the piano seems to have been
regarded as just one possibility among others. Many sources could be
quoted to illustrate this point. One of the earliest, and probably the best
known, is Carl Philipp Emanuel Bach (1714–88), who wrote in 1753:

Figure 1.3 Clavichord by Christian Gotthelf Hoffmann, Ronneburg, 1784.

something remains to be said about keyboard instruments. Of the many kinds, some of which remain little known because of defects, others because they are not yet in general use, there are two which have been most widely acclaimed, the harpsichord and the clavichord. The former is used in ensembles, the latter alone. The more recent pianoforte, when it is sturdy and well built, has many fine qualities, although its touch must be carefully worked out . . . It sounds well by itself and in small ensembles. Yet, I hold that a good clavichord, except for its weaker tone, shares equally in the attractiveness of the pianoforte and in addition features the vibrato and *portato* which I produce by means of added pressure after each stroke. It is at the clavichord that a keyboardist may be most exactly evaluated.[26]

C. P. E. Bach must have written this after several years' experience of Silbermann's pianos at Frederick the Great's court. Further evidence for the limited progress of the piano in the region comes from Jacob Adlung, who spent all of his adult life in Erfurt, not far from Gera, where Friederici worked, and even closer to Rudolstadt, where Silbermann had sent a piano in the early or mid 1740s. In 1758 Adlung wrote that he had not yet

Figure 1.4a Square piano by Zumpe, London, 1766.

Figure 1.4b Detail of Zumpe piano showing (inside the case, to the left) the sustaining handstop which raises the bass dampers from the strings, the small, leather-covered hammers and (at the top of the photograph) the wooden levers on which the dampers are mounted.

seen a piano, although he was aware that the instrument was known in a number of places, and he knew of Friederici.[27]

The slow progress of the piano is underlined by Charles Burney's account of his journey to Germany and Austria in 1772 which reveals much concerning keyboard history and performance. Over a period of several months he heard many keyboard players, both in public and in private, but there are relatively few accounts of performances on the piano. Only harpsichords and harpsichordists are mentioned in his account of Coblenz and Frankfurt. In Ludwigsberg Burney met Christian Friedrich Schubart (1739–91) who 'played on the clavichord, with great delicacy and expression' and then later in the day 'played a great deal on the Harpsichord, Organ, Piano forte, and Clavichord'.[28] In Munich Burney heard several harpsichord performances, but none on the piano, and in Vienna, out of a total of some fifteen accounts of keyboard playing in public and in private, only one was on a piano: a 'child of eight or nine years old' played 'upon a small, and not good Piano forte'.[29] In Czaslau Burney heard clavichords and in Dresden a harpsichord, but it was only when he arrived in Berlin that he heard pianos again. Agricola 'received me very politely; and though he was indisposed, and had just been blooded, he obligingly sat down to a fine *piano forte*, which I was desirous of hearing and touched it in a truly great style'.[30] Of Johann Philipp Kirnberger (1721–83), however, Burney noted that

> the harpsichord, which was his first, is likewise his best instrument . . . He played at my request upon a clavichord, during my visit, some of his *fugues* and church music . . . After this he had the complaisance to go with me to the house of Hildebrand, the best maker of harpsichords, and piano-fortes, in Berlin.[31]

The mention of Hildebrand as a piano maker is interesting, since it demonstrates that by this time other makers besides the Silbermanns and Friederici had set up in business. Indeed, a brief article published in 1769 reports that Johann Andreas Stein (1728–92), who was to become one of the most important late-eighteenth-century piano makers, had already been working to improve the piano for the previous ten years.[32] Stein had worked with the Strasbourg Silbermanns in 1748 and 1749 and is usually associated with the so-called 'Viennese' action (see chapter 2).

England

The early history of the piano in England is sketchy. According to Charles Burney 'The first [piano] that was brought to England was made by an

English monk at Rome, Father Wood, for an English friend (the late Samuel Crisp . . .)'.[33] Crisp spent some time in Italy in the late 1730s and it seems likely that Father Wood, of whom nothing is known, made a copy of a Cristofori-type piano. The action of Wood's piano cannot have been very sophisticated since 'the touch and mechanism were so imperfect that nothing quick could be executed upon it, yet the dead march in Saul, and other solemn and pathetic strains, when executed with taste and feeling by a master a little accustomed to the touch, excited equal wonder and delight to the hearers'.[34] Burney relates how Crisp sold the piano to Fulke Greville for 100 guineas and elsewhere describes how he became accustomed to the touch of the instrument during a prolonged stay in Greville's house, which must have been in the late 1740s.[35] Again, according to Burney, this piano remained unique in England 'till Plenius . . . made a piano-forte in imitation of that of Mr. Greville. Of this instrument the touch was better, but the tone very much inferior.'[36] Roger Plenius (1696–1774) came to England having worked for some time in Amsterdam. He was in London by 1741 and the records of his bankruptcy in 1756 show that in December 1741 he borrowed £1100, presumably to set up in business. After making his copy of Greville's piano Plenius evidently asked Burney to demonstrate it in public, but Burney declined because 'I had other employmt^s wch I liked better than that of a shewman'.[37] Presumably this discussion took place after Burney returned to London from Greville's estate and before he went to live in Kings Lynn, that is, in the years 1749–51, or after Burney again returned to London in 1760.

Meanwhile an English cleric, William Mason journeyed to Hanover where he purchased a combination piano/harpsichord. On 27 June 1755 he wrote to his friend Thomas Gray: 'Oh, Mr Gray! I bought at Hamburg such a pianoforte, and so cheap! It is a harpsichord too of two unisons, and the jacks serve as mutes when the pianoforte stop is played, by the cleverest mechanism imaginable.'[38] Unfortunately, no details of this instrument survive.

In 1763 Frederic Neubauer advertised 'harpsichords, piano-fortes, lyrachords and claffichords' for sale in London.[39] No records survive to show whether or not he sold any instruments, but the mention of pianos in the same advertisement as lyrachords possibly suggests the work of Plenius: the lyrachord was a peculiar invention of his, and he had probably made a piano by this time.

From 1766 there is incontrovertible evidence of piano making in London in the form of some existing square pianos by the German *émigré* Johann Christoph Zumpe (*fl.*1735–83), who had settled in London in about 1760 (Figs. 1.4a and 1.4b). Zumpe began to make pianos in the mid

1760s and within a very short time his instruments, as well as similar models by other makers such as Johann Pohlman (fl.1767–93), had become extremely popular. This was doubtless partly due to their price – half that of a single manual harpsichord and much less than a grand piano (see below) – as well as their touch sensitivity, though that was limited by today's standards. A nineteenth-century member of the Broadwood family summed up the characteristics of these instruments well:

> They were in length about four feet, the hammers very lightly covered with a thin coat of leather; the strings were small, nearly the size of those used on the Harpsichord; the tones clear, what is now called thin and wiry; – his object being, seemingly, to approach the tones of the Harpsichord, to which the ear, at that period, was accustomed . . . Beyer, Buntebart and Schoene – all Germans – soon after this introduction by Zumpe, began making Pianos, and by enlarging them, produced more tone in their instruments.[40]

Johann Christian Bach (1735–82) quickly took advantage of the new interest in square pianos. On 17 April 1766 the London *Public Advertiser* announced the publication of Bach's 'Six Sonatas for Piano Forte or Harpsichord' Op. 5, which were presumably intended for performance on Zumpe's instruments. Bach also seems to have become an agent for Zumpe: on 4 July 1768 his bank account at Drummond's shows a payment of £50 to Zumpe (enough, probably for three pianos – see the prices quoted below) and Bach helped Madame Brillon in Paris to acquire an English piano sometime before Burney visited her in 1770.[41]

The grand piano took rather longer than the square to come into popular use in England. Americus Backers (fl.1763–78) was the first maker of significance. He probably began to make grands in the late 1760s, and an instrument of his dated 1772 still exists (Fig. 1.5).[42] By the time Backers made this instrument he had refined the action to the extent that other makers of English grands such as John Broadwood (1732–1812) copied its essential details. The 1772 Backers is bichord throughout (unlike some of his later pianos – see Burney's letter below) and has the two pedals that were to be standard on English grand pianos thereafter; a damper or sustaining pedal and a *una corda* pedal. Backers appears to have made about sixty pianos before his death in January 1778 and for most of this time he seems to have been the only maker of grand pianos in London. One of his instruments was probably rented by J. C. Bach, who made a payment of ten guineas to Backers on 17 February 1773. Backers also earned Burney's respect, judging from the latter's comments which also sum up the state of the English piano industry in 1774. Burney wrote to Thomas Twining on 21 January:

Figure 1.5 Grand piano by Americus Backers, London, 1772.

[Ba]ckers makes the best Piano Fortes, but they come to 60 or 70 £, with 3 unisons – & of the Harpsichord size – Put *them* out of the question, & I think Pohlman the best maker of the small sort, by far. *Z*[*u*]*mpe WAS* the best, but he has given up the business. – Pohlmann then for 16 or 18 Guineas makes charming little instruments, sweet & even in Tone, & capable of great variety of piano & forte, between the two extremes of pianissimo & fort^mo. Those for 16 Gn^s only go to double G, without a double G♯; but for the 2 Gn^s more he has made me two or three with an octave to double F & F♯ with a double G♯.[43]

The piano was adopted for public performance relatively quickly in England. The first recorded occasion was 16 May 1767, when Charles Dibden (1745–1814) accompanied Miss Brickler in a 'favourite Song from Judith . . . on a new instrument called piano-forte' at Covent Garden.[44] The first solo performance seems to have been a piano concerto played by James Hook (1746–1827) on 7 April 1768, possibly on a Backers grand.[45] Within just a few years, most of the prominent keyboard players in London were performing in public on the piano. There were notable exceptions, however. Ironically one was Muzio Clementi (1752–1832), the so-called 'father of the pianoforte'. Despite the fact that his publications of the 1770s all stipulate the piano or harpsichord on their title pages, six out of seven public performances that he gave in the period 1775–80, and for which it is possible to identify the keyboard instrument, were given on the harpsichord.[46]

The piano may have featured relatively early in professional concerts in London. In a domestic setting, however, and outside of the capital, the harpsichord persisted much longer. This is illustrated in the number of harpsichords still made in the 1770s and 1780s by firms such as Broadwood (see also chapter 2). Some insight into domestic music making is also to be found in the account books of Thomas Green, a keyboard tuner in Hertford: although he tuned a piano as early as 1769, he continued to tune and purchase harpsichords right up to the end of his career in 1790.[47]

France

Apart from some drawings of hammer actions submitted to the Académie Royale in Paris in 1716 by Jean Marius, the first reference to a piano in France is an advertisement dated 20 September 1759 which describes in some detail the 'newly-invented harpsichord called *piano et forte*'.[48] Nine months previously, the keyboard player Johann Gottfried Eckard (1735–1809) had arrived in Paris with Johann Andreas Stein, both having visited the Silbermann workshop in Strasbourg *en route*. Perhaps Eckard, who stayed in Paris, had begun to act as Silbermann's agent. Whether or not this was so, there is clear evidence that Silbermann's pianos became known in Paris in the 1760s. An advertisement for one of his pianos, with transposing device, appeared in the *Avant Coureur* in April 1761. In 1769 an article in Hiller's *Nachrichten* reported that 'Mr. Daquin . . . organist at Notre Dame' had a Silbermann piano which he compared with his harpsichord: 'the harpsichord is the bread, and the fortepiano a delicate dish, of which one will soon be sick'.[49] Later eighteenth-century dictionary articles also relate how Silbermann's pianos were especially well known in France.

Two grand pianos of the 1770s by J. H. Silbermann survive, and it was probably for this type of instrument that Eckard published the first music for the piano in France – his Op. 1 Sonatas, which were advertised in the French press on 28 April 1763. The title page mentions only the harpsichord but an explanatory note inside mentions the possibility of harpsichord, piano or clavichord. His Op. 2 was advertised for harpsichord or piano in the following year. By this time, in addition to Silbermann's imported instruments, there is evidence of grands being produced in Paris by local makers: an inventory detailing the belongings of Claude-Bénique Balbastre's (1727–99) wife, of 1763, mentions a 'clavecin with hammers' by François-Etienne Blanchet (c.1730–66),[50] in whose workshop was found a similar, but unnamed, instrument in 1766.[51] Blanchet's work was continued by Pascal Taskin (1723–93), who was making grand pianos at least as early as the mid 1770s, and some of whose pianos survive.[52] Other Parisian makers followed, such as Jacques Goermans (1740–89).[53]

Makers of square pianos in London quickly made inroads into the Parisian market: J. C. Bach acted as an agent for Zumpe in the sale of at least one square piano (see above, p. 17) and we know from Burney that Zumpe himself had been in Paris in 1770.[54] Burney himself advised Diderot on the cost of a Zumpe square which was quoted at the apparently inflated price of twenty-eight guineas.[55] The number of imports from England at this time can be judged from the comments in the French press. The *Avant Coureur* of 2 April 1770 reported a performance on a new piano designed by Virbès, describing the instrument as 'in the shape of those from England'. The same newspaper printed a poem entitled 'L'Arrivée du forte piano' ('The arrival of the forte piano') which read:

> What, my dear friend, you come to me from England?
> Alas! How can we declare war on her? [56]

In 1773 the French music publisher Cousineau announced that he had 'several excellent English pianos' for sale,[57] and a number of later sources made it clear that a large proportion of pianos sold in France in the 1770s and 1780s came from England.

Far from attempting to resist this trend, some French keyboard makers themselves imported English square pianos. In 1777 Pascal Taskin evidently owed money – sufficient for two square pianos – to Frederick Beck (fl.1756–98) in London,[58] and in 1784 the same maker ordered four more pianos from Broadwood.[59] Such was the popularity of English squares that by the time of the Revolution the vast majority of pianos owned by the nobility were made by Zumpe, his successor Schoene and others such as Beck and Pohlman.[60] In the face of this flood of imports a number of French makers began to produce copies of English square pianos. The first appears to have been Johann Kilian Mercken (1743–1819) – a 1770 piano of his survives. Mercken was followed by several other Parisian makers, one of whom was Sebastian Erard (1752–1831), whose firm was to become very influential in the subsequent history of the piano (see chapters 2 and 3).

The impression gained from a study of the introduction of the piano into France is that square pianos became very popular as domestic instruments, presumably on account of their size and low cost, while grand pianos took much longer to be preferred over harpsichords. Perhaps this is not surprising in view of the magnificence of many mid-eighteenth-century French harpsichords which still survive. Certainly the French were strongly attached to the harpsichord as we have seen from Daquin's remarks, as well as comments such as those by Voltaire, who considered the piano to be a tinker's instrument compared with the harpsichord.[61] It is unsurprising therefore that the piano only gradually came to be preferred in public performance. Despite the fact that a piano was first heard in public in Paris as early as 1768, the harpsichord still featured on more occasions than the piano a decade later at the Concert Spirituel. From 1780 onwards, however, the piano was used as the main keyboard instrument.

2 Pianos and pianists *c*.1770–*c*.1825

DAVID ROWLAND

In 1830 Friedrich Kalkbrenner (1785–1849) wrote:

> The instruments of Vienna and London have produced two different
> schools. The pianists of Vienna are especially distinguished for the precision,
> clearness and rapidity of their execution; the instruments fabricated in that
> city are extremely easy to play, and, in order to avoid confusion of sound,
> they are made with mufflers [dampers] up to the last high note; from this
> results a great dryness in sostenuto passages, as one sound does not flow into
> another. In Germany the use of the pedals is scarcely known. English pianos
> possess rounder sounds and a somewhat heavier touch; they have caused the
> professors of that country to adopt a grander style, and that beautiful
> manner of *singing* which distinguishes them; to succeed in this, the use of
> the loud pedal is indispensable, in order to conceal the dryness inherent to
> the pianoforte.[1]

His remarks could easily have been made twenty or thirty years previously, since his description summarises – albeit in a highly generalised
fashion – so many of the essentials of piano making and playing for much
of the period covered by this chapter.

'Viennese' and English grand pianos

Most English grand pianos of the late eighteenth century look much like
the Backers grand of 1772, illustrated in Fig. 1.5. The anonymous and
undated grand of Fig. 2.1 is typical of instruments made in the last two
decades of the eighteenth century in southern Germany and Austria
(generally referred to as 'Viennese' pianos). These two instruments therefore illustrate the essential differences in appearance of pianos by
members of the English and 'Viennese' schools.

The English piano looks heavier, and is square at the tail, whereas the
'Viennese' piano is more elegant, in this instance with a double bentside
(the S-shaped piece of wood on the long side of the piano to the right of
the performer). Eighteenth-century 'Viennese' pianos have knee levers
rather than the pedals found on English grands. Internally, the two types
of instrument have important differences too. The 'Viennese' piano has a
substantial base board (the underside of the piano) upon which the inter-

Figure 2.1 Grand piano, c.1795, Stein school, South Germany.

nal bracing system is built. The strength of an English piano case is derived largely from a system of internal bracing which holds the sides of the instrument (which are thicker than the 'Viennese') together. The action of the two types of instrument differs fundamentally (Figs. 2.2a–2.3b). 'Viennese' hammers are very light and are usually mounted on the key mechanism itself, pointing towards the performer. English hammers are mounted on a separate frame and point away from the performer. Both actions, however, have escapement mechanisms and in both types of piano the hammers are covered with leather (in the case of Fig. 2.3a, multiple layers of leather). The damping systems are placed above the strings in both types of piano, but the 'Viennese' system is more effective, as Kalkbrenner later pointed out, and continues up to the highest note, whereas most English pianos have an undamped upper register.

It is impossible to be certain when and where pianos with 'Viennese'

Figure 2.2a 'Viennese' grand piano action by Rosenberger, Vienna, c.1800.

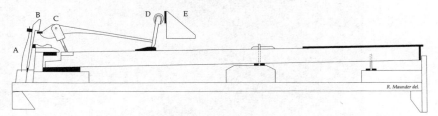

Figure 2.2b Diagram of the action in Figure 2.2a. A. Escapement spring; B. Escapement lever; C. *Kapsel*; D. Hammer; E. Check rail.

actions were first made: relatively few eighteenth-century instruments of this kind still exist, and they are usually undated. Johann Andreas Stein, also a maker of organs, clavichords and a variety of combination instruments (such as harpsichord/pianos), was initially the best-known maker of 'Viennese' pianos. He produced them from at least the 1780s and possibly earlier. Several of his pupils set up their own businesses in southern Germany in the last decade or so of the century, and he must have had a sizeable workshop judging by the number of references to his workmanship in late-eighteenth-century journals. Stein died in 1792 but his business was continued by his daughter, Nannette (1769–1833), and son, Matthäus (1776–1842), who both moved to Vienna in 1794. Nannette was married to Johann Andreas Streicher (1761–1833).

In Vienna, Nannette Streicher (who continued to include her father's name on her instruments for at least another thirty years) was in competition with many other piano makers. Among them was Anton Walter (1752–1826), who began to make pianos in Vienna probably around 1780. Walter's action was similar to that of Fig. 2.2a, with a hammer check rail whose function is to catch the hammer as it returns to its resting position (the English action of Fig. 2.3a has individual checks for each

Figure 2.3a English grand piano action by Broadwood, London, 1798.

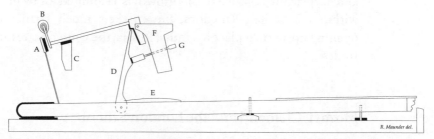

Figure 2.3b Diagram of the action in Figure 2.3a. A. Check; B. Hammer; C. Hammer rest rail; D. Escapement lever; E. Escapement spring; F. Hammer pivot rail; G. Escapement adjustment.

hammer). The Stein–Streicher version of the 'Viennese' action differed in certain respects from Walter's; for example, it had no check rail. Walter's pianos were renowned for their robustness, characterised by a strong tone, especially in the bass, and a heavier touch than some other 'Viennese' makers. His instruments were comparatively expensive, but seem to have been preferred by at least some of the leading pianists in the city at the end of the century.[2] Wolfgang Amadeus Mozart (1756–91) acquired one of Walter's pianos in the early 1780s: the instrument, which still exists, has no maker's inscription, but there is little doubt that it is by Walter, given its similarities to other known Walter pianos.[3] When Carl Czerny (1791–1857) first visited Ludwig van Beethoven (1770–1827) in 1801 he found a Walter piano in the composer's room, and Beethoven is known to have been in negotiation with Walter for a piano on another occasion.[4]

In England, following Backers's introduction of the grand piano in London around 1770, other makers such as Joseph Merlin (1735–1803) and Robert Stodart (*fl*.1775–96) – both, incidentally, makers of combination piano/harpsichords – set up in business. The most important figure, however, was John Broadwood. At first, Broadwood made harpsichords with his mentor Burkat Shudi (1702–73). He then started to make square pianos, probably in 1770, no doubt eager to capitalise on the market already exploited so successfully by Zumpe. He began to make grands somewhat later, and by the early 1780s Broadwood's workshop was producing harpsichords, grand and square pianos, with an increasing emphasis on the piano side of the business. Wainwright identifies 1783 as the year 'that the pianoforte began to overhaul the harpsichord in popularity', though the latter continued to be made in large numbers for several years afterwards.[5] Along with the growth in popularity of the piano came a boom in business – by the end of the century the firm was making in excess of one hundred grands a year, as well as square pianos and harpsichords. Much of this growth is accounted for by increased sales within the United Kingdom, but markets much farther afield were opening up, in such places as India, Russia, the United States and the West Indies.

Mozart, Clementi and the London School

Kalkbrenner (see the quotation above) recognised a London and a Viennese school of playing in 1830 (see p. 22), but he was by no means the first to categorise pianists according to the cities in which they performed. As early as 1802, an article appeared in the *Allgemeine musikalische Zeitung* which identified a group of pianists whose names were closely associated with London: Muzio Clementi, Johann Baptist Cramer (1771–1858) and Jan Ladislav Dussek (1760–1812).[6] Ironically, none of them was British, but each had settled in London for some years towards the end of the eighteenth century, during which time they worked together as pianists, composers, teachers and businessmen. No such close-knit school can be said to have existed in eighteenth-century Vienna, though there were several important individuals such as Leopold Koželuch (1747–1818), who arrived in Vienna in 1778. However, by far the most important keyboard player in the region at the time was Mozart.

Mozart's early experience of keyboard instruments must have been extremely varied.[7] As a very young child, travelling around Austria and southern Germany in the early 1760s, it is unlikely that he would have played any pianos: harpsichords and clavichords still appear to have been the only normally available keyboard instruments in those regions at the time. While it is just possible (but by no means proven) that he encountered some of the first pianos in Paris, London, Holland and Belgium in 1763 and 1764, he played the harpsichord for most, if not all, of the time in Italy in the early 1770s. Back home in Salzburg, there is no evidence that there were pianos except for a square dated 1775 which was owned by Archbishop Colloredo. In fact, the earliest conclusive account of Mozart playing a piano dates from the winter of 1774–5, when he performed on an 'excellent Fortepiano' in the home of one Mr Albert in Munich.[8] After this, he played the harpsichord, clavichord and piano, depending on what was available, although once he had settled in Vienna and acquired his Walter piano there can be little doubt that this was the instrument for which he composed.

Mozart's keyboard music was evidently written for a variety of instruments. The sonatas may all have been composed for the piano, but some of the variations (for example, the C major variations K179) were possibly written for harpsichord. Several of the early concertos were almost certainly for harpsichord (K175, K238, K242, K246), some others are debatable, while those written in Vienna are certainly for piano. Of these, at least two (K466 and K467 of 1785) appear to have been composed with the pedal piano in mind.[9] The evidence – a letter from Mozart's father, a concert announcement and accounts of those who visited Mozart – shows clearly that Mozart used a pedalboard with independent action and strings which was situated underneath his Walter piano (Fig. 2.4). The pedalboard has long since been lost and the only evidence in the music itself for its use is the presence of some bass notes in the first movement of the D minor Concerto K466. It is impossible to play these notes and the chords above them with the left hand alone (Ex. 2.1). Exactly what else Mozart played with his feet in this concerto or in other works, and indeed which works he played on the pedalboard, remain largely matters of conjecture; but the reinforcement of the bass register which results from a use of the pedals makes a significant difference to the way in which Mozart's music is perceived.

Mozart was particularly admired for his expressive playing, which was praised by no less a pianist than Clementi, following a competition staged between them in 1781. One of the most noteworthy aspects of Mozart's expressive performance was his use of *rubato*; not the constant changing of tempo which is adopted by many pianists today, but a technique whereby the two hands do not quite synchronise. Mozart himself explained it in a letter to his father of 1777 in which he pours scorn on Nannette Stein's playing:

Figure 2.4 Reconstruction by Richard Maunder of Mozart's Walter piano with pedalboard.

> she will never acquire the most essential, the most difficult and the chief
> requisite in music, which is, time, because from her earliest years she has
> done her utmost not to play in time . . . Everyone is amazed that I can always
> keep strict time. What these people cannot grasp is that in tempo rubato in
> an Adagio, the left hand should go on playing in strict time. With them the
> left hand always follows suit.[10]

The way in which some of Mozart's published music is written suggests
that he sometimes notated a *rubato* (Ex. 2.2), although even this amount
of rhythmic detail must surely have been inadequate to express the subtlety of Mozart's playing.

This kind of *rubato* featured in the playing of a number of later
pianists, notably Fryderyk Chopin (1810–49) (see chapter 4) and can be
heard in many twentieth-century recordings (see chapter 5).

The same letter contains remarks by Mozart on other elements of
technique. Commenting on Nannette's performance he says:

> instead of sitting in the middle of the clavier, she sits right up opposite the
> treble, as it gives her more chance of flopping about and making grimaces.
> She rolls her eyes and smirks. When a passage is repeated, she plays it more
> slowly the second time. If it has to be played a third time, then she plays it
> even more slowly. When a passage is being played, the arm must be raised as
> high as possible, and according as the notes in the passage are stressed, the
> arm, not the fingers, must do this, and that too with great emphasis in a

Ex. 2.1 Mozart, Piano Concerto in D minor, K466, first movement,
bars 88–91 (piano part).

Ex. 2.2 Mozart, Rondo in A minor, K511, bars 85–7.

heavy and clumsy manner. But the best joke of all is that when she comes to
a passage which ought to flow like oil and which necessitates a change of
finger, she does not bother her head about it, but when the moment arrives,
she just leaves out the notes, raises her hand and starts off again quite
comfortably.[11]

We should be careful about the conclusions we draw from such a passage.
Nannette was only eight at the time, yet she grew to be very well respected
as a performer, as was her teacher (whom Mozart also criticises). Perhaps
Nannette's performance was bad; but it is also possible that she had been
trained in a school of playing that Mozart disliked and found easy to cari-
cature. However, what is certain from this letter is that Mozart's ideal
technique was based on finger movement only, with an evenness in
certain passage-work, which should 'flow like oil'.

When Clementi recalled his meeting with Mozart in 1781 he confessed
himself to have been amazed at Mozart's lyrical playing.[12] Mozart was less
generous: he regarded Clementi as a 'mere *mechanicus*'.[13] Other contemporary writers, however, were dazzled by Clementi's virtuosity and
his playing of fast movements generally – a prominent feature of the
'London' school's style: 'Clementi's greatest strength is in characteristic

Ex. 2.3 Steibelt, *Mélange* Op. 10, p. 6. ⊘ denotes the use of the pedal which, according to the preface to the work, 'imitates the harp' and ⊘ denotes the use of the sustaining pedal. The symbol + signifies the release of the pedal.

and pathetic Allegros, less in Adagios.' The same author goes on to describe Dussek's and Cramer's style: 'Dussek played truly excellent, brilliant Allegro movements with great speed, but played the Adagio very tenderly, agreeably and ingratiatingly; Cramer commanded such speed less well, but had an extremely neat and magical style', which the author found difficult to describe, but which was very 'singular' nonetheless.[14]

Among the elements of Dussek's and Cramer's techniques which later authors singled out for particular mention was their use of the pedals. However, although these pianists undoubtedly contributed much to early pedalling techniques, it was Daniel Steibelt (1765–1823) who had first indicated the use of the pedals in two printed works which were published in Paris in 1793.[15] The nature of most of these markings suggests that pianists were at that time using the pedals for little more than to create a particular tone quality or effect lasting for several bars at a time (Ex. 2.3).

Indeed, this was all that could be achieved on the numerous early pianos which had handstops rather than knee levers or pedals to operate the sustaining and other devices. Some of the earliest pedal markings in the works of other composers suggest a similar approach to Steibelt's, such as the indication to raise the dampers throughout the first movement of Beethoven's 'Moonlight' Sonata Op. 27 No. 2. As Beethoven's pupil Czerny remarked about a passage in the slow movement of Beethoven's Third Piano Concerto which the composer played with con-

Ex. 2.4 Steibelt, Concerto Op. 33, p. 12 (indications for the use of the sustaining pedal).

stantly raised dampers, this kind of performance worked on eighteenth-century pianos with their relatively small resonance, but it was not viable on later instruments.[16]

Pedalling began to be indicated in printed music by members of the 'London' school shortly after Steibelt's arrival there in the winter of 1796–7. The markings of Dussek and Cramer (but not those of Clementi), as well as those in Steibelt's London works, show how sophisticated their technique had by then become. It is common in these works to see the sustaining pedal depressed for half a bar, or a single beat, for the purposes of creating a certain richness in part of a phrase, or for enabling the pianist to play in a more *legato* style (Ex. 2.4).

The pedalling technique in these works is still a long way removed from the kind of constant pedalling that became fashionable in the second quarter of the nineteenth century, but it represents a significant development from earlier eighteenth-century techniques and marks the end of performances 'on harpsichord or pianoforte' that were advertised on so many keyboard works of the late eighteenth century. By the end of the 1790s the piano is undoubtedly the only option for the music of the London School. The new pedalling techniques of the late 1790s also gave rise to significant new figurations in compositions of the period (see chapter 8).

Grand pianos *c.*1790–1825

The period from about 1790 to 1825 was one of intense activity for piano makers, during which the initiative moved between three major piano-making centres, London, Vienna and Paris.

Most pianos made in London before the 1790s had a five-octave range, from FF to f³, although there were exceptions such as Burney's six-octave Merlin piano of 1777. It appears to have been Dussek who prompted Broadwood to add a further half octave to the standard five-octave range, to take the treble up to c⁴. A letter of Broadwood of 1793 states that 'We now make most of the Grand Pianofortes in compass to CC in alt. We have made some so for these three years past, the first to please Dussek, which being much liked Cramer Jr. had one off us so that now they are become quite common.'[17] The piano in question may have been that which Broadwood sold to Dussek on 20 November 1789.[18] By 1792, Broadwood was making six-octave pianos.[19] This was achieved by adding the half octave in the bass (down to CC) that was found on some earlier English harpsichords.

English pianos were vigorously marketed on the continent. French, German and Austrian newspapers contain advertisements for English pianos in the 1780s and 1790s. Members of the London School played their part too, in their continental tours of the late 1790s and early 1800s. Dussek, for example, was contracted to Clementi, who in 1798 had become a partner with James Longman in a firm of piano makers and music publishers following the demise of Longman & Broderip. Dussek sold a number of Clementi's pianos on the continent.[20] Clementi himself toured Germany, Russia, Italy and Austria in the years 1802–10, selling pianos as he went.[21] He set up a large piano warehouse in St Petersburg with his pupils John Field (1782–1837), Ludwig Berger (1777–1839) and Alexander Klengel (1783–1852), and formed business partnerships with firms such as Breitkopf und Härtel and Artaria. All of this activity placed considerable pressure on some continental makers to keep up with the latest developments in London, while other continental makers were already making changes of their own.

The different compasses of German and Austrian pianos at the end of the eighteenth century are difficult to summarise. Some makers preserved the five-octave range FF–f³ into the nineteenth century while others exceeded that range at a considerably earlier date. In 1789 and 1790, for example, the Speier *Musikalische Real-Zeitung* advertised the work of two of Stein's pupils, Johann Georg Kuppler in Nürnberg and J. C. Bulla in Erlang. Both makers were selling pianos with ranges from FF to a³ – just over five octaves.[22] Other continental makers at the time commonly used the range FF–g³. Joseph Heilmann of Erfurt (son of the better-known Matthäus Heilmann of Mainz) advertised six-octave pianos from FF to f⁴ in 1799 while at the same time continuing to make five-octave pianos[23] – it was common for makers to produce more than one model at a time. In Vienna the compass used by makers seems to have stayed around five octaves until just after 1800. Streicher, however, appears to have extended the range from five and a half to six octaves very quickly – probably by 1803 – perhaps as a direct response to English competition.

The six-octave compass of continental and English pianos differed. For some years Broadwood used the six-octave compass down to CC, whereas continental instruments (including French pianos) had six octaves beginning an interval of a fourth higher, at FF. The situation was even more complicated, however, because some English and Irish makers (notably William Southwell (1756–1842), in the closing years of the eighteenth century, and Clementi, from *c.*1810) used the 'continental' six-octave compass. This confused state of affairs posed obvious problems for composers who wished to write music for the international market, and it is noteworthy that almost all works from around the turn of the century stay within the five and a half octaves, range FF–c^4, which was manageable on both English and continental extended-compass instruments. There were some exceptions, however, notable among which is the early use of a 'continental' six-octave compass in one of Steibelt's Op. 16 sonatas published in Paris around 1795. An easy resolution of the incompatible six-octave compasses was to combine them in a six and a half octave compass, from CC to f^4. This happened before 1810 on the continent, and shortly afterwards in London.

Other differences characterised English and continental pianos in the early nineteenth century. In Paris from around 1800 – where Sebastian Erard had begun to make pianos based on the English model – and in Vienna from a few years later, it became customary for pianos to have four pedals (knee levers being generally abandoned at about this time). In addition to the sustaining and *una corda* pedals, which were the only two normally found on London pianos, continental instruments also used the 'moderator' – a strip of material interposed between the hammers and strings which produces a muffled sound (Fig. 2.6). On 'Viennese' pianos a bassoon effect was also made possible by means of a strip of parchment or silk which was placed against the bass strings to produce a buzzing sound (Fig. 2.7). (The moderator was the usual device for muting the sound on 'Viennese' pianos in the eighteenth century: the *una corda* was introduced on these instruments only in the nineteenth century.) The French also used the bassoon, but on some of their instruments there was instead a lute pedal which brought a strip of material into permanent contact with the strings, thereby reducing their vibration, to make a dry, plucking effect. On some extravagant continental instruments there were also drums, bells, triangles and cymbals operated by pedals, or a combination of several pedals and a few knee levers; but there is strong evidence to suggest that professional pianists treated these 'extras' with disdain.[24]

Figure 2.5 Grand piano by Graf, Vienna, *c.*1820.

However, by about 1830 in France, and about 1840 in Vienna, the number of pedals was reduced to the same two found on English pianos – sustaining and *una corda*.

Other developments in the construction of grand pianos in the early decades of the nineteenth century, and a description of domestic pianos, are discussed in chapter 3.

Figure 2.6 Moderator device on a 'Viennese' grand piano *c.*1800 – tongues of material are interposed between the hammers and strings. To the right of the hammer can also be seen a metal spacer which helps to keep open the space between the soundboard and the wrestplank. The damper rail can be seen at the top of the picture, above the strings.

Figure 2.7 Bassoon device on a grand piano by Streicher, Vienna, 1823.

Pianists in Vienna and Paris

A number of pianists came to prominence in Vienna following Mozart's death. Beethoven was the most famous: having settled in the city in 1792 he quickly established himself as a leading performer until deafness forced him progressively to retire from public performance during the early years of the nineteenth century. In the years 1795–9 Beethoven had a serious rival in Joseph Wölfl (1773–1812), but like many pianists of his generation, Wölfl did not stay in any one city for very long, and departed for Prague, Dresden, Leipzig, Berlin and Hamburg on his way, eventually, to Paris and London. The other pianist of note at the time was Johann Nepomuk Hummel (1778–1837), one of Mozart's pupils, whose style of playing differed markedly from Beethoven's (see below).

Before examining Beethoven's style of performance, some attention must be given to the pianos that he played and for which he wrote. Much controversy has surrounded the instruments of his which survive – an Erard grand of 1803, a Broadwood grand of 1817 and a Conrad Graf (1782–1851) grand of 1825.[25] Beethoven's ownership of these pianos is not in doubt: it is their significance for the performance of his music that is in question. Beethoven found the action of the Erard unsatisfactory and sent it back to Streicher's workshop for adjustment. By 1810 he considered the piano 'quite useless'.[26] The compass of the Broadwood must have been considered rather odd when it arrived in Vienna in 1818. It had six octaves, from CC to c^4, a peculiarly English compass, as we have seen; and Beethoven was already writing music for the full six and a half octaves which had been available to him in Vienna for a decade. By the time the Graf piano arrived in 1825, Beethoven had written all of his keyboard music and had only two years to live, so the instrument's significance is limited.

So which pianos did Beethoven prefer? A strong case has been put forward suggesting that Beethoven maintained a preference for 'Viennese' instruments throughout his life.[27] Prior to his arrival in Vienna he appears to have developed a preference for Stein's pianos. There were several of them in Bonn in the late 1780s[28] and Beethoven was uneasy about performing on at least some pianos by other makers, if a report from Mergentheim in 1791 is to be believed: 'Beethoven did not perform in public, probably the instrument here was not to his mind. It is one of Späth's make, and at Bonn he plays upon one by Stein.'[29] When Beethoven arrived in Vienna he would have found pianos by many local makers as well as a few imported instruments (mostly squares). During his early days in the city he hired a piano: no further details exist as to its type. In 1794 Nannette and Matthäus Stein, and Johann Andreas Streicher moved to Vienna and renewed their friendship with Beethoven, prompting a large body of correspondence between them, and prompting Beethoven to use their pianos on numerous occasions. Nevertheless, despite his relationship with them, Beethoven appears also to have used pianos by other Viennese makers: the presence of a Walter piano in his apartment in 1801 has already been noted, and his correspondence shows how he also used a piano by Johann Schanz (*c*.1762–1828) and had dealings with a variety of makers on his own account as well as on behalf of others.[30]

Beethoven's preference for 'Viennese' pianos was strong, yet he also had an affinity with members of the London School and their music. He knew some of them personally and imitated certain aspects of their compositions. Czerny, for example, observed that the finale to the Piano Sonata Op. 26 was in that 'perpetually moving style, as are many of the sonatas by Cramer, whose sojourn at Vienna prompted Beethoven to the composition of this work'.[31] In performance, Beethoven seems to have taken some of the more robust elements of the London School and combined them with his own somewhat rough character. Consequently, his playing was contrasted with Hummel's more refined style: 'Hummel's partisans accused Beethoven of mistreating the piano, of lacking all cleanness and clarity, of creating nothing but confused noise the way he used the pedal.'[32] We have already seen how the use of the sustaining pedal was particularly developed by the London School. Beethoven may not have been so adventurous as the likes of Dussek, but he was clearly more inclined to use it than was Hummel. Hummel's aversion to a liberal use of the sustaining pedal is a theme that recurs in his piano tutor of 1828, in which he also calls into question the necessity for the *una corda* pedal, which had been available on the earliest English grand pianos, but was not found on 'Viennese' pianos until after 1800. Beethoven, however, indicates the use of the *una corda* in his music far more than any other pianist of his generation: other performers were rather more circumspect regarding its use because of the change in timbre which resulted, as well as the tendency for the piano to go out of tune when only one string was hit with the full weight of the hammer. A further peculiarity of Beethoven's pedalling is the absence of any markings for the moderator pedal in his music. Some Viennese composers such as Franz Schubert (1797–1828) occasionally indicated the moderator in their music, but there is no evidence that Beethoven ever used it.[33]

Literally hundreds of piano tutors were published at the end of the eighteenth and beginning of the nineteenth centuries, most of them for the domestic amateur market. Hummel's is one of the relatively few tutors aimed at a more professional readership and it is one of the most conservative of his generation. In addition to expressing concerns about pedalling, Hummel comments on other performing trends. One of these was the increasingly fashionable tendency towards rhythmic flexibility – a tendency of which Mozart had complained in Nannette Stein's playing. Hummel was highly critical of performers who distorted the rhythm 'by the capricious dragging or slackening of the time, (*tempo rubato*), introduced at every instant and to satiety'.[34] Beethoven had been inclined to do this in some small measure. His pupil Ferdinand Ries (1784–1838), himself a prominent nineteenth-century pianist and composer, recalled how Beethoven 'in general . . . played his own compositions most capriciously, though he usually kept a very steady rhythm and only occasionally, indeed very rarely, speeded up the tempo somewhat. At times he restrained the tempo in his crescendos with a ritardando, which had a beautiful and most striking effect'.[35] Carl Maria von Weber (1786–1826) also espoused a flexible approach: 'the beat, the tempo must not be a controlling tyrant nor a mechanical, driving hammer; it should be to a piece of music what the pulse beat is to the life of a man'.[36]

By the 1820s the pianists who embraced these more progressive trends most wholeheartedly began to group themselves around Paris, where the most significant developments in piano design were also taking place (see chapter 3). Franz Liszt (1811–86) is typical: having received lessons in Vienna from Czerny, he used Paris as a base from which to tour from 1823, and settled there more permanently after the death of his father in 1827. Elements of his technique are discussed in chapter 4. Another important, but slightly older, performer of the 1820s whose style can be discussed here was Friedrich Kalkbrenner. (It was he who offered to teach the young Chopin when the latter arrived in Paris in 1831 – the offer was declined.) Like Hummel, Kalkbrenner also published a piano tutor aimed at the professional market. Unlike Hummel, however, Kalkbrenner included in his work the most up-to-date practices. The *una corda* pedal, for example, which many in the 1820s still viewed with suspicion, was wholeheartedly recommended because it 'produces a marvellous effect in all diminuendo passages, and may be used when a composer has marked a diminuendo, morendo, or pianissimo'.[37] In Kalkbrenner's music the *una corda* is often indicated at the end of a phrase, in which case it would have been used at the same time as another effect: 'all terminations of *cantabile* phrases should be retarded'. Kalkbrenner also goes on to suggest changes of tempo in other places: 'when a frequent change of harmony occurs, or modulations succeed each other rapidly, the movement must be retarded'.[38] This should happen several times in each piece, if the musical examples in his tutor are to be regarded as typical.

We should be uneasy about generalising too much about a period of performance history during which pianists moved frequently from country to country, but by the end of the period under discussion in this chapter it appears that most of the progressive figures in piano making and performance were centred in Paris while the conservatives were to be found in German-speaking lands. London had in the meantime receded in importance.

3 The piano since *c*.1825

DAVID ROWLAND

The concert grand to *c*.1860

Piano making in the years *c*.1825–60 was characterised by the development of ever more powerful and sonorous instruments. In order to achieve their aims, makers continued to experiment with all aspects of piano design and as each small change was made in one part of the instrument, modifications were inevitably required elsewhere. So, for example, greater string tension necessitated a stronger frame and heavier hammers, which in turn led to a deeper touch. However, a deeper touch made fast note repetition more difficult, so a new kind of action was invented. It was a combination of hundreds of such developments (each of them painstakingly patented by makers, and listed by piano historians)[1] that led to the emergence, around 1860, of grand pianos which were essentially the same as those used on concert platforms today.

A wooden structure was sufficient to cope with the string tension on early grand pianos. Nevertheless, small amounts of metal were used by some makers to strengthen the most vulnerable parts of the piano's structure. The first Broadwood grands, for example, from the 1780s, had small hoops of metal between the wrestplank (the block of wood which holds the tuning pins) and belly rail (the substantial wooden frame member that runs across the width of the piano and supports the end of the soundboard nearest the player) in order to prevent the gap closing through which the hammers pass on their way to hit the strings. Viennese makers soon adopted the same practice having first used wooden supports for the same purpose.[2] (Fig. 2.6 shows a metal support for this purpose on a 'Viennese' piano of *c*.1800.) Broadwood experimented with additional metal bracing in the form of bars 'to resist the treble strain in 1808, and again in 1818, but was not successful in fixing them'.[3] One of the most significant additions of metal to the grand piano was the compensation frame, invented by two Englishmen, James Thom and William Allen. This was patented in 1820 and consisted of metal tubes made of the same materials as the strings over which they were placed – brass in the bass and steel in the treble – in order to provide greater tuning stability (the tubes were intended to expand and contract in response to changes in temperature at the same rate as the strings beneath) (Fig. 3.1). Erard patented an identical scheme in Paris in 1822. The effects of the compensation frame

Figure 3.1 Grand piano by Stodart, London, *c.*1822.

on tuning stability were debatable, but the additional strength that it gave to the structure of the instrument was undeniable. Other makers quickly began to use a number of solid metal braces above the strings of grand pianos (Fig. 3.2): Broadwood evidently began to do so at least by 1823.[4]

Having provided longitudinal strength to the grand piano, makers quickly turned their attention to the next weak point – the hitchpins around which the strings pass at the end of the piano opposite the keyboard. Until the 1820s the hitchpins had been set in wood, but in 1827 Broadwood patented a small hitchpin plate – a single metal plate into which were set all of the hitchpins. The longitudinal metal bars above the strings were fastened to the metal hitchpin plate, which was in turn screwed into a wooden block beneath (Fig. 3.3). Broadwood's patent was quickly followed by similar ones of Pleyel (1828), Pape (1828) and Erard (1839).

The next part of the instrument to be strengthened was the wrest-plank. This proved difficult, since the tuning pins themselves could not be

Figure 3.2 Metal bracing on a grand piano by Erard, London, 1840–1.

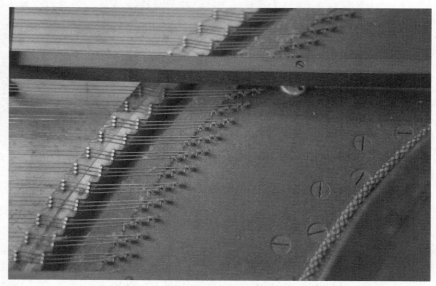

Figure 3.3 Metal hitchpin plate on a grand piano by Erard, London, 1840–1.

set into metal. Consequently a variety of different methods of strengthening the wrestplank – which was liable to split under the increasing string tension – were attempted in the 1830s and 1840s.

While English and French makers progressively adopted metal in grand pianos during the 1820s and 1830s, their Viennese counterparts persisted with wooden framing: Graf's surviving pianos, for example, which are dated between 1812 and 1842, have only wooden bracing.[5] Nevertheless, many of these 'Viennese' pianos are very robust – less prone to twisting under the tension of the strings than some English and French pianos. Despite the continuing success of the wooden bracing system, however, some of the more progressive Viennese makers such as Streicher began to use systems of metal bracing in the 1830s.[6]

For most of the first half of the nineteenth century grand pianos were considered essentially wooden structures, strengthened in varying degrees by the addition of metal. But at the Great Exhibition of 1851 the essential 'woodenness' of pianos was fundamentally challenged by instruments whose main strength lay in their metal framework:

> Messrs. Erard exhibited, in 1851, a full-sized grand instrument, the
> peculiarity of which was, that, in addition to the metallic string-plate and
> longitudinal tension bars, the wrest-block was also of metal, being formed of
> a frame-work of brass, in which was fixed a strip of beech-wood to receive
> the wrest-pins. This, in conjunction with the longitudinal bars and the
> string-plate, formed an entire metallic framing, extending from one end of
> the instrument to the other.[7]

As the description makes clear, this was a combination of all the previous metal additions making up a composite metal frame. However, a more radical solution had already been patented in 1843 by Jonas Chickering (1798–1853) of Boston. This was the complete cast-iron frame for grand pianos, in which the entire frame was cast as one piece, rather than assembled from a number of smaller metal components. Chickering's cast-iron frame for grands was the climax of American developments, most notably the invention of a cast-iron frame for a square piano (the result of a number of attempts to strengthen square pianos with metal) by Alpheus Babcock (1785–1842), also of Boston, in 1825: during the second quarter of the century Boston emerged as one of the most progressive centres of piano development.[8]

As we shall see later in this chapter, the use of the cast-iron frame was to be very significant in taking the initiative in piano development away from Europe to the United States. As the Americans modernised and streamlined their manufacturing processes, many European makers became entrenched in their traditional views. The debate can already be seen in a number of mid-century sources as, for example, in Edward Rimbault's history of the piano, published in London in 1860:

> We agree . . . that the growing tendency to the use of too much metal in the
> construction of pianofortes is injurious to the quality of the tone. It also
> adds greatly to the weight of the instrument, and consequently diminishes
> its portability and general usefulness. Nevertheless, the use of metal up to a
> certain point has its advantages; in fact, owing to the increased weight of the
> strings, it cannot now be dispensed with.[9]

Another development which became associated with the American grand piano was cross-stringing – an arrangement whereby the bass strings pass either over or underneath the remaining strings of the piano. Cross-stringing had been applied to the upright piano as early as 1828, in a patent by Henri Pape (1789–1875) in Paris. Its use at such an early date was brought about by the demand for increasingly compact pianos, in which the length of the bass strings was severely restricted so long as they remained in a vertical position. Pape's solution was to place the bass strings diagonally across the instrument, in front of the rest of the strings, which continued to run more or less vertically. There was no comparable string-length problem on grand pianos and makers continued to string their instruments in the traditional way until it was realised that a better tone was achieved by moving the bridge for the bass strings further towards the centre of the soundboard. This necessitated a cross-stringing arrangement without, however, significantly increasing string length. Following the development of cross-stringing by a number of makers of upright and square pianos and a few experiments on grands,[10] Henry Steinway (1797–1871) patented a system for grands in 1859 which used cross-stringing as well as a cast-iron frame. The 'Steinway system' was to provide the basis for the design on which modern grand pianos are made. It was the cause of much debate at the 1862 London exhibition. Some European makers quickly adopted the American innovations while others remained sceptical of its advantages: Broadwood, for example, did not cross-string grands until 1895.[11]

The progressive use of thicker strings at higher tensions demanded heavier hammers and the merits of various kinds of hammer coverings occupied makers for most if not all of the nineteenth century. Various forms of leather had been used on the majority of pianos in the early history of the instrument and by the 1820s grand piano hammers were generally covered with several layers of the material (see Fig. 2.3a). Around this time, however, Pape developed a felt covering which was more durable than had previously been available, and which he patented in 1826.[12] Other makers in France and England followed Pape and for some time it was customary for hammers to have a final covering of felt on top of several layers of leather. This arrangement was still common at the time of the Great Exhibition, according to an account of materials used in the construction of pianos which lists buffalo leather as the 'under cover-ing' for bass hammers, while 'saddle' was used in the tenor and treble with felt as the 'external covering'.[13] However, while English and French makers experimented with felt, makers of 'Viennese' pianos, with their lighter action, continued to use leather: for example, all Graf's extant instru-ments, made before he sold his business in 1842, have 'hammer heads ...

covered with several layers of brown leather, ranging from as many as six in the bass to three in the treble'.[14]

If some European makers remained conservative in their use of felt, a number of their American counterparts were pressing forwards to develop methods of covering hammers by machine. The benefits of this system were that a set of hammers could be covered quickly, and therefore cheaply, with a consistency that was virtually impossible to achieve if the process were done by hand. The technical problems that needed to be overcome were the production of suitable felt and the development of a machine to fix the felt to the wooden base of the hammer. Following initial developments in Germany in the 1830s, a number of Americans developed systems, culminating in the work of Alfred Dolge (1848–1922) in the 1880s which enabled hammers to be covered with a single, thick layer of felt, rather than the multiple layers of earlier decades.[15] In developing his hammer-covering business Dolge epitomised a new trend in piano manufacture – the development of a piano components industry in which parts of the instrument, such as actions, hammers or frames, were made in one factory and purchased wholesale by makers who then assembled the components into the finished product in much the same way as the production of the modern motor car.[16]

Throughout the nineteenth century both the 'Viennese' and English actions continued to be made. At the Great Exhibition, for example, it was noted that all of the pianos from Vienna had an action which was 'altogether different from the English mechanism'.[17] By this time, however, the 'Viennese' action's popularity was in sharp decline because, as Sigismund Thalberg (1812–71) put it in his report on the pianos at the exhibition, 'now . . . we have an action, the invention of the late Sebastian Erard, which gives a more powerful blow than the old grand action [Thalberg's term for the English action], and a far more rapid and delicate effect than the old Vienna action – thus combining the advantages of both systems'.[18] Thalberg was referring to Erard's double escapement action which was patented in 1821 and which enabled the performer to repeat notes without the necessity of the key returning to its resting position. With this action, as Thalberg pointed out, makers could use heavier hammers and a greater depth of touch without sacrificing the responsiveness which players demanded. Similar actions were quickly adopted by other makers in France, England and Germany, and Erard's pianos became popular all over Europe – a fact which the firm was extremely eager to point out in their own publicity literature.[19] Before long, the 'Viennese' action was more or less confined to makers in Vienna itself. Graf, for example, persisted with it in all of the instruments he made before selling his business in 1842. Streicher, however, began to experiment with various kinds of action while continuing to make 'Viennese' grands in the conventional way. He patented a down-striking action in 1823 which was evidently popular judging from the amount of coverage it received in the press as well as its use in a number of surviving instruments.[20] In the mid 1830s the *Allgemeine musikalische Zeitung* reported that Streicher was also making his own version of the English action in his workshop alongside the 'Viennese' and down-striking models.[21] Streicher's manufacture of alternative actions evidently persisted for a long while, since pianos with English and 'Viennese' style mechanisms survive from at least as late as *c*.1870. Indeed, some makers continued to make pianos with 'Viennese' actions well into the twentieth century: Bösendorfer included it in standard models until 1909[22] and other makers used it later still.

Keyboard compass continued to vary in the period. Erard's seven-octave range of 1822, from CC to c^5, proved unsatisfactory according to the company's own literature of 1834, which stated that Erard had by then returned to the six-and-a-half octave range CC to f^4 because of the poor quality of sound at the extremities of the keyboard.[23] Most other makers were producing pianos with a similar or identical range of six and a half octaves by the 1830s; but at the same time, some makers were beginning to extend the compass further. Graf evidently added two extra notes (up to g^4) in the late 1820s – which was then to become the standard range for most makers until the late 1840s – while a few makers took the keyboard a little higher still to a^4. Shortly before the Great Exhibition some of the most influential makers again adopted a seven-octave compass, most commonly from AAA to a^4 (such as Erard, Collard and Kirkman) but sometimes from GGG to g^4 (Broadwood). William Pole, in his description of the pianos at the Exhibition, also noted that 'one in the Exhibition, made by Mott, has seven and a half octaves, from F to C; and M. Pape, of Paris, has made them eight octaves from F to F; but it is doubtful whether more than six and a half will be generally used'.[24] In the event, Pole's final comment was proved wrong: a seven-octave compass from AAA to a^4 was adopted as standard on concert instruments until the 1870s, when a further three notes were added in the treble to take the keyboard up to c^5, thus establishing the range that has been used by most makers to the present day.

Grand pianos after 1860

The iron-framed, cross-strung grands made by Steinway and its imitators from the 1860s onwards are essentially the same as the pianos used on concert platforms today. This is not to say, however, that instruments of the 1860s sound the same as their modern counterparts, or that no developments have occurred since then. On the contrary, grands from this earlier period tend to sound brighter and are not quite so powerful as modern instruments on account of small changes in design, such as those which affected hammer coverings.

One significant development was Steinway's addition of a third pedal, patented in 1875. The third ('sostenuto') pedal 'catches' the dampers of any notes that are being played at the moment it is depressed: the dampers of any other notes played after the pedal has been activated continue to work as normal. This principle of selective sustaining (in addition to the 'normal' sustaining pedal) had been a concern of European makers in earlier decades. The Parisian maker Xavier Boisselot was the first to invent such a device in 1844, and others followed with schemes of varying complexity. One of the more difficult to operate was designed by Eduard Zachariae of Stuttgart whose invention 'divides the row of dampers by four cleft pedal feet into eight sections'.[25] None of these schemes enjoyed any degree of success, however, and the principle of selective sustaining gained ground significantly only after Steinway's patent of 1875. Following the third pedal's acceptance in America, a few European makers adopted it. Others remained sceptical of its value, however, such as Broadwood, who dismissed it in a pamphlet of 1892: 'THE THIRD PEDAL . . . being of no value in the concert room, and liable to get out of order, is not adopted by John Broadwood and Sons.'[26]

The third pedal was not adopted wholeheartedly by makers in Europe: Steinway themselves did not include it on pianos made in their Hamburg branch and Bösendorfer began to use it only after the second world war, as a result of requests from American dealers.[27] Japanese makers, however, adopt it as a matter of course on their instruments and it looks to have become a permanent feature of the concert grand, whether or not pianists choose to use it!

Since the 1870s there have been few deviations from the normal concert grand compass of seven and a third octaves (AAA–c^5). Some seven-octave instruments continued to be made after that date (AAA–a^4) but by far the most important exceptions to the normal compass are the eight-octave keyboard (CCC–c^5) found on the largest of Bösendorfer's pianos from the early years of the twentieth century to the present day, as well as the seven-and-a-half-octave compass (FFF–c^5) available on smaller grands by the same maker. A small repertory exists which uses these extra notes,[28] but the additional compass has not found general acceptance among makers.

Aside from developments in the instrument itself, one of the most important aspects of piano history since the mid nineteenth century has been the rise and fall of national piano industries within world markets. In the second half of the nineteenth century many of these developments can be traced in the literature of the various trade exhibitions held around the world: the Great Exhibition in London has already been referred to on a number of occasions; of equal significance to the piano's history were the London and Paris exhibitions of 1862 and 1867 respectively. Steinway exhibited at both of these and as a consequence its innovations were immediately seized upon and copied by the more progressive European makers. Germany led the way, notably with newer companies such as Bechstein and Blüthner (both founded in 1853), although some older firms also adopted the new technology – Streicher, for example, exhibited an iron-framed, overstrung piano in 1867. The English and French were, on the whole, more reactionary. Firms which had exerted considerable influence earlier in the century, such as Broadwood and Erard, continued to be sceptical of the latest developments in both piano design and industrial practices: a visitor to Erard's factory in 1894, for example, noted that 'each hammer was still being individually covered three times by hand before the outer covering was applied',[29] in contrast to the machine covering processes used in America and Germany. Such practices were wasteful and increased costs, and Erard's firm went into sharp decline. Pleyel, by far Erard's biggest competitor in France earlier in the century, fared rather better by adopting new technology and practices; but nobody in Europe could rival the growth of the German piano industry and by the end of the nineteenth century almost all virtuosos played American or German instruments.[30]

The continued prominence of Steinway in the twentieth century is a tribute to the firm's products as well as its industrial practices and marketing. The durability of all of the various Steinway models is attested by the high prices that second-hand instruments nearly a century old still command. Intense competition has never been far away, however. In 1936, for example, when the BBC anonymously selected a number of grand pianos for broadcasting use, it was Bösendorfer's instruments which were judged best in the full-sized and small-grand categories, whereas Steinway's and Challen's medium-sized grands were preferred.[31] Competition later came from the Far East. A Japanese maker exhibited a square piano at the Paris exhibition of 1878, and in the decades that followed Japanese apprentices studied American and German instruments – Yamaha hired a Bechstein consultant in the early stages of their enterprise.[32] To begin with, firms such as Yamaha and Kawai (the two most prominent Japanese makers) concentrated on the cheaper domestic market, although they did make some grands. Later, grands by both makers offered serious competition to Steinway, Bösendorfer and others on the concert platform. However, it is probably in the market for medium-sized grands that Yamaha and Kawai have made the greatest impact: with instruments costing between a third and a half of the equivalent Steinway, these makers have progressively killed off their British competitors and the German industry.

Domestic pianos

In his report of the pianos at the Great Exhibition, Thalberg wrote:

> the increase of the number of pianos compared with the population is every year more rapid, a circumstance which is not observed in regard to other musical instruments . . .
>
> The social importance of the piano is beyond all question far greater than that of any other instrument of music. One of the most marked changes in the habits of society, as civilisation advances, is with respect to the character of its amusements. Formerly, nearly all such amusements were away from home and in public; now, with the more educated portion of society, the greater part is at home and within the family circle, music on the piano contributing the principal portion of it. In the more fashionable circles of cities, private concerts increase year by year, and in them the piano is the principal feature. Many a man, engaged in commercial and other active pursuits, finds the chief charm of his drawing-room in the intellectual enjoyment afforded by the piano.
>
> In many parts of Europe this instrument is the greatest solace of the studious and solitary . . .
>
> . . . this influence of the piano . . . extends to all classes; and while considerable towns have often no orchestras, families possess the best possible substitute, making them familiar with the finest compositions.[33]

Even so, the mass ownership of pianos was in its relative infancy, as Cyril Ehrlich points out:

> By the early twentieth century perhaps one Englishman in 360 purchased a new piano every year, a proportion at least three times higher than in 1851 and exceeded only in the United States where it was 1:260. In Germany the ratio was 1:1000, and in France 1:1600 . . . by 1910 there were some two to four million pianos in Britain – say one instrument for every ten to twenty people.[34]

Piano ownership peaked in the early twentieth century, but was soon to decline. Production was seriously affected by the first world war, after which the piano faced intense competition from at least two important sources – the motor car, which made 'a greater visible show' than the piano and absorbed a significant proportion of the family budget, and the gramophone, which was a cheaper and easier way of bringing music into the home.[35]

The nineteenth and twentieth centuries have seen a wide variety in the design of domestic pianos. Around 1825 the square was undoubtedly the favourite type. Such instruments were more or less straightforwardly developed from their eighteenth-century predecessors, although increased keyboard compass (not necessarily to the full extent of the largest contemporary grands) and heavier stringing had necessitated a heavier construction and the introduction of metal in various ways. Broadwood, for example, began using metal hitchpin plates on squares in 1821,[36] several years before their introduction on grands, and a number of makers began to use metal bars in various ways to strengthen the frame. Babcock's invention of the cast-iron frame for squares in 1825 has already been mentioned.

Square pianos were made in large numbers. Around 1790 Broadwood was making some 200 a year, but the figure rose to about ten times that number by the 1840s.[37] In 1842 squares accounted for almost two-thirds of Broadwood's total annual output of pianos (including various grands and uprights). When the firm stopped making them in 1866, the last instrument was numbered 64161[38] (see Fig. 3.4). Broadwood had numerous competitors, both large and small, such as Clementi (later Collard) and many other makers, several of whose instruments survive today. Despite its popularity, however, the days of the square piano were numbered: already in the 1840s production was falling sharply and at the Great Exhibition only a handful of squares were seen. Their place had been taken by dozens of uprights from all over Europe, particularly France. Square pianos remained popular in America, however, where large, seven-octave cross-strung squares with cast-iron frames were produced in the second half of the nineteenth century. The success of these models can be gauged by the numbers made by Steinway: in 1866, for example, 97 per cent of the firm's pianos were squares. Popularity declined sharply in the 1880s, however, in the face of competition from greatly improved uprights, and in 1896 only 1 per cent of Steinway's output were squares, whereas uprights accounted for 95 per cent of total production.[39]

The development of the upright piano was a long process which saw a variety of models come and go as makers tried to overcome some fundamental design problems. To begin with, makers did little more than turn a grand on its end, supporting it on a stand, with the strings running vertically upwards from the level of the keyboard. Both del Mela and Friederici made instruments like this in the mid eighteenth century (see chapter 1), and they were followed by Stodart, Clementi, Broadwood and others in Europe at the end of the century and at the beginning of the nineteenth

Figure 3.4 Broadwood square piano, 1858. This piano was used by the company until 1925 and was frequently hired out to Buckingham Palace.

(Fig. 3.5). The problem with these instruments lay chiefly in their height – in excess of eight feet – although the invention of an action to strike vertically-arranged strings also posed difficulties: consequently, relatively few instruments of this design were ever made. At the beginning of the nineteenth century makers conceived the idea of running the strings of an upturned grand from just above floor level. Either the wrestplank could be placed at the bottom of the instrument, as in the continental 'giraffe' pianos which were popular in the early decades of the century, or it could be placed at the top, which made tuning easier. Either way, a new kind of action had to be invented allowing the strings to be struck towards one or other end, not in the middle, on a level with the rest of the key mechanism. The 'sticker' action was therefore used in English pianos, in which the hammers are mounted at the top of a long piece of wood attached at the other end to the rest of the action, which is at key level (Figs. 3.6 and 3.7). These 'cabinet' pianos were more successful than upright grands; Broadwood continued to make them until the 1850s. On continental giraffe pianos the hammer was situated below the level of the keys.[40]

Cabinet and giraffe pianos were sizeable pieces of furniture, and during the entire period of their manufacture makers were struggling to produce smaller pianos with vertical stringing. The ancestors of the

Figure 3.5 Upright grand piano by Jones, Round and Co., London, c.1810.

modern upright began to be made around 1800. Aside from William Southwell's attempt to make an upright in 1798 by turning a square piano on its side,[41] the first significant instruments in the line of the modern upright were made in 1800: the 'Ditanaklasis', by Matthias Müller (1770–1844) of Vienna, and the 'Portable Grand Pianoforte', by John Hawkins (1772–1855) of Philadelphia. Müller's instrument was about five feet tall, and Hawkins's was a little shorter.[42] In both instruments the strings run more or less vertically from floor level and both have novel actions to deal with the problem of striking a vertical string. Several other

Figure 3.6 Cabinet piano by Broadwood, London, *c.*1825.

makers began to make instruments of a similar size shortly after the beginning of the century and they acquired a variety of names, 'cottage piano' and 'pianinino' being two of the most common (Fig. 3.8). One of the fundamental problems of these small instruments, as it had been on earlier square pianos, was the length of the bass strings compared with their grand counterparts: shorter bass strings need to be thicker, but overly thick strings produce a 'clanking' sound. The solution on squares had always been to use 'wound' strings, in which the mass was increased

Figure 3.7 Action of cabinet piano by Broadwood, London, *c*.1825. The hammers can be seen just above the wooden rail at the top of the photograph.

by winding one string around another. The best solution on any keyboard instrument, however, was always to maximise the length of the bass strings: Pape did just this by using a system of cross-stringing in his uprights of 1828.

In addition to improvements in stringing, the upright's action received much attention in the early decades of the nineteenth century: many of these developments are described by Harding in her chapter on the development of the upright piano.[43] Wornum was associated with a

Figure 3.8 'Cottage' piano by Dettmar & Son, London, c.1820.

number of improvements, not least the 'tape-check' action used on its
pianos in the 1840s, which had, however, previously been used by others.
This action used a short strip of material, or tape, to prevent the hammer
rebounding onto the strings. It proved to be very successful and the
actions of most modern uprights are based on it.

The history of the upright piano since the 1840s mirrors in so many
ways the history of the grand. By the end of the nineteenth century the
market leaders of iron-framed, cross-strung uprights were Steinway and
Bechstein, although a host of inferior instruments were available at a wide
variety of prices. In the twentieth century the Japanese captured a large
percentage of markets with their cheaper, but reliable instruments.
Within the last two decades, however, even the Japanese have had to give
way to other makers from the Far East, particularly South Korea.

As well as squares and uprights, small grand pianos should also be included in this section on domestic instruments. It could be argued that 'domestic' grand pianos have been made since about 1800: when the compass of concert instruments extended to five and a half, then six octaves and beyond, makers continued to produce grands with less than the full compass and it was still possible to purchase five-and-a-half-octave grands twenty years after six-octave instruments were first made. In the Great Exhibition a number of the smaller grands exhibited had only six and a half or six and three-quarters octaves and were called 'short' or 'semi' grand. However, these instruments were still large compared with the 'baby' grands of less than five feet in length which were particularly popular in the first quarter of the twentieth century in America, and a little later in Europe.

4 The virtuoso tradition

KENNETH HAMILTON

That night Sylvia took me to a friend's house, where some Belgian musicians played chamber music . . . They played Mozart's G minor piano quartet with Mark Hambourg at the keyboard. Hambourg was a pianist of the old virtuoso school; his percussive tone and his freelance treatment of the work was wholly unadaptable for Mozart.[1]

Mark Hambourg's (1879–1960) cavalier approach to Mozart, as recalled by Artur Rubinstein (1887–1982), typifies one popular image of the Romantic virtuoso pianist: stylistically insensitive, contemptuous of textual fidelity and, to cap it all, too loud – especially in chamber music. Rubinstein heard Hambourg in 1915, but equally harsh criticisms of the 'virtuoso school' had been penned at least as far back as the nineteenth-century heydays of Liszt and Thalberg, whose concert triumphs served as models for many later pianists. Even today, some critics seem unable to utter the word 'virtuosity' without the appendages 'empty' or 'meretricious'. This contrast between playing that somehow metaphysically exposes the soul of music without drawing attention to technical accomplishment, and playing in which tasteless display is paramount echoes Mozart's two-hundred-year-old criticism of Clementi as 'a mere *mechanicus*'.[2] Of course, in a fundamental sense this contrast is misleading. No player, however elevated his interpretative ability, can communicate his intentions without a sound instrumental technique (unless he becomes a conductor), and most of the great Romantic pianists were both interpreters and virtuosos of the highest order.

The golden era of Romantic pianism lasted roughly one hundred years, the famous musical duel between Liszt and Thalberg in 1837, and the death of Paderewski (the most highly paid concert pianist of all time) in 1941 being convenient, if slightly arbitrary, markers at either end.

Liszt and Thalberg

The evening of 31 March 1837 witnessed an unusual, and long-awaited, entertainment at the Parisian salon of Princess Christina Belgiojoso, a svelte Italian aristocrat of wide-ranging artistic interests, extensive financial resources and paradoxically left-wing politics, a combination as fashionable then as it is today. Her social coup had been to persuade both

Liszt and Thalberg, contenders for the title of 'greatest pianist in Europe', to perform at a charity concert in aid of indigent Italian refugees. For over a year the Parisian newspapers had fanned the flames of rivalry between the two musicians, despite the fact that their personal relations were not always unfriendly.

Franz Liszt was the greatest prodigy as a pianist since Mozart. Born in Raiding, Hungary, of humble background, he had studied under Beethoven's pupil Carl Czerny and was a veteran of international concert giving by his mid teens. Sigismond Thalberg was, by contrast, an illegitimate scion of the German aristocracy, whose masters were Hummel and Ignaz Moscheles (1794–1870). By 1834 he had already toured extensively and been appointed court pianist to the Habsburg emperor in Vienna, but it was the tremendous impression he made on Parisian audiences in 1835–6 that set the seal on his fame. Liszt, though hitherto a resident of Paris, had eloped with the Countess d'Agoult to Switzerland; Thalberg temporarily had the field, if not completely to himself, then at least cleared of his most threatening competitor.

Thalberg's playing was characterised by an intense cultivation of the *legato cantabile* style, and his unostentatious manner contrasted vividly with Liszt's wild rhapsodic virtuosity. The satirical sculptor Jean-Pierre Dantan made comic statuettes of both players, and managed to capture for posterity something of the visual aspect of their performance styles (Figs. 4.1, 4.2). Thalberg's demeanour is grave and concentrated, nothing about his statuette suggesting any unnecessary movement whatsoever. Only his hands seem at all remarkable, when the viewer notices that each has more than the regulation five fingers. Liszt's statuette is akin to the depiction of a tornado at the keyboard, all flailing arms and dishevelled hair. He too has a distinctly unconventional number of fingers. When Liszt was unwise enough to express irritation at the amount of hair Dantan had endowed him with, the sculptor made a second statuette with even more, this time completely covering his face. Liszt made no further comments.

Although the styles of the two pianists were so vastly different that comparison was scarcely possible, Thalberg's enormous success with his Fantasy on Rossini's *Moïse* (Moses) (1835) prompted a lively debate in the musical world about their respective merits. The *Moses* Fantasy was a showcase for Thalberg's so-called 'three-handed' writing (Ex. 4.1), where a melody in the middle register is decorated by arpeggio figuration in bass and treble, cunningly arranged to give the impression that three hands are indeed needed to perform the whole thing simultaneously. The effect, though adumbrated in the works of Francesco Pollini (1762–1846) and others, had appeared in his first *Don Juan* Fantasy, performed in Vienna in

Figure 4.1 Statuette of Thalberg by Jean-Pierre Dantan.

1833–4. The audience included a fascinated Czerny, who admitted that even the most experienced pianists present could not initially work out how it was done.[3] Liszt, initially isolated in Switzerland, was worried that Thalberg's popularity would eclipse his own, and wrote a damning article about Thalberg's music in the *Revue et gazette musicale*. This, however, was temperate compared with his private correspondence, where he described the hapless Thalberg as 'a con-trick' and 'a failed nobleman who makes an even more failed artist'.[4] (Evidently Thalberg's rumoured

Figure 4.2 Statuette of Liszt by Jean-Pierre Dantan.

aristocratic ancestry had also touched a raw nerve.) A newspaper war of words ensued, with the critic François-Joseph Fétis taking Thalberg's part, but hostilities were brought to an end with Princess Belgiojoso's charity soirée. Liszt performed his Fantasy on a cavatina from Giovanni Pacini's *Niobe*, Thalberg his *Moses* Fantasy. The pianists acquitted themselves well, and it was finally realised that both were masters in their own domain. Newspaper reviews counselled that Thalberg could benefit from a little of Liszt's spirit and energy, while Liszt would be improved by the addition of a little of Thalberg's repose, which might have prevented him banging the pedal so loudly with his foot during the more vigorous passages of his *Niobe* Fantasy.

Liszt soon took Thalberg's arpeggio effects into his repertory, the G major study from the *Grandes études* (later titled *Vision*) displaying the full panoply of arpeggio writing. A few years later, the Fantasy on Bellini's *Norma* would effectively out-Thalberg Thalberg, as he himself admitted. A perusal of Thalberg's other piano music shows him to have been a com-

Ex. 4.1   Thalberg, *Grand Fantasia For The Piano Forte On The Celebrated Prayer in Rossini's Opera Mosé in Egitto . . .*
Op. 33, bars 262–3 [1839].

petent but unimaginative composer, at his best producing nothing more than an insipid imitation of Chopin (for example the Twelve Studies Op. 26), at his worst producing an atrocity like the *Marche funèbre*, Op. 56, in which the contrast between the attempted solemnity of the music and the poverty of its invention might at least move an audience to tears of laughter, if not emotion. Although Thalberg's concert repertory largely consisted of his own music, he was admired for his interpretations of Chopin by no less a musician than Robert Schumann (1810–56). In this, at least, his fine pianistic gifts were married to music of comparable quality. As a teacher he was less active than either Chopin or Liszt. His one eminent pupil, Charles-Wilfred de Bériot (1833–1914) became a professor at the Paris Conservatoire where Enrique Granados (1867–1916) and Maurice Ravel (1875–1937) were his students. An almost painless way of comparing Thalberg's compositional skills with that of his contemporaries is by a glance at the gargantuan *Hexaméron*, a set of variations on 'Suoni la tromba' from Bellini's *I puritani*, originally intended to be the centrepiece of Princess Belgiojoso's soirée, but not finished in time. This composite work consists of variations by Thalberg, Liszt, Johann Peter Pixis (1788–1874), Henri Herz (1803–88), Czerny and Chopin, with an introduction, interludes and finale by Liszt rounding off the whole. It was one of Liszt's favourite war-horses during his tours of the 1840s, usually in an arrangement for piano and orchestra. The piece is occasionally still performed, mostly for its curiosity value, and proves that posterity is, for once, correct in singling out Chopin and Liszt for immortality. Their contributions are embarrassingly better than the miserable clichés trotted out by the other four composers.

The only respect in which Thalberg surpassed Liszt was the extent of his concert tours, which took in North and South America (in 1855–6) as well as Europe. Liszt had also been offered engagements in America with the prospect of earning phenomenal sums of money, but by the 1850s had given up his life as a travelling virtuoso. It was left to Anton Rubinstein

(1829–94), and later Ignacy Paderewski to capitalise fully on the opportunities offered in the new world after Thalberg's successes. Although confined to Europe, Liszt's tours of the 1840s took in Moscow, St Petersburg and Constantinople as well as all other major capitals. In 1848 he finally gave up his gypsy life to devote himself to composition in Weimar. The 'Glanz-zeit' ('glory-days') of the 1840s had, however, been enough to establish his reputation as the greatest of Romantic pianists. Liszt still performed fairly frequently after 1848, giving, for example, the first performance of his E♭ piano concerto in 1855, with Berlioz conducting, but most of his subsequent concerts were for charity. Charity concerts were not subjected to the intense criticism that professional performances often elicit, and 'virtuosity', Liszt explained to Eduard Hanslick, 'requires youth'.[5]

The concert world of the nineteenth century

The success of Liszt and Thalberg would have been impossible without the improvement to piano design achieved during the first few decades of the nineteenth century (detailed in chapter 3). The introduction of iron bracing, the double escapement action, and the use of heavier hammers and thicker strings created a greater volume of tone and a more penetrating sonority. The piano of Mozart's day was incapable of producing enough sound to fill a large hall, let alone opera houses like La Scala, Milan, where Liszt performed in 1837–8. The striving for ever-increasing volume eventually led to the cast-iron frame, popularised by Steinway's in the 1860s. Only with this could the pianist play as loudly as possible without danger of serious mishap. In old age Liszt recalled the problems he faced during his tours of the 1830s and 1840s:

> In those times pianos were built too light. I usually had two grands placed on the platform, so that if one gave out it could be replaced without delaying the recital. Once – I think it was in Vienna – I crippled both grands, and two others had to be brought in during the intermission.[6]

No doubt the possibility of witnessing the smashing-up of an expensive piano helped to sell tickets for Liszt's recitals, but a more potent incentive was the growth of amateur piano playing among the newly emergent middle classes of Europe, nowhere more obvious than in Paris. The bourgeoisie had been the chief beneficiary of the 1830 July revolution, and their predilection for the piano as a domestic instrument had already given work to a remarkable number of instrument makers. According to Fétis, 320 piano makers worked in Paris by 1830, and 139 in the French *départements*.[7] Although these figures probably represent individual workers rather than companies, they are still astonishingly high, considering that Paris was a city of under one million inhabitants. Fifteen years later, the manufacturers had succeeded in creating a situation where there were an estimated 60,000 pianos in Paris, and around 100,000 persons capable of playing them to some extent.[8] Not surprisingly, pianists flocked to Paris like the elect to the New Jerusalem. By 1839 the city could boast, as either permanent or sporadic residents, Liszt, Chopin, Thalberg, Herz, Pixis, Theodor Döhler, Jacob Rosenhain, Pierre-Joseph-Guillaume Zimmermann, Henri Bertini and Charles Alkan, along with a host of other, tyro virtuosos.

The context in which the public heard these master pianists was strikingly different from that of the present-day formal recital. Its respectful audience offers polite applause to the white-tied pianist on his first appearance, and maintains silence until the end of each individual piece, when the applause is then repeated to a formal bow from the performer. Such an event would have seemed bizarrely funereal throughout most of the nineteenth century. To begin with, solo recitals were relatively rare. The term 'recital' had first been used by Liszt for a number of his 1840 London concerts. He himself believed that a concert he gave in Rome towards the end of 1839 was the first true solo recital and announced with pride to his friend Princess Belgiojoso that he could say, after Louis XIV, that 'Le concert c'est moi' ('I am the concert!').[9] This Rome recital was short by modern standards, consisting of a few transcriptions and character pieces, all by Liszt himself. Even after 1840, the solo concert was hardly a normal part of the musical scene. Most concerts were in the nature of variety acts, with a number of performers sharing the stage either solo or in ensemble. When Liszt toured Britain in 1841 he did so as part of a troupe of artists presenting a mixed programme, which included not only his own solo contributions but also comic songs such as 'Wanted, a governess'. Though Liszt was usually spared the indignity of accompanying ditties like this, he did act as accompanist for other, more elevated, offerings, as well as performing his trademark improvised fantasia on themes suggested by the audience.

Today the art of improvisation is alive and well in the world of the jazz or even the cocktail pianist, but the idea of improvising in public would now strike fear into the heart of many classical pianists, whose attempts at improvisation are usually restricted to covering up particularly catastrophic memory lapses. Liszt was unusual in showcasing his improvisational ability to such an extent, but in the nineteenth century the talent was expected of any decent performer. Czerny, writing in 1836, commented:

> It is akin to a crown of distinction for a keyboardist, particularly in private
> circles at the performance of solo works, if he does not begin directly with
> the composition itself, but is capable by means of a suitable prelude of
> preparing the listeners, setting the mood, and also hereby ascertaining the
> qualities of the pianoforte, perhaps unfamiliar to him, in an appropriate
> fashion.[10]

In more formal public concerts, the soloist often played a modulatory
prelude between pieces, a practice that survived well into the twentieth
century. As late as 1938, when Josef Hofmann (1876–1957) gave a famous
recorded recital in the Casimir Hall, Philadelphia, this art was still alive,
Hofmann improvising sometimes reflectively, sometimes humorously
between works. At one point the audience laughs at a particularly strident
bass octave interjected jokingly before the next piece, Chopin's fourth
Ballade![11] So much for the awed hush expected of modern audiences
before the performance of a masterwork. Even the sacred Beethoven was
not immune. Liszt's pupil Hans von Bülow (1830–94), the first (and, one
hopes, the last) pianist to play all five of Beethoven's late sonatas in a single
recital, gave an extempore introduction to each sonata – the one for the
'Hammerklavier' consisted of a chordal build-up on the dominant
seventh of B♭, leading straight into the opening theme.

Pianists were not averse to preluding verbally as well as musically.
Pieces were normally announced from the platform, and some performers in smaller halls even milled around the audience between pieces to
chat to their friends and to gauge their reaction. Friedrich Wieck
(1785–1873) described a particularly theatrical incident at one of Liszt's
concerts in April 1848:

> He played the Fantasy on a C. Graff, burst two bass strings, personally
> fetched a second C. Graff in Walnut wood from the corner and played his
> Étude. After breaking yet another two strings he loudly informed the public
> that since it didn't satisfy him he would play it again. As he began he
> vehemently threw his gloves and handkerchief on the floor.[12]

Audiences, for their part, could be equally vocal. Especially captivating
passages were applauded, wherever they appeared in the piece. Bülow
proudly told his students that he had always been given a good round of
applause for his opening solo in Beethoven's 'Emperor' Concerto.[13] (As
this applause presumably drowned out most of the subsequent orchestral
tutti, the need for a so-called 'double' exposition in many concertos might
need to be understood in a new light.) A public largely made up of
amateur pianists could usually be relied upon to notice particularly fine
displays of technical accomplishment, and to reward them accordingly.
To be doubly certain of applause, Bülow also advised that in sections con-

sisting of, for example, daring leaps, the pianist should always get one or two wrong deliberately. This would ensure that everyone in the audience could have no doubt just how difficult the passage was. After all, what was the point of jumping hurdles that no-one realised were there?[14]

A nineteenth-century virtuoso could expect the audience to respond to his choice of repertory as well as to his skill in performing it. In many ways the reaction was similar to that found at present-day pop concerts. Requests would be shouted out for favoured items. One notorious incident concerned a chamber-music recital in Paris in 1841. Charles Hallé was in attendance:

> The programme given in the 'Salle du Conservatoire' contained the 'Kreutzer' Sonata, to be played by Liszt and Massart, a celebrated and much esteemed violinist. Massart was just commencing the first bar of the introduction when a voice from the audience cried out 'Robert le Diable!!' At that time Liszt had composed a very brilliant fantasy on themes from that opera, and played it always with immense success. The call was taken up by other voices, and in a moment the cries of 'Robert le Diable!' 'Robert le Diable!' drowned the tones of the violin. Liszt rose, bowed, and said 'Je suis toujours l'humble serviteur du public, mais est-ce qu'on désire la fantaisie avant ou après la Sonate?' ['I am always the humble servant of the public, but do you want the fantasy before or after the sonata?'] Renewed cries of 'Robert, Robert!' were the answer upon which Liszt turned half round to poor Massart and dismissed him with a wave of the hand, without a syllable of excuse or regret. He did play the fantasy magnificently, rousing the public to a frenzy of enthusiasm, then called Massart out of his retreat, and we had the 'Kreutzer', which somehow no longer seemed in its right place.[15]

This was not an isolated demonstration. A little later Liszt was again forced to play the Fantasy on Meyerbeer's *Robert le Diable* by an enthusiastic audience before he commenced a performance of Beethoven's 'Emperor' Concerto conducted by Hector Berlioz (1803–69). Richard Wagner (1813–83), who was then in Paris as a correspondent for a German newspaper, wrote that one day Liszt would no doubt be expected to play his fantasy on the Devil before St Peter and the assembled company of angels – as his very last performance.[16]

If Liszt was the pioneer of the solo recital, it was the next generation of pianists that established it in the more extensive form familiar today. Of particular significance was Anton Rubinstein, one of the nineteenth century's greatest pianists and a prolific composer. His 'historical recitals', which took in music from the late renaissance to his own time, served as a template for twentieth-century pianists, many of whom retain a fondness for programmes which traverse a few hundred years of music in chronological order. The main difference is the sheer length of the recital.

Rubinstein, Bülow, Busoni, Arthur Friedheim (1859–1932) and others thought nothing of performing for nearly three hours in a single evening. Bülow's programme of the last five Beethoven sonatas, mentioned above, also had an encore – the 'Appassionata'!

Undoubtedly, the fact that playing from memory was not absolutely *de rigueur* for these pianists allowed them to tackle longer programmes with greater confidence. Bülow frequently played from music, especially in his last years, and Rubinstein, whose ability to play from memory was legendary, also suffered legendary memory lapses. In any case, even when they had the score in front of them, many Romantic pianists did not feel the need to pay slavish attention to it, for the golden era of the piano was also the era of the composer–virtuoso.

The pianist as composer

A highly significant feature of pianism in the Romantic era is that virtually all pianists were composers as well as performers. Of course, even today there are few pianists who do not have some attempts at composition hidden in their attic, but for most of the Romantic virtuosos compositional activity was an integral part of pianism. The most extreme example is Chopin, who rarely performed in public, and when he did almost always played nothing but his own music. His reputation as one of the greatest of pianists is inseparably linked with his reputation as a composer. For Liszt and Thalberg the situation was similar – we have already mentioned that Liszt's first solo 'recital' was entirely made up of his own original pieces or arrangements. As the nineteenth century progressed, the balance between the pianist as composer and the pianist as interpretative artist changed somewhat. The recital programmes of Paderewski or Hofmann were largely made up of other composers' music. Nevertheless, Paderewski composed his (remarkably fine) piano concerto chiefly for his own performance, while few of Hofmann's concerts were complete without one of his own character pieces, such as *Kaleidoscope*, thrown in as an encore.

In some respects, these performers' roles as composers crossed over into their interpretations of other repertory. Anton Rubinstein advised his piano students to learn a piece of music exactly as the composer wrote it. If, after having mastered the work, the student thought that some improvements could be made, then he should feel free to make them. The result of this approach can be seen in such publications as Ferruccio Busoni's (1866–1924) fascinating edition of Bach's Goldberg Variations, where the last four variations are rewritten as a free fantasy in a pianistic

Ex. 4.2 J. S. Bach, Goldberg Variations, final aria, bars 1–4.

Ex. 4.3 Busoni's arrangement of Ex. 4.2.

style that owes far more to Busoni than to Bach. The final return of the theme is also rearranged, shorn of ornamentation and played forcefully in block chords (Exx. 4.2, 4.3). For Busoni, this was a more fitting use of the powers of the nine-foot grand piano than Bach's delicate conception.

Sergey Rachmaninoff's (1873–1943) magnificent recording of Chopin's B♭ minor sonata also makes important changes to the original text, most notably the way in which he treats the Funeral March – a long crescendo followed by a decrescendo (with the Trio an interlude in the middle). This derives from Anton Rubinstein's interpretation of the piece and ignores Chopin's own dynamic indications. Such reinterpretations of dynamics stop short of Busoni's wholesale recomposition in the Goldberg Variations, but go considerably further than most pianists nowadays in imposing a different climactic structure upon the music. Very few of the Romantic pianists who recorded the Funeral March could resist some form of reinterpretation. Raoul Pugno (1852–1914, a pupil of Chopin's pupil Mathais) in his 1903 recording gives a similar interpretation to that of Rachmaninoff. Paderewski, though more faithful to Chopin's dynamics, cannot resist rewriting the bass in the recapitulation of the march, producing an effect akin to the tolling of a deep bell – a wonderful idea, even if it does have nothing to do with Chopin.

Pieces like the Funeral March, with an ostinato rhythm, were particular targets for rewriting. Busoni was one of the most inventive of the usual suspects. His piano roll of Chopin's 'raindrop' Prelude treats the central section as one long, gloomy crescendo, while in the A♭ Polonaise (according to the edition of his pupil Guido Agosti) he rewrote the central part of the trio, with its famous octave bass, to produce a continuous build up of sonority rather than the two separate crescendos indicated by Chopin. He also added octaves in the middle, where Chopin had unaccountably left them out. Busoni was certainly influenced in this by Liszt's octave crescendo in *Funérailles*, and he transferred the dynamic structure of the Liszt piece onto the similar passage of the Chopin. Ironically, as this section of Liszt's *Funérailles* was itself inspired by Chopin's A♭ Polonaise, we have here a peculiar example of anachronistic cross-fertilisation, prompted by Busoni's desire to raise the rafters with his, no doubt very impressive, octaves.

These alterations to Chopin and Bach are prime examples of the intermingling of performance and composition in the Romantic era. This musical approach was, of course, one that existed long before the first generation of Romantic pianists. In fact, it is the musical culture of the late twentieth century, with its emphasis on textual fidelity, and on the relegation of the performer's role to that of a sometimes strait-jacketed interpreter – all underpinned by the division, in music conservatories and colleges, of students into separate composition and performance streams – that constitutes a radical break with previous eras of music.

A large part of the responsibility for this lies with the growth of a 'standard' repertory of concert music that pianists, and other performers, are now required to master. Most of this music is at least one hundred years old, and considered a distinct category from contemporary music, which occupies an isolated, and often less popular, niche. The performance of a pianist's own compositions now seems rather inappropriate, perhaps even arrogant, in the same programme as the masterpieces of the past. Yet when Liszt played Schumann, for example, he was performing contemporary music beside which his own compositions took their natural place. The general style in which he played his own compositions, and those of other composers with whom he had a particular connection, was passed to two generations of students, the younger of which helped to bring Romantic pianists into the recording age. Only Theodor Leschetizky (1830–1915) had a comparable number of distinguished pupils and it is to the legacy of Liszt and Leschetizky that we must look for definite information on Romantic performance styles.

How they played

Leschetizky, like Liszt, was a pupil of Czerny. His students included Hambourg, Ignacy Friedman (1882–1948), Benno Moiseiwitsch (1890–1963), and Paderewski. Although primarily a gifted teacher, Leschetizky's own playing can be heard on piano rolls, which feature, among other things, Mozart's C minor Fantasy K475 and Chopin's D♭ Nocturne Op. 27 No. 2.

Despite the much-discussed inadequacy of the piano roll recording method, we can gain from these performances a fairly good idea of Leschetizky's own style of playing. The Mozart is treated in a much more respectful manner than Rubinstein's description of Hambourg, reminding us that Leschetizky also taught the arch-classicist Artur Schnabel (1882–1951), but the Chopin displays the two prime techniques often categorised as late-Romantic 'mannerisms', namely frequent arpeggiation of chords and the asynchronisation of bass and treble. In other words, Leschetizky, the Czerny pupil, played in a left-hand-before-right style easily as extensive as that of his most successful student Paderewski. Leschetizky probably thought that this style was quite appropriate to Chopin, for he had been particularly impressed by what seems to have been a similar approach in the playing of the Chopin pupil Julius Schulhoff (1825–98). He described the impact of hearing Schulhoff in the 1850s in effusive terms:

> That melody standing out in bold relief, that wonderful sonority – all this
> must be due to a new and entirely different touch. And that cantabile, a
> legato such as I had not dreamed possible on the piano, a human voice rising
> above the sustaining harmonies! I could hear the shepherd sing, and see
> him.[17]

This obsession with a singing tone on the piano was a theme of much nineteenth-century pedagogical writing and no doubt the chief stimulus for what Percy Grainger (1882–1961) described as a 'harped' or highly arpeggiated piano style.

The most detailed attempt to notate this manner of playing is Grainger's own *Rosenkavalier ramble*, where the individual voicing of each chord, and the speed of the spread, is meticulously indicated (Ex. 4.4). Romantic pianists, however, tended to spread chords whether indicated or not, especially in lyrical works. If we compare modern performances of Chopin's E♭ Nocturne Op. 9 No. 2, or Schubert's A♭ Impromptu with the recordings by Paderewski, we hear two completely different sound worlds. Paderewski arpeggiated chords so frequently that a chord played together was almost a special effect. Moreover, in the noc-

Ex. 4.4 Grainger, *Rosenkavalier ramble*, bars 1–6.

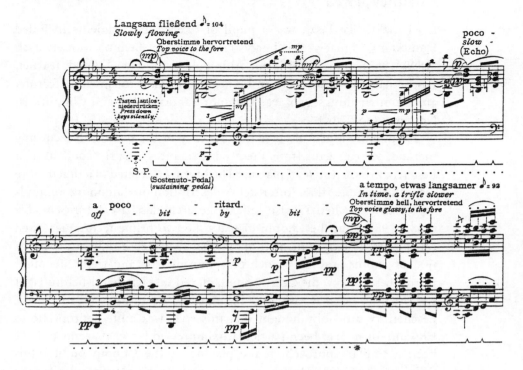

turne virtually every left hand bass note is played before the melody note with which, according to the notation, it ought to synchronise. The effect is not only to emphasise the melody (for no other note is thus struck simultaneously with it) but also to give it a greater singing quality, for the piano strings are already resonating with the pedalled bass note, providing a cushion of sound on which to place the tune. Although Paderewski is an extreme example of this style of playing it was used frequently by many pianists at the turn of the century, and probably long before. The performance of Chopin's Op. 9 No. 2 recorded by Vladimir de Pachmann (1848–1933) is very similar to Paderewski's. Interestingly, when Paderewski was playing under par, his chief worry was not wrong notes, of which there were almost enough to make another piece, but that he could not produce a singing tone.

From the 1830s onwards a large part of the pianist's repertory had consisted of opera or song transcriptions, encouraging direct imitation of vocal models in the production of piano tone. In 1853 Friedrich Wieck, whose daughter Clara (1819–96) had already established herself as one of the finest nineteenth-century pianists, entitled his *magnum opus* on piano teaching *Piano and song*, while Sigismund Thalberg published *The art of singing applied to the piano* around the same time. This consisted of a collection of transcriptions prefaced by a short dissertation on *cantabile* playing, the importance of which was ringingly endorsed in a preface, which included the comment that 'it is by the force of melody, and not of harmony, that a work endures successfully through all ages'.[18] Notwithstanding Artur Rubinstein's denigration of Hambourg's 'percussive' touch, an attention to tonal beauty and melodic projection is one of the few things common to all Romantic pianists who have left recordings.

Although Leschetizky did at least leave an impression of his playing on piano rolls, Fryderyk Chopin died long before that method or Edison's cylinder recording was available. In contrast to Liszt, we do not even have any recordings by distinguished pupils. Chopin's most promising student, Karl Filtsch (1830–45), died at a tragically young age, and it was left to students like Karol Mikuli and Georges Mathias to transmit what they remembered of Chopin's teaching to pianists such as Raoul Koczalski and Pugno, who then transferred some of their art to disc. As far as direct information on Chopin's teaching and performing is concerned, the best present-day compendium is Jean-Jacques Eigeldinger's indispensable *Chopin: pianist and teacher* (Cambridge, 1986) which collects together the most important sources.

It is a moot point whether the type of playing favoured by Schulhoff – which so impressed Leschetizky and became the basis of his style – was actually based on Chopin's teaching, or was an independent development. When Schulhoff came to Weimar in the 1850s to perform before Liszt and his students, William Mason (1829–1908) remarked on his beautiful *cantabile* tone, adding that the basic sound was much more attractive than Liszt's. Despite this, he maintained that Liszt's playing was of an infinitely superior intellectual and emotional range.[19] We might assume from this that Liszt's approach to *cantabile* tone, and thus his use of arpeggiation, was different from Schulhoff's. There seems nevertheless to be no way of proving this one way or the other, short of dabbling in spiritualism and asking the question directly.

Liszt's playing was never recorded – rumours of an Edison cylinder that occasionally crop up are surely without foundation – but his art lives on in his music for piano, which displays the most acute and inventive ear for keyboard sonority of any Romantic composer. In this he was approached only by Chopin, who nevertheless rarely strove for the orchestral effects constantly suggested by Liszt's writing. Initially inspired by the example of Paganini on the violin, Liszt freed virtuoso writing from an over-reliance on brilliant finger-work. His own technique, and his music, united what had hitherto been specialities of individual pianists: the octaves of Alexander Dreyschock (1818–69) (who reputedly played the left hand of Chopin's 'Revolutionary' Study in octaves, but found a scale in single notes something of a trial); the solo left-hand writing of Theodor Döhler (seen especially in the early version of Liszt's *Petrarch sonnet 104*); the wide accompaniment stretches of Adolf Henselt (1814–89); and the *legato* arpeggio style of Thalberg. To this core he added a fondness for wide leaps in both hands which far surpass anything found in the music of Henri Herz. All the elements are found in the twelve *Transcendental studies* of 1837–51, but are seen in perhaps their most extravagant form in *Reminiscences de Don Juan* (1841), described quite aptly by Busoni as a pianistic summit. However astounding Liszt's technical capabilities were, they would now be only of historical interest had they not been wedded to a musical imagination of the highest order. Now that more of his music has become part of the standard repertory than ever before, it has become easier to evaluate the astonishing range of his gifts both as a pianist and composer.

Liszt's work as a teacher of the next two generations of pianists ensured his continued influence on pianism well into the twentieth century. In addition to the redoubtable Hans von Bülow, the first wave of Liszt students in the 1850s included Carl Tausig (1841–71), William Mason and Karl Klindworth (1830–1916). All died too early to leave recordings, but most of the second generation of students – Emil Sauer, Alexander Siloti, Arthur Friedheim, Eugène d'Albert, Moriz Rosenthal, Frederic Lamond, Bernhard Stavenhagen, Jószef Weisz, Arthur de Greef, Conrad Ansorge and José Vianna da Motta among them – can be heard on record. Their playing all demonstrates, to varying degrees, the typically Romantic traits of frequent chordal arpeggiation and asynchronisation of the hands. Although the individuality of these players is at least as marked as that which they have in common, these familiar features of turn of the century pianism – found also in the playing of most of the Leschetizky students mentioned towards the beginning of this section – must surely reflect something of Liszt's approach to the keyboard.

There has rightly been much discussion over whether the playing of a pupil can tell us much about the playing of a teacher (the problem of Schulhoff, for example, was mentioned above). Pianists are often exaggeratedly proud of their pedagogical pedigrees – as if musical talent were passed on by apostolic succession – and all of Liszt's best pupils had gone beyond the stage of thoughtless imitation. Moreover, with a pianist like Rosenthal, whose teachers included Mikuli, Liszt and Rubinstein, the question of what he learned from whom becomes ludicrously complicated. It does, however, appear to me that it is possible, by listening to a selection of recordings of Liszt's pupils, to gain a good idea of the *broad stylistic range* within which he expected most piano music, including his own, to be interpreted. This is especially significant because so many features of the playing of Liszt's pupils differ from performances today. With a pupil like Arthur Friedheim, who admired Liszt to the point of idolisation, we may hear closer echoes of Liszt's own playing, although the exact extent of these must always remain a matter of opinion.[20]

Fortunately we also have a large amount of written information on Liszt's playing and teaching, the main source being Lina Ramann's *Liszt-Pädagogium*, reprinted some time ago with an excellent introduction by Alfred Brendel, in addition to the diaries of August Göllerich, and memoirs by other Liszt students such as Carl Lachmund, Lamond and Sauer.[21] One of the most moving of all sources is Frederic Lamond's radio broadcast from the 1940s of his memories of Liszt's teaching. Lamond's awe and admiration for Liszt are still evident in his voice after nearly sixty years. 'He could be very strict!'

Taken together, the written sources show that Liszt's playing changed considerably in his old age from that of his virtuoso years. Gone were the wild gestures, and many of the extensive alterations to the score. Beethoven and Chopin, in particular, were regarded as sacrosanct, and interpreted with a keen fidelity. Liszt had given the first public performance of Beethoven's 'Hammerklavier' sonata in 1836. According to Berlioz he played it exactly as written – unusual enough in those days to be remarked upon. Hans von Bülow's Beethoven edition shows that he did, in fact, make some minor alterations to the last page, but there can be little doubt that Liszt pioneered the art of faithfully interpreting masterworks at the same time as he was giving demonstrations of the art of Romantic exaggeration. The contradictions were fundamental to the man. Although Arthur Friedheim was notoriously unhappy with his recordings, if we listen to his first movement of Beethoven's 'Moonlight' Sonata, we do indeed hear a remarkably simple, straightforward, even 'modern' performance, in contrast to Paderewski's indulgent Romanticism in the same piece. Perhaps Friedheim is passing down something of Liszt's teaching here? (We know that Liszt used to make fun of Anton Rubinstein's wayward performance of the 'Moonlight'.) Friedheim's added turns and ornaments in his piano roll of Liszt's *Harmonies du soir* also sound strikingly similar to descriptions of Liszt's own treatment of his more lyrical works. A full discussion of this topic would require a book on its own, but as suggested above, by critical listening to the recordings of Liszt's pupils, we can at the very least get some general idea of a Liszt style.

If this stylistic ambit does indeed seem wide – from the dash of d'Albert to the aristocratic poise of Sauer – it is because in the final analysis variety and individuality were the chief hallmarks of Romantic pianism. The virtuoso tradition emphasised the uniqueness of the inter-preter along with that of the composition, and it could be argued that the difference between the styles of, say, Paderewski and Hofmann was almost as great as the differences between the separate pieces on their pro-gramme. The concert world of today may have lost some of the more questionable fits of caprice exhibited by the great virtuosos of the past – Vladimir de Pachmann's spectacular rallentando at the end of Chopin's C♯ minor Waltz sounds as if the audience might die of old age before he gets to the final note – but in consequence it has also made a sacrifice of interest, spontaneity and sheer panache.

5 Pianists on record in the early twentieth century

ROBERT PHILIP

The experience of recording

The modern recording studio is a very different place from the studios of the early twentieth century, and the process of making records has changed very greatly. Until the introduction of tape recording around 1950, pianists, like other musicians, recorded onto a wax disc one side at a time. The maximum length was about four and a half minutes by the 1930s, shorter in the early days. Recordings could not be edited, and they could not even be played back at the time without destroying the wax master. Before the advent of electrical recording in the mid 1920s, the frequency range was very limited in both bass and treble, making a concert grand piano sound more like a small upright.

The first important pianists to make records were Alfred Grünfeld in Vienna in 1899, and Raoul Pugno in Paris in 1903. But for several years into the twentieth century the principal work of the studios was vocal recording. Because the acoustic recording horns were very directional, the piano used for accompaniment was raised up to the same level as the singer's head. In 1902, Caruso's accompanist Salvatore Cottone played on an upright piano set up on a platform of packing cases. Pugno's recordings were made under similar conditions.[1] Even when solo piano recording became established, and grand pianos were routinely used in the studio, the pre-electric recording still had limitations. Busoni left a vivid description of his first experience of recording Liszt's arrangement of the waltz from Gounod's *Faust* in 1919:

> They wanted the Faust waltz (which lasts a good ten minutes) *but it was only to take four minutes!* That meant quickly cutting, patching and improvising, so that there should still be some sense left in it; watching the pedal (because it sounds so bad); thinking of certain notes which had to be stronger or weaker in order to please this devilish machine; not letting oneself go for fear of inaccuracies and being conscious the whole time that every note was going to be there for eternity; how can there be any question of inspiration, freedom, swing, or poetry?[2]

For many musicians, making records remained a very unnerving experience right through the era of 78 rpm recordings, until the advent of tape editing. Rachmaninoff's view was widespread: 'When the test records are made, I know that I can hear them played back at me, and then everything is all right. But when the stage is set for the final recording, and I realise that this will remain for good, I get nervous and my hands get tense.'[3] Restrained pedalling, which Busoni mentions, is a feature of many pre-electric piano recordings. The only disc published from Busoni's first session in 1919, Chopin's Etude in G♭ major Op. 10 No. 5 ('Black Keys'), is clear and delicate, with very little pedalling. Similarly, Paderewski's earliest recordings, which date from 1911 and include Chopin's nocturnes in F major and F♯ major Op. 15, are much more lightly pedalled than his later, electrical recordings.

Fred Gaisberg of the Gramophone Company, who made the first recordings of Paderewski at his home in Switzerland, wrote,

> Paderewski, from the first, diffidently consented to record and never
> completely reconciled himself to the ordeal. He always doubted whether a
> machine could capture his art. Today, knowing better what Paderewski was
> and the limitations of the gramophone, I am inclined to agree with him. His
> art involved such broad and unrestrained dynamics – the faintest *pianissimo*
> crashing into a great mass of tone. In other words, he painted on a vast
> canvas, and the gramophone could only reproduce a miniature of his mighty
> masterwork.[4]

Paderewski continued to make records until 1938, so Gaisberg (who was writing in 1946) was referring not just to his pre-electric recordings, but to later, electrical recordings which were able to capture much more of the tonal and dynamic range of the piano. This raises some important points about piano recordings. Why are most of Paderewski's recordings so unsuccessful in conveying his power? There are other pianists recorded in the 1920s and 1930s – Sergey Rachmaninoff, Josef Hofmann, Josef Lhévinne (1874–1944) and Percy Grainger, for example – who, within the limitations of the recordings, sound immensely powerful. Even Pugno's primitive 1903 recordings at least suggest a commanding musical personality. Paderewski's records often convey charm and elegance, particularly the early ones, and occasionally remarkable dexterity (as in Liszt's 'La Leggierezza', 1923), but few of them suggest real power. And yet Paderewski's financial success as a concert pianist was greater than that of any other pianist up to that time. Admittedly Paderewski had an impressive stage presence, enhanced by his fame as a world figure (he became prime minister of independent Poland in 1919). Not surprisingly, none of that is conveyed by the recordings. Also, Paderewski was already fifty-one when he made his first recordings in 1911, and in his late seventies when he made his last records. Therefore, he never made records in his prime. The same is true of Pachmann. When he played Chopin's B minor Sonata in London in 1911, his playing was 'a reminder of what it had been in past years'. [5] In other words, he was already well past his best. So we have to be very careful in our assessment of early recordings of pianists. What was the reputation of the pianist at the time of the recording? How might the pianist's normal performance have been adapted for purposes of recording (notably by restraint in pedalling)? And, a question which applies to recordings of all dates, what are we missing by not being able to see the pianist? It is only since the advent of recordings that we have been able to separate the sound of a performance from the complete experience of being in the presence of the musician.

The recording studio is a very different environment from the concert platform. In the late twentieth century, with digital sound and sophisticated editing techniques, the demand for clarity and accuracy imposes restraints on tempo, but minor slips can be corrected without having to repeat a long section. In the days of 78 rpm recording, there was not the same concentration on absolute accuracy, and tempos were often faster than would nowadays be considered compatible with poise and clarity. Virtuoso piano music was frequently recorded with extraordinary panache. But mistakes could not be edited out, and given the nervousness of many pianists in the studio, we must allow for the possibility that they may in many cases have given somewhat restrained performances in the studio compared with their concert performances.

If studio recordings do not give the whole picture of a pianist, they do at least reproduce, within their limitations, the actual sound of a musician performing. In the early years of the century there was an alternative, which avoided the limitations of the gramophone but imposed limitations of its own. This was the 'reproducing piano', a highly sophisticated development of the pianola, which recorded onto a roll of paper not only the timing of each note of a performance, but also the speed of the hammers and the use of the pedals (Fig. 5.1). Holes were then cut in the roll, corresponding to the recorded marks, so that when it was played back a pneumatic mechanism operated the hammers, reproducing the original performance as accurately as possible. Most of the prominent pianists in the first three decades of the century made piano-roll recordings for one or more of three makes of reproducing piano: Welte-Mignon, Duo-Art and Ampico. Of these, Welte-Mignon was the first in the field, and Ampico was the most sophisticated.

In the days when the gramophone was unable to record anything like the full dynamic and tonal range of a piano, many leading concert pianists expressed their enthusiasm for the reproducing piano, and approved rolls which they recorded as true to their performance. Painstaking restoration of the original machinery has produced some remarkable results in recent

Figure 5.1 Steinway grand piano with 'Duo-Art' reproducing mechanism, 1925.

years. The real value of piano rolls nevertheless remains controversial. Though all three of the principal makes of machine can make a clear distinction between the dynamic levels of melody and accompaniment, Duo-Art and Welte-Mignon are more limited than Ampico in their ability to render the precise volume of each note in a complicated texture. As a result, they often sound rhythmically clumsy. On the other hand, the Ampico system, though capable of greater subtlety, has been criticised for the extent to which it tidies up the performances by ironing out rhythmic irregularities in rapid passages. Comparisons reveal that Ampico rolls do sometimes give an impression of superhuman dexterity which is not borne out by gramophone recordings (in the playing of Josef Lhévinne, for example). One question which applies to all three types is whether it can be wholly satisfactory to record the behaviour of the hammers on one piano, and then transfer this information to a different piano with different acoustical properties, and with hammers in a different condition. Delicate adjustment of the playback mechanism is needed to achieve a plausible result, and it can never be known how close the reproduction is to the original performance on the original instrument.

The undoubted value of piano rolls is to increase our knowledge of pianists who did not survive into the period of electrical gramophone recordings. Busoni is perhaps the most important example. According to Ferruccio Bonavia, he 'commanded a wider range of tone than any other living pianist',[6] so the short pieces which he recorded for the pre-electric gramophone so uncomfortably in 1919 and 1922 could hardly be expected to give a complete picture. Some of his piano rolls do convey considerable power, and help us to gain a more complete impression of his playing, even if the details cannot be trusted.

Composer–performers

The early years of recording captured some important composer–pianists. The first was Johannes Brahms (1833–97), playing part of his Hungarian Dance No. 1 in G minor, and recorded on an Edison cylinder in 1889. The original cylinder was lost, and in all transfers made so far the piano is barely audible above the roar of the surface noise. With a little imagination it is possible to infer considerable panache, and a certain swagger in the rhythm, but little else. On the other hand, the virtuoso dash of Camille Saint-Saëns (1835–1921) is very clear, including an impressive command of rapid repeated notes (in, among other works, an improvised cadenza to his 'Africa', recorded in 1904). Edvard Grieg (1843–1907) plays 'To Spring' with considerable expressive freedom and narrative force (considering the limitations of the 1903 recording). Claude Debussy (1862–1918) accompanies Mary Garden in extracts from *Pelléas et Mélisande* in 1904, but the music of the accompaniment is too sparse to give much impression of his playing.

We can, however, gain a very vivid impression of how Debussy liked his music to be played from the recordings of Ricardo Viñes (1875–1943), made in the early 1930s. Viñes was closely associated with both Debussy and Ravel, and premiered many of their works. Poulenc, who was taught the piano by Viñes, wrote, 'No-one could teach the art of using the pedals, an essential feature of modern piano music, better than Viñes . . . [he] somehow managed to extract clarity from the very ambiguities created by the pedals.'[7] Clarity is indeed one of the most striking characteristics of Viñes's recordings. Even the most complex textures are crystal clear, no doubt partly because of the subtle pedalling, but also because of the sensitive judgement of balance between the different layers of the texture, as in the 1930 recording of 'Poissons d'or', which Debussy dedicated to Viñes. His rhythmic subtlety is also extraordinary, particularly the way he highlights melodic fragments not just by volume, as a modern pianist would, but by the slightest hint of rhythmic separation from the textures above or below it, by playing notes fractionally early or late.

As far as the modern listener can judge, Viñes's recordings convey much of the quality described by his contemporaries. Fortunately, the same is true of the greatest of twentieth-century composer–pianists, Rachmaninoff. He began recording in 1919, but it is in his electrical recordings from the late 1920s onwards that his full powers as a performer are conveyed. Rachmaninoff had a severe stage presence, and some critics have found his recordings cold. Certainly there is nothing self-indulgent or full-blown about them. Compared with modern performances of his works, they are austere, partly because of his tempos. The opening of the Third Piano Concerto, for example (recorded 1939/40), is substantially faster than in most modern performances ($\downarrow = 144$). Instead of the heavy melancholy which modern pianists affect, Rachmaninoff plays it as a simple folk song. Most of the tempos in his famous 1929 recording of the Second Concerto are similarly very fast by modern standards.[8] Another feature which distinguishes Rachmaninoff's playing from that of other pianists who have recorded his music is his style of *rubato*. For the modern pianist, the expressive playing of Romantic music involves taking great care to give full weight and time to every phrase and every chord. Richness of texture and a leisurely pacing are the norm. Modern flexibility most often consists of a yet more leisurely rendering of important turns of phrase. The flexibility of Rachmaninoff's phrasing is quite different. His pace is volatile, but it speeds up as much as it slows down. His *rubato* involves not just taking time for important phrases, but of lengthening individual notes and shortening others. His most famous melody, from the Variations on a theme of Paganini, provides a good example (Ex. 5.1). The modern pianist will almost certainly take time over each of the upbeat groups. Rachmaninoff also takes his time, but he does not distribute that time evenly. In the first group of semiquavers (bar 2 of the variation), the first three notes are long, but the fourth is short, giving quite a sudden impulse into the next bar. There is a similar effect in bar 3 and, more subtly, in bars 4 and 5. This sort of rhythmic unevenness is generally avoided by the modern pianist, but it is a particular feature of Rachmaninoff's playing. It gives a wonderful 'speaking' character to his phrasing, providing added emphasis to crucial notes of the phrase, but without the added weight of (what is now) a conventional allargando. He applies a similar technique to the principal theme in the slow movement of his second concerto.

The other major composer–pianist to have recorded extensively, Béla Bartók (1881–1945), played with great energy and freedom. In the introduction of Beethoven's 'Kreutzer' Sonata (recorded at a public recital

Ex. 5.1 Rachmaninoff, Rhapsody on a theme of Paganini, variation 18, bars 1–6. Rachmaninoff's *rubato*.

with Joseph Szigeti in 1940), the first chord of the piano entry is virtually the only one in the whole introduction in which all the notes are played simultaneously. Here, and similarly in the theme of the slow movement, almost every chord is slightly arpeggiated, with the bass note leading. In Scarlatti's Sonata in G, L286/Kk427 (recorded 1929) the rapid semiquavers are dashed off with great vigour, but without modern rhythmic clarity. Because the detailed rhythm is not explicitly clear, the sudden accents which punctuate the piece come as unpredictable stabs. Bartók also recorded a large number of his own solo works. The impression which his playing of them made on contemporaries was startlingly varied. When he came to London in 1922, Percy Scholes reported 'a hard, cold rattle of a keyboard, violently attacked in chance combinations of keys and notes, with the stiffened metal muscle of a jerkily rhythmic automaton'.[9] On the other hand Otto Klemperer thought Bartók 'a wonderful pianist and musician. The beauty of his tone, the energy and lightness of his playing were unforgettable. It was almost painfully beautiful. He played with great freedom, that was what was so wonderful.'[10] It is difficult to know how much of Scholes's criticism is directed at the music, and how much at the playing. From the perspective of the late twentieth century, Klemperer's view of Bartók's playing is more comprehensible. He certainly played with considerable force in pieces such as *Allegro Barbaro* (recorded 1929), but with much less suggestion of the automaton than in most modern performances. In the opening theme, the speed of semiquavers varies considerably, tending to accelerate when they are continuous, and played fast where they end a phrase. Far from sounding mechanical, this suggests the fluid movement of a dancer. As in his Scarlatti, Bartók often plays his own music with an impressionistic rather than clinical approach to detail. In the first movement of the Suite Op. 14 (recorded 1929), slurred groups of semiquavers in the opening theme are played as fast and light swirls, again suggesting dance movement (Ex. 5.2). Later in the piece, accented long notes are emphasised by being played later than the bass. There are many examples of this technique in Bartók's recordings, notably in *Mikrokosmos* No. 100 ('In the style of a folksong', recorded 1940), where two contrapuntal strands are subtly separated by this kind of dislocation. In the fourth movement of the Suite, there is a striking example of *rubato* in which a sighing effect is created by alternately lengthening and shortening notes, in the manner much favoured by Rachmaninoff (Ex. 5.3). There is nothing in the score (apart from the general instruction *dolcissimo*) to suggest to the modern pianist that Bartók had such *rubato* in mind. It is a technique which Bartók uses in many subtle ways throughout his recordings.

Performers and repertory

Over the first half of the twentieth century, a huge number of pianists recorded a vast range of music, but in the early years of the gramophone the recorded repertory was very limited.

A convenient landmark in the history of the marketing of piano recordings is the year 1911, in which Paderewski made his first recordings of Chopin. By then, a number of renowned pianists had already made records in the eight years since Raoul Pugno entered a Paris studio, including Pachmann, Alfred Cortot (1877–1962), Wilhelm Backhaus (1884–1969), Hambourg, and d'Albert. Almost all of the pieces which they recorded lasted for one, or at most, two four-minute sides. Short works by Chopin, Mendelssohn, Grieg, Liszt, Joachim Raff (1822–82) and others were the order of the day, with occasional popular eighteenth-century pieces. In 1910 Backhaus recorded Grieg's concerto, with the New Symphony Orchestra conducted by Landon Ronald. This was the first recording of a concerto, but it was cut to fit onto two single-sided discs (approximately a quarter of its original length).

Before the first world war, therefore, piano recording, which was still

Ex. 5.2 Bartók, Suite Op. 14, first movement, bars 1–12.

Ex. 5.3 Bartók, Suite Op. 14, fourth movement, bars 22–3. Bartók's *rubato*.

very much second to vocal recording in importance, was restricted to short pieces or cut-down longer ones, almost all of them from the popular nineteenth-century repertory. It is easy for a record collector to get the impression that this was what pianists of the time played, but it is important to realise that the limitations were imposed more by the caution of the recording industry than by the tastes of the pianists. A comparison with concert programmes of the time shows that the gramophone was only dipping its toe hesitantly into a much broader repertory. For example, reports in *The Musical Times* for 1911 include the following: in London Rosenthal played Schumann's Concerto 'with great lucidity' and Pachmann gave his first performance there of Chopin's B minor Sonata; Pugno not only gave solo recitals, but also played all the Beethoven violin sonatas with Eugène Ysaÿe (1858–1931). Other London recitalists included Harold Samuel, William Murdoch (his first appearance), Leopold Godowsky, Alfred Cortot, Benno Moiseiwitsch, Harold Bauer, Emil Sauer, Irene Scharrer, Myra Hess, Percy Grainger, Teresa Carreño, Leonard Borwick, Fanny Davies and Adela Verne (the last three were all pupils of Clara Schumann). Donald Tovey played the second Brahms concerto with Elgar and the LSO, and Brahms's cello sonatas with Pablo Casals. In Dresden Rachmaninoff 'obtained a great success' with his new Piano Concerto No. 3, which he repeated in London 'with great brilliance'. In Berlin Carl Bernhard Philipsen gave the premiere of Arnold Schoenberg's (1874–1951) Piano Pieces Op. 11. In Budapest Debussy played his own compositions and 'aroused great interest'. The centenary of the birth of Liszt was celebrated: in Berlin Busoni gave a series of six concerts of Liszt, for which he supplied analytical notes; a Liszt Festival in Budapest included Liszt's pupils d'Albert, Friedheim, Lamond, Rosenthal and Sauer. At the festival in Heidelberg, Busoni played the Second Piano Concerto, and Saint-Saëns played a recital including Liszt's transcription of his *Danse macabre*. In Dresden, Max Reger (1873–1916) played his own Piano Concerto in F minor, and the solo part in Bach's Brandenburg Concerto No. 5. At the second Bach Festival in Leipzig, he played the Goldberg Variations.

It was many years before this breadth was reflected in gramophone recordings. Long works continued to be cut routinely until the advent of electrical recording in the mid 1920s, and record companies were conservative in their choice of repertory, however distinguished the pianist. For example, having recorded the first of Bach's 48 Preludes and Fugues for Columbia in 1922, Busoni offered to record the complete set. His offer was turned down, and the complete work was not recorded until more than a decade later, by Edwin Fischer.

By 1936, when the first attempt at a comprehensive encyclopedia of recordings was published,[11] electrical recording had been in existence for eleven years, and much piano repertory had been recorded. Even so, the situation for a record collector was nothing like that of a CD collector in the 1990s. There were still substantial gaps, and many standard works had been recorded only once or twice, so that there was little or no choice of performer. Schumann's *Kinderszenen* had been recorded by Cortot, Moiseiwitsch, Fanny Davies and Ernö Dohnányi, and there were many arrangements of 'Träumerei'. For *Carnaval* there was Rachmaninoff, Godowsky, Cortot and Szreter. But there was no complete recording of the *Fantasiestücke*, and although there were four recordings of 'Aufschwung', even 'Warum?' was restricted to an old acoustic recording by Paderewski. Of Chopin's sonatas, there were seven recordings of No. 2, with its famous Funeral March, two of No. 3 (Cortot and Grainger), but none of No. 1. Schnabel's famous HMV 'Beethoven Society' series of all that composer's sonatas was gradually being issued, and these were proving phenomenally successful (collectors had spent £80,000 on the first three volumes by 1935).[12] There were many duplicate performances listed of the popular sonatas – including Kempff, Backhaus, Murdoch, Lamond, Hambourg and Szreter for the 'Pathétique', Kempff, Backhaus, Lamond, Bauer, Friedman, Hambourg, Evelyn Howard-Jones and Szreter for the 'Moonlight'. But for the lesser-known sonatas, it was Schnabel or nothing. Backhaus led the field in Brahms; his were the only recordings so far of the First Piano Concerto, the Scherzo in E♭ minor, the Intermezzi Op. 76 No. 7, and Op. 118 Nos. 1, 4 and 6. Those who got to know the piano music of Beethoven and Brahms from recordings therefore came to associate these composers with particular styles of playing: Schnabel's lucid and volatile Beethoven, and Backhaus's big, rather plain Brahms. The playing of gramophone records on the radio reinforced this association. Less exclusively, Cortot led the available recordings of Chopin. His complete recording of the Ballades was already his second. (In a survey in *The Gramophone* in 1928, readers had voted Cortot's first recording of Chopin's Preludes as the fourth most popular electrical recording, the highest position for a piano record.) Only two of Schubert's sonatas are listed in the 1936 encyclopedia: No. 9 in A major, played by Myra Hess, and No. 11 in G, by Lev Pouishnoff and Franz Josef Hirt. Ten of Mozart's piano concertos had been recorded, the D minor K466 and the A major K488 twice each, but there was not yet a recording of the now-popular C minor concerto K491. A number of pianists had recorded Bach on the piano. As well as Edwin Fischer's complete '48', several of the preludes and fugues, and other works by Bach, had been recorded by Samuel, Backhaus, Howard-Jones and Kempff.

By the mid 1930s, therefore, much of the piano repertory had been recorded, but the gaps meant that pioneering recordings were appearing almost every month. For many works, collectors could hear one interpretation and one only. For music which had not yet been recorded, the situation was as it always had been: they could get to know a work by playing it themselves, or wait for an opportunity to hear it played by amateur or professional performers (in the flesh or on the radio). Despite the great expansion of the gramophone industry since the introduction of electrical recordings, records were not yet the principal means of enlarging a listener's repertory.

Teachers and pupils

Among the many pianists who made records in the first half of the twentieth century were a number who studied with important teachers of the late nineteenth century – Liszt, Clara Schumann, Anton Rubinstein, Theodor Leschetizky, and several pupils of Chopin. These in turn taught a younger generation of pianists. Recordings make it possible for the first time to trace the influence of teachers from one generation to another, and to examine the differences and similarities between fellow pupils.

Pupil–teacher relationships are very varied, and recordings do not reveal a simple pattern of influences. This is hardly surprising. No pianists, before or after the invention of the gramophone, made their reputations by playing exactly like their teachers, or even as their teachers instructed. The picture is further complicated by the fact that many early twentieth-century pianists studied with more than one teacher. Leschetizky's pupils included Paderewski, Friedman, Hambourg, Moiseiwitsch and Schnabel, all of whom made recordings. There are also piano rolls (but not gramophone recordings) of Leschetizky himself. The differences between these pianists are much more striking than their similarities, but recordings of Friedman, Hambourg and Moiseiwitsch do have in common a wonderfully subtle layering of textures. In Hambourg's performance of the 'Mélodie' from Gluck's *Orfeo ed Eurydice* (recorded 1929), the very soft accompaniment allows the melody to project although played very quietly, so that it acquires a floating, gently singing quality. Friedman similarly plays Chopin's Nocturne in E♭ Op. 55 No. 2 with a very quiet accompaniment, so that the melody sings without being pushed, and details in the accompaniment tell with only the subtlest emphasis. Moiseiwitsch plays Rachmaninoff's Prelude in B minor Op. 32 No. 10 with the most beautiful shading of phrases and balancing of the inner voices (Moiseiwitsch's playing was particularly admired by Rachmaninoff). Friedman, Hambourg and Moiseiwitsch also share a very subtle approach to *rubato* and the rhythmic dislocation of chords. Slight arpeggiation of chords, and anticipation of important notes in lower parts are used very selectively.

Schnabel stands somewhat apart from other Leschetizky pupils, partly because of the repertory which he recorded, notably the recording of all Beethoven's sonatas (recorded 1932–5), mentioned above. He is often characterised as the great 'Classical' pianist, as opposed to the 'Romantics' Friedman, Moiseiwitsch and Hambourg. Certainly he gives the impression of a highly analytical mind, through performances in which every phrase and every paragraph seem to have a precise place in the whole structure. This is achieved partly by a volatile response to the changing character of the music, and partly by the characterising of rhythmic details, underlining the differences between the accented and the unaccented, the short and the long, and distinguishing points of repose and points of transition. In practice, this means almost constant subtle changes of pace from phrase to phrase, and a very flexible approach to the relationship between long and short notes. What he did have in common with other Leschetizky pupils was a command of subtly layered textures, which enabled him to clarify Beethoven's counterpoint in an extraordinary way. (His pupil Clifford Curzon remembered how Schnabel stressed the importance of balancing precisely each note of a chord against the others.)[13] He also shared with many pianists of his generation a preference for fast tempos in fast movements, even when this meant occasional loss of precision. His attempt to play Beethoven's 'Hammerklavier' Sonata at something like the composer's metronome markings is famous (recorded 1935). Other examples of Leschetizky pupils playing with great brilliance include Moiseiwitsch in Weber's *Perpetuum Mobile* (recorded 1922), and Hambourg in the finale of Beethoven's Sonata in C Op. 2 No. 3 (recorded 1926), which he takes at extraordinary speed ($\bullet = 152$) and with the jig rhythm lightened by short and snappy quavers.

The most famous and successful pupil of Leschetizky was Paderewski, but his recordings, which are very mixed, present something of a puzzle to the modern listener. Throughout his recording career his performances reveal a bewildering mixture of considerable charm and what now sounds like clumsiness. In his very first year of recording (1911) he made records of two Chopin nocturnes. Apart from the light pedalling, which has already been mentioned, the Nocturne in F♯ major Op. 15 No. 2 has delicate decoration, and quite subtle and selective use of dislocation, with important melody notes played after the bass. On the other hand, the Nocturne in F major Op. 15 No. 1 is rhythmically much looser, with almost constantly delayed melody notes sounding dangerously like routine. Paderewski's use of dislocation is particularly striking in Chopin's Mazurka in C♯ minor Op. 63 No. 3 (recorded 1930). Where the melody is played in canon (from bar 65), Paderewski uses this technique to give independence to the two parts.[14]

There were therefore considerable differences between the pupils of Leschetizky. In particular, Schnabel and Paderewski had little in common. Because Leschetizky himself made only piano rolls, it is impossible to judge quite what his playing sounded like. But it is clear that he used as much dislocation of bass and treble as Paderewski at his most extreme.

The most distinguished example of a pianist who studied with a pupil of Leschetizky is Clifford Curzon, who was taught by Schnabel. Curzon said that Schnabel taught him to let the music 'breathe',[15] and his sense of timing and placing of detail do, within the constraints of a more modern style, have something in common with Schnabel. But since Schnabel's own style was highly individual, and very different from that of other Leschetizky pupils, Curzon cannot in any useful sense be considered 'a grand pupil' of Leschetizky.

There are similar problems with the 'Liszt Tradition'. Liszt's pupils included Moriz Rosenthal, Arthur de Greef, Arthur Friedheim, Frederic Lamond, Emil Sauer and Eugène d'Albert, all of whom made records. None of these were in their prime by the time they made records. Lamond retains a fair amount of brilliance in his recordings of Liszt. His tempos are very volatile, not only in Liszt and Chopin but also, more surprisingly to modern ears, in Beethoven. D'Albert's *rubato* includes much uneven pairing of notes (in the manner adopted more subtly by Rachmaninoff). All of these Liszt pupils make much use of dislocation between melody and bass. In Brahms's Capriccio in B minor Op. 76 No. 2 (recorded 1928), Lamond produces an extraordinary 'gallumphing' effect by the continual anticipation of the bass. In Sauer's recording of Liszt's Concerto No. 1 (recorded 1938), he not only dislocates melody and bass in the piano part, but also creates accents by playing melody notes ahead of the orchestra. Friedheim (in Liszt's Hungarian Rhapsody No. 2, recorded *c*.1917) and Rosenthal (in Liszt's *Soirées de Vienne*, recorded 1936) show the light and snappy playing of short notes, a characteristic of so many pianists of their generation.

Rosenthal is, to the modern listener, probably the most impressive Liszt pupil on record. His later recordings show him limited by old age (for example, in Chopin's Sonata in B minor, recorded 1939), with the dislocation becoming unsubtle. But a 1930 recording of Chopin's Berceuse reveals a wonderfully delicate and fluid lyricism. Ex. 5.4 gives some idea of Rosenthal's rhythmic adjustments in the opening bars of Chopin's Nocturne in E♭ Op. 9 No. 2 (recorded 1936). The smooth and quiet melodic line seems to float independently above the bass, because of the subtlety with which Rosenthal places it in relation to the rhythm of the accompaniment.

The problem for anyone wanting a simple family tree of teachers and pupils, is that Rosenthal studied not only with Liszt, but also with Liszt's pupil Carl Tausig, and with Chopin's pupil Karol Mikuli. When he appeared in Vienna at the age of twenty-one, he made a mark as a fiery virtuoso in the Liszt mould, but Eduard Hanslick disliked the 'unlovely violence with which the keys were pounded in fortissimo passages'.[16] It was later that he developed a reputation for the delicacy of his soft playing. It would be neat if Rosenthal acquired his gentle qualities from Mikuli, and his brilliant virtuosity from Liszt. But his three years with Mikuli were from the age of nine, before he studied with Liszt.

A number of pianists who made records studied with pupils of Chopin. Like Rosenthal, Alexander Michalowski and Raoul Koczalski both studied with Mikuli, one of Chopin's most important pupils. Michalowski's recordings include Chopin's Polonaise in A major

Ex. 5.4 Chopin, Nocturne in E♭, Op. 9 No. 2. Rosenthal's *rubato*. \ indicates note played late.

(recorded *c*.1907), played very vigorously, but with light dotted rhythms. He also recorded two versions of the 'Minute' Waltz, one a 'straight' version, played with considerable dash, the other, more surprisingly, a virtuoso rearrangement of the kind which was popular in the early years of the century. Koczalski is perhaps the most important link with the 'Chopin School', because, unlike his fellow pupils Rosenthal and Michalowski, he did not move on to other teachers after studying with Mikuli. (He was, however, only eleven when he finished studying with Mikuli, and did not make his first recordings until about twenty-seven years later.) Koczalski is also the most impressive of pianists in the Chopin line to have recorded. The Scherzo in B♭ minor (recorded *c*.1936) is much lighter than most modern performances, volatile in tempo, very clear in texture, with sparing use of the sustaining pedal, and with beautiful, free *rubato* in the melody of the second theme, over an accompaniment which maintains a strong forward impulse.

Alfred Cortot and Marguerite Long were also taught by a disciple of Chopin, Emile Decombes.[17] In the 1930s and 1940s Cortot was probably the most widely admired of all Chopin players, but his style was very individual. The singing of his melodic lines had a particular intensity (greater than that of any of the Leschetizky pupils), and his approach to tempo was very flexible. But his precise pinpointing of the character of each moment nevertheless creates an impression of command over the whole structure of the music. No-one has played Chopin's twenty-four Preludes with such mercurial beauty, and yet with such a sense of the set as one continuous work (he recorded it three times, but the 1933–4 version is the most impressive). His 1931 recording of Chopin's Sonata in B minor contains many detailed tempo changes and points of emphasis (very different from the more straightforward, muscular brilliance of Percy Grainger in 1925), and is memorable for moments of exquisite shading and lyricism. But the work as a whole also hangs together. Cortot's responsiveness to musical character made him particularly suited to the music of Schumann.

There was, however, an official 'Schumann tradition', passed down from Clara Schumann to her pupils, who included Fanny Davies, Adelina de Lara and Mathilde Verne. The playing of Davies and de Lara now seems rather plain, certainly much plainer than that of Cortot, with a great deal of loose co-ordination between the hands. In de Lara's recordings, all made in her late seventies, some of this might be attributable to old age. But Davies, who was in her fifties, shows a similar style in, for example, the opening piece of *Kinderszenen* (recorded 1929), with the bass anticipating the melody on almost every beat, in a somewhat routine manner.

Mathilde Verne did not record, but she was well known as a teacher. Her pupil Moura Lympany (*b*.1916) remembers in her autobiography Verne's strict instruction that she should play the opening of Schumann's Concerto at a constant pace, without slowing down for the principal theme. Lympany herself does not take this instruction literally in her recording from the 1950s, but she does play the principal theme unusually fast. On the other hand, Fanny Davies (1928) plays it more slowly. The question arises which of them (if either) represents the tradition handed down from Clara Schumann. As for the old-fashioned rhythmic loose-ness, which is so much a feature of Davies's and de Lara's playing, there is no trace of it in Lympany. By the time she rose to prominence in the 1940s, the dislocation of bass and treble had become seriously unfashionable, and one of the lessons of the gramophone is that changing fashion has a more powerful influence on the style of a young pianist than the tradi-tions of a teacher.

Modern rhythmic discipline was also characteristic of Solomon (1902–88), probably the greatest British pianist of the century. He too studied with Mathilde Verne, though only as a child prodigy. He later described the experience as 'terrible, terrible', and denied that he learned anything more than basic playing technique from her.[18] Perhaps his contact with the Schumann school did encourage a certain reserve and absence of show, though these qualities may have owed more to Lazare Lévy with whom Solomon studied at the Paris Conservatoire as a young adult (Clara Haskill, another pupil of Lévy, shared these qualities). Solomon's *rubato* was always restrained, his tempos were never self-indulgent. But these were not negative qualities in Solomon. His playing was notable for its power, clarity and delicacy, achieved with a seemingly effortless technique.

One early twentieth-century pianist who declared himself against the rhythmic separation of the hands was Josef Hofmann. As early as 1909 he advised amateur pianists: 'this "limping", as it is called, is the worst habit you can have in piano playing...'[19] Hofmann was the only private pupil of Anton Rubinstein in Moscow. His recordings show an extraordinary technique, a very wide range of tone colour and dynamics, and a singing *legato*. In public recital, where, according to those who heard him, the 'real' Hofmann was to be heard, he took liberties which now sound anything but modern. The recording of his 1938 recital at Casimir Hall, Philadelphia, includes virtuoso display pieces, delivered with glittering panache, and two substantial works of Chopin: the Ballade in F minor played with powerful contrasts of volume and tempo, and the Polonaise in E♭ minor, much more wilful in its flexibility, with a portentous, slow introduction.

Sergey Rachmaninoff and Josef Lhévinne, who were influenced by Rubinstein, though not actually taught by him, both had in common with Hofmann a commanding technique – surprising in Rachmaninoff, who had never intended to make a career as a concert pianist. Rachmaninoff's highly individual style of *rubato* has already been discussed. Both he and Lhévinne shared Hofmann's generally modern approach to the rhythmic relationship between the hands, but they also exercised a much stricter control of tempo than Hofmann. In Lhévinne's recordings, the impression is of very firm projection of tone, and a steely brilliance in virtuoso passages, as in Schulz-Evler's arrangement of 'The Blue Danube' (recorded 1928). (The Ampico piano rolls of Lhévinne playing this and other pieces, which were first issued on LP in the 1960s, were adjusted to give a feathery lightness to the playing, which is not borne out by the studio recording.) Like Rachmaninoff, and unlike Hofmann, he uses subtle anticipations and delays to emphasise melody notes, as in a marvellously glittering performance of Liszt's arrangement of Schumann's 'Frühlingsnacht' (recorded 1935).

The most prominent heir to this 'Russian school' was Vladimir Horowitz (1904–89), who was taught by another student from Rubinstein's classes, Felix Blumenfeld. Horowitz revered Hofmann, and has more in common with him than with Rachmaninoff or Lhévinne, combining a phenomenal technique with a huge range of tone, touch and dynamics, and a very free approach to tempo. His early recordings, made in the early 1930s, already reveal the disturbing mixture of qualities which persisted throughout his career, alternating between powerful athleticism and sudden moments of calm beauty.

Finally, it is worth mentioning the 'English school' of piano playing, which developed in the early twentieth century. Tobias Matthay was an important figure, teaching, among others, Myra Hess, Irene Scharrer, Harriet Cohen and Harold Craxton. Hess in turn taught Stephen (Bishop) Kovacevich, Craxton taught Denis Matthews, Peter Katin and Noel Mewton-Wood. The sobriety and lack of display of Matthay's pupils had something in common with the Clara Schumann school. Finesse and quiet intensity of tone were characteristic of both Hess and Scharrer. Scharrer's few recordings include some beautifully poised performances of the gentler works of Chopin. Hess's recordings range from Bach and Scarlatti through Mozart, Beethoven, Brahms and Schumann to a few twentieth-century works, notably the Sonata of her friend Howard Ferguson (recorded 1940). Harriet Cohen was especially noted as a friend and champion of Arnold Bax (1883–1953), and she was also chosen by Edward Elgar (1857–1934) to record his Piano Quintet in 1933.

But if there was an English school, it extended beyond the pupils of Matthay. Solomon (taught as a child by Mathilde Verne and as an adult by Simon Rumchiysky and Lazare Lévy), Lympany (taught by Verne), Kathleen Long (a pupil of Herbert Sharpe) and Clifford Curzon (a pupil of Schnabel) shared with the Matthay pupils a tendency to understatement which was far removed from a Hofmann or a Horowitz, and had more in common with Schnabel or Edwin Fischer. At their best they had a quiet intensity and sensitivity, and it was these qualities which made them all fine chamber musicians.

Trends of the century

However detailed the information which has come down to us, establishing the styles in which pianists of the eighteenth and nineteenth centuries played is to some extent a matter of conjecture. With the advent of recording, we can actually hear how pianists played eighty or ninety years ago, and, by the same token, we can hear how modern playing developed. A number of general features of early twentieth-century piano playing have been mentioned in this chapter. Chief among them is a tendency, compared with today, for pianists early in the century to play with lightness of rhythm. This takes the form of a habit of playing short notes, such as semiquavers in a fast movement, faster and more lightly than modern pianists. Dotted rhythms are often 'overdotted' and very snappy, groups of semiquavers are dashed off, sometimes as mere swirls, and continuous semiquavers often accelerate in a manner which would now be thought uncontrolled. There is much less emphasis than today on achieving the firm placing of every detail. Despite the great differences between early twentieth-century pianists, this general approach to rhythm can be heard in piano playing from all countries and all schools – Russian (Rachmaninoff), Hungarian (Bartók), German (Schnabel), French (Cortot), English (Kathleen Long) and Spanish (Viñes).

The trend over the century has been away from this lightness of rhythm, which has come to be regarded as too casual, towards a greater emphasis on clarity and precise weighting of detail, and the setting and controlling of a tempo which allows this to be achieved. Modern pianists play Rachmaninoff more slowly and with heavier emphasis than the composer did; modern Bartók playing is more sharp-edged and literal in its note values than Bartók's own. For eighteenth- and nineteenth-century repertory, there is a growing number of specialists who play on period instruments in a generally lighter style than conventional modern pianists, but not even they play Beethoven or Schumann with the dash or volatility of Schnabel or Cortot.

This change in style and approach can be traced in the careers of individual pianists who recorded over a long period. Artur Rubinstein's flexibility of tempo in Chopin's Concerto in F minor was more extreme in 1931, more measured in 1960. Similar comparisons apply to Kempff in Beethoven's Sonata Op. 110 (1936 and 1964) and Backhaus in the 'Pathétique' Sonata (1927 and 1958). Claudio Arrau came to be regarded as one of the most searching of pianists, but his recordings of Schumann's Concerto (*c.*1945 and 1963) and Chopin's Ballade in A♭ major (1939 and 1955) show that his performances became not only generally slower in the later recordings, but also more heavy in rhythmic detail, more inclined to linger, and less inclined to accelerate. There are similar comparisons with many pianists, and they illustrate not just the changes in a maturing musician, but a more general shift in style to which all musicians, to a greater or lesser extent, responded.

The styles of *rubato* used by many pianists in the early twentieth century were very different from what we are accustomed to in the late twentieth century. There was considerable argument about the subject, and disagreement about what kind of flexibility was appropriate in piano playing. Some writers concentrated on the form of *rubato* which is still most familiar today – a momentary rallentando followed by a return to tempo. Argument here centred on the idea of 'compensation'. Tobias Matthay, a noted piano teacher and theoretician, wrote that any time 'borrowed' in the rallentando should be 'payed back' in the accelerando, so as to maintain 'the Tempo outline'.[20] A similar principle of balance in *rubato* was put forward by Josef Hofmann.[21] Others, including Paderewski and Wanda Landowska, while agreeing that the momentary rallentando and accelerando was the basis of *rubato*, rejected the idea that they must balance each other. [22]

Less familiar to modern pianists is the idea of *rubato* which is based not on fluctuation in tempo, but on the lengthening and shortening of individual notes. Leschetizky, according to his pupil George Woodhouse, emphasised 'rhythm and nuance – those revealing accents, hoverings, the hundred and one subtleties of phrasing which give life and soul to musical form', and complained of the modern *rubato* which 'tends inevitably to reduce expression to whimsical play upon tempo'.[23] One of the consequences of this approach is that a melody played with *rubato* may part company from its accompaniment, as Frederick Niecks writes: 'Where there is an accompaniment rhythmically distinct from the melody, the former should be in strict time, while the melody, within certain limits, may proceed on her course with the greatest freedom.' [24] This will sound familiar to anyone who has read descriptions of the *rubato* of Liszt and Chopin.

Recordings demonstrate that, in practice, styles of *rubato* in early twentieth-century pianists were extremely varied. Mention has been made several times of the old-fashioned habit of rhythmically separating bass and treble, most often by playing notes in the melody late, or by spreading chords. This stylistic device is too easily dismissed by some modern writers as old-fashioned sloppiness.[25] The most extreme examples, by Paderewski, Pachmann and others, can certainly sound extraordinarily unthinking to unaccustomed modern ears. But recordings demonstrate that it was a very widespread habit, not only among the famous recitalists, but also among musicians who were not concert pianists. Elgar, Beecham, Landon Ronald, Ernest Newman, as well as many accompanists in recordings of singers, can be heard playing the piano with virtually no chords played together, in a manner which even amateur pianists would now consider laughable. This rhythmic device gradually fell out of fashion during the 1930s and 1940s, so that from the 1950s onwards almost no professional pianists, except the very old, were heard using it, except as a very occasional and subtle effect.

Other kinds of *rubato* – momentary rallentando and accelerando, or the lengthening and shortening of individual notes – have changed over the century, becoming less abrupt and more gradual. The *rubato* of many early twentieth-century pianists has the effect of highlighting notes or phrases so that they stand out in relief. This is true of the delayed notes of Paderewski, the *tenuti* of Rachmaninoff and Bartók, and the detailed tempo-changes of Cortot and Schnabel. The modern tendency is to avoid sudden emphasis, the principle being that any *rubato* should be approached and left smoothly. Modern *rubato*, compared with the old, therefore tends to take time, and to add to the trend towards slower tempos and more measured emphasis.

These stylistic changes can be summarised as a gradual shift over the century towards a more deliberate, and in some ways more literal, interpretation of the score. In this, pianists were part of a wider movement which affected musicians of all kinds. The lightness of rhythm in the early part of the century is just as noticeable in recordings of violinists, string quartets and orchestras. The spreading of chords was part of a more general rhythmic style, which included a (to modern ears) loose approach to rhythmic discipline in ensembles. The suddenness of much old *rubato* is paralleled by the sudden emphasis of old string-players' portamento. The freedom of a melody over its bass is, in origin, an imitation of the sort of freedom which singers (such as Adeline Patti) and string players (such as Ysaÿe) used to exercise.

It is important to realise, therefore, that trends in piano playing are part of trends in musical performance as a whole. Our ability to hear those trends preserved over a century in recordings is a new experience. It enables us not only to analyse the past, but also to realise that modern styles, however natural or inevitable they may seem at the time, are no more than points in the continuous evolution towards the styles of the future.

6 The acoustics of the piano

BERNARD RICHARDSON

Introduction

The underlying acoustical principles of sound production on the piano are very straightforward. When a key is depressed, it causes a small, felt-covered hammer to be thrown against a set of strings tuned to a specific note of the scale. The key incorporates an escapement mechanism which detaches the hammer from the key just before striking the strings so that they receive a single, unimpeded blow from the hammer. The exchange of momentum causes the strings to vibrate, and it is these vibrations which are the origin of the musical sound. The strings do not radiate sound directly, however, because they are much too small to interact with the surrounding air. Instead, they are coupled to a soundboard, a lightweight plate of wood, which is specifically designed to vibrate in sympathy with the strings. It is the structural vibrations of the soundboard which induce pressure changes in the air, rather in the manner of a loudspeaker cone, to create the sound we hear.

This is, of course, just the start of the story. This simple explanation of the mechanical action of the piano invites more questions than it answers. Why do different pianos have different sound qualities? What is the function of double and triple stringing? What control does the performer have on the final sound quality of an instrument? In searching for the answers to these questions, we discover that the piano has a few hidden secrets of surprising complexity, and we have to marvel at the ingenuity of the craftsmen who have played their part in the development of the modern instrument and at the skill of the technician who keeps a piano at the peak of its performance.

This chapter will examine in detail the vibrations of the strings and soundboard and the all-important string–hammer interaction.[1] It will also look briefly at the perception of musical sounds, at tuning and temperaments, and at more esoteric issues such as piano touch. It begins, however, by discussing the general construction of the modern piano and the various factors which influence its sound and playing qualities.

Piano construction

Keyboard stringed instruments differ most notably from their smaller cousins such as violins and guitars by having one musical oscillator (one set of strings) per semitone of the scale. This, coupled with the considerable degree of mechanical detachment of the player from the strings, is what makes sound production on the piano so easy. At the same time, the increased mechanisation makes the piano look very complicated, but it can, nevertheless, be conceptually broken down into its functional parts.

Fig. 6.1 shows a plan view of a concert grand piano. Most modern instruments have a playing range in excess of seven octaves. The piano shown here is a 'standard' set up with 88 keys operating a total of about 240 strings in the pitch range AAA to c^5.[2] In the bass region there is just one string per note, but the middle and treble ranges use first two and then three strings per note; multiple stringing helps increase the sound output. The fundamental frequencies of the string vibrations range from 27.5 Hz to just over 4000 Hz, a range which spans all but the top two octaves of the limits of human hearing. (The abbreviation Hz stands for Hertz, or cycles per second.) The musical pitch of a vibrating stretched string depends on its length, tension and mass. In order to tension the strings, they are stretched tightly across a massive iron frame (clearly visible in Fig. 6.1) between hitchpins and tuning pins (see Fig. 6.2). The latter can be adjusted to alter the string tension and thus tune the instrument. The higher the tension of the strings the larger the driving force at the bridge, and in the modern piano each string might be at a tension of 1000 Newtons (about 100 kg weight) with the frame supporting an astonishing total of 20 tonnes. The string tensions in the piano are considerably higher (by a factor of at least ten) than those found in most other stringed instruments, which is one reason why it is such a powerful instrument. The bass strings need to be long and heavy; they might be as much as 2 m long and made from a heavy steel core overwound with one or two layers of thick copper wire. The copper wrappings increase the mass of the string whilst retaining its flexibility, a necessary requirement, as will be discussed later, for a 'good' musical oscillator. At the treble end of the scale, the strings are very short (minimum about 50 mm) and made from plain steel wire of diameters 0.8–1.2 mm.

The vibrating length of each string is not governed by the dimensions of the frame but by the distance between a bridge at one end and some kind of rigid termination at the other – either an agraffe, *capo d'astro* bar or a raised nut (Fig. 6.2) – which is attached to or is an integral part of the iron frame. Attachment to the heavy frame helps to minimise energy losses at this end of the string. The bridge, on the other hand, is mounted

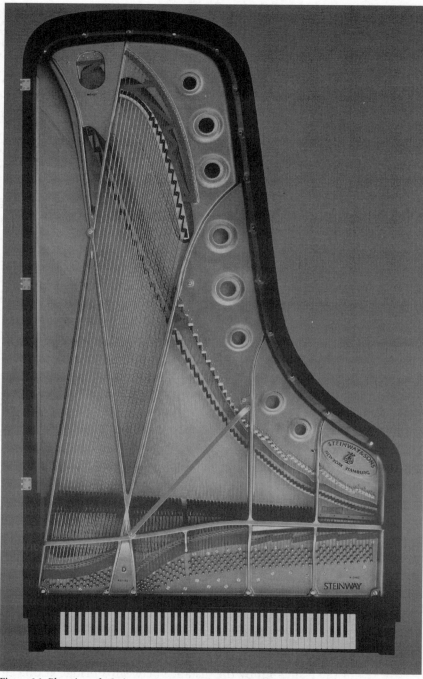

Figure 6.1 Plan view of a Steinway concert grand piano, model D (9 foot).

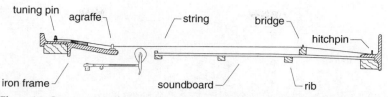

Figure 6.2 Cross-section of a piano showing the principal parts. Adapted from Askenfelt, *The acoustics of the piano*, p. 12.

directly on the compliant soundboard, and it is the tiny induced movements of the bridge and soundboard that are responsible for generating the sound we hear. The bridge is usually in two portions. The long bridge, which can be seen sweeping along the length of the soundboard in Fig. 6.1, carries the mid to high range of notes. A separate, shorter bridge is provided for the bass strings. This design feature is known as 'overstringing' (or 'cross-stringing') and allows the bass strings to terminate at a more reactive part of the soundboard. The strings make a slight 'break' across the bridge creating downward pressure on the soundboard; this is necessary to prevent the strings being dislodged by the blow of the hammer. The soundboard itself is a large, thin panel, usually made of spruce, and supported on the underside by ribs glued across the board. The soundboard and iron frame are attached to a wooden framework which is in turn attached to the case. The framework and case are very heavy and their acoustical role is fairly passive, except for their influence on the sound radiation from the soundboard.

The general layout of the modern grand piano has changed little from Cristofori's original design of the early eighteenth century, which itself was based on harpsichords of that period. Thus the shape of the case, the form of the bridge and layout of the strings and keys firmly echo its smaller predecessor. Much of the piano's development has basically been one of scale, literally in the case of the playing range, which originally encompassed only four octaves. The iron frame, introduced in the early nineteenth century, allowed the string tension, and hence the power of the instrument, to be dramatically increased. Furthermore, it was dimensionally stable, unlike the former wooden frames, and tuning accuracy could be guaranteed for much longer periods. The iron frame was therefore swiftly adopted by many manufacturers. The iron frame also allowed the successful construction of the upright piano. While there are subtle differences in the mechanical action of the key mechanisms which make uprights less responsive for professional use, the general construction and acoustical principles are, of course, the same as found in the grand piano. The more compact size of the upright, however, undoubtedly led to its

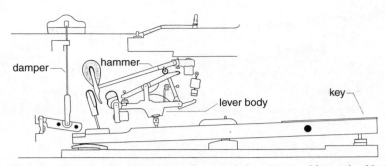

Figure 6.3 Side view of the action of a modern grand piano. Reprinted from Askenfelt, *The acoustics of the piano*, p. 40.

adoption in domestic environments and to the extraordinary popularity of the piano towards the end of the nineteenth century.

The early nineteenth century also saw a flurry of experimentation with hammers and the action. The first effective felt covering was developed by 1826, and felt has been used ever since. The properties of hammers will be discussed in the next section. The action is the mechanism which converts the player's key-stroke into a hammer blow at the string. Basically, it is a system of levers which amplify the velocity of the key so that the hammer travels some five times faster than the key (Fig. 6.3). The action also incorporates the damper mechanism, which prevents the strings vibrating when not required (the line of dampers is the only part of the action to be seen in Fig. 6.1). The action is undoubtedly the most complex, and intriguing, part of the piano. Cristofori's original piano had small leather-covered hammers with a simple escapement mechanism which disengaged the hammer from the key just prior to striking the string, allowing it to fall back to a resting position without rebounding against the strings. Simple escapement mechanisms such as this proved satisfactory throughout the eighteenth century, but as the component parts of the action became heavier, and the key-depth increased in the nineteenth century, a new mechanism was needed which could be re-primed quickly to allow the playing of rapidly repeated notes. The double-repetition action of Erard, patented in 1821, achieved this and is still extensively used in modern grand pianos. With this mechanism, the key need not be completely lifted to re-prime the hammer. It is also highly responsive to the nuances of the player. The action of the grand piano is much assisted by gravity; the same is not true of the action in upright pianos. Though similar in essence, the latter is functionally less responsive, there being no counterpart to the Erard double-repetition action. Diagrams and details of the operation of piano action can be found in a number of texts,[3] but the best way to comprehend the operation of this intriguing mechanism is to get inside your piano and have a look for yourself!

The final mechanisms of interest are the pedals. The left pedal is the *una corda* or 'soft' pedal. In grand pianos, the keyboard is shifted so that the hammers strike one fewer string in the middle and treble ranges. Reducing the number of strings which are struck reduces the loudness of the instrument and also has some more subtle effects on the sound quality. In uprights, the soft pedal moves the hammers nearer to the strings so that the striking momentum is reduced, again to aid in the production of a quieter sound. The right pedal, the sustaining pedal, simply raises all the dampers so that when keys are released the strings continue to sound. The raised dampers also encourage sympathetic string vibrations giving extra 'resonance' to the sound. Some pianos include a third pedal. In the modern grand piano this is likely to be a 'sostenuto' pedal; this operates a clever mechanism which keeps raised all the dampers that are raised when the pedal is depressed, allowing those strings to continue ringing even after the keys have been released, but which allows the pianist to play further notes without sustain. Some pianos intended primarily for domestic use incorporate a 'practice pedal'. Depressing this introduces a strip of soft felt between the hammers and strings (a more extreme revision of the early moderator), effectively softening the hammer and considerably reducing the loudness of the instrument.

Strings and hammers

When the string is struck by the hammer, it becomes locally distorted. There is nothing to restrain this local distortion, so it starts to travel in both directions away from the hammer creating *waves*, much in the same way that a stone thrown into a pond creates ripples which travel away from the initial disturbance. The speed of propagation (c) of the waves depends on the tension (T) and mass per unit length (m) of the string according to the equation $c = \sqrt{T/m}$. Wave speeds on piano strings can be as much as 400 metres per second. When the waves arrive at the agraffe and bridge they are reflected. In the former case, almost all the energy returns, but in the latter, a little of the energy of the wave is transferred to the soundboard (some of which in turn gets converted into sound energy) and the rest returns towards the hammer. The waves travel back and forth along the string applying some type of 'pulse' at the bridge once per round trip, and the induced soundboard vibrations create cyclic pressure variations in the air (Fig. 6.4a). Since each wave travels a total

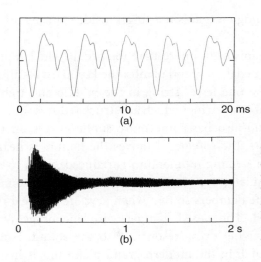

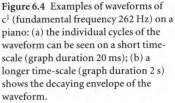

Figure 6.4 Examples of waveforms of c^1 (fundamental frequency 262 Hz) on a piano: (a) the individual cycles of the waveform can be seen on a short time-scale (graph duration 20 ms); (b) a longer time-scale (graph duration 2 s) shows the decaying envelope of the waveform.

distance of twice the length of the string, the repetition rate of the driving force applied at the bridge is given by a second equation

$$f = \frac{1}{2L}\sqrt{\frac{T}{m}}$$

where L is the length of the string. The *pitch* of the sound is effectively determined by the frequency f. This formula, often known as Mersenne's law, is used by piano designers in choosing appropriate string lengths, tensions and gauges. It is clear from the presence of the square root that changes in the length of the string have a larger effect on pitch than do corresponding changes in the tension or mass of the string.

Ideal-string modes

The mental picture created above of pulses rebounding between the end points of the string is physically accurate. However, there is an equivalent way of considering these motions in terms of the *modes of vibration* of the string. It is useful to consider the string vibrations in this way because it gives greater insight into the sound signals received by the ear.

The reader can get a feel for string modes by playing with a 'slinky spring' stretched between two hands (as in Fig. 6.5). The spring vibrates in an identical way to a string, but the lower tension and increased mass slows down the motion so that it can actually be seen. Instead of letting the spring vibrate freely, it can be forced to vibrate by gently moving one hand up and down. When the spring is vibrated at just the right rate, at a *resonance* frequency, individual modes are excited, and lots of movement is produced for very little effort. In its *fundamental* mode (top picture of Fig. 6.5), the whole spring simply oscillates up and down. The frequency

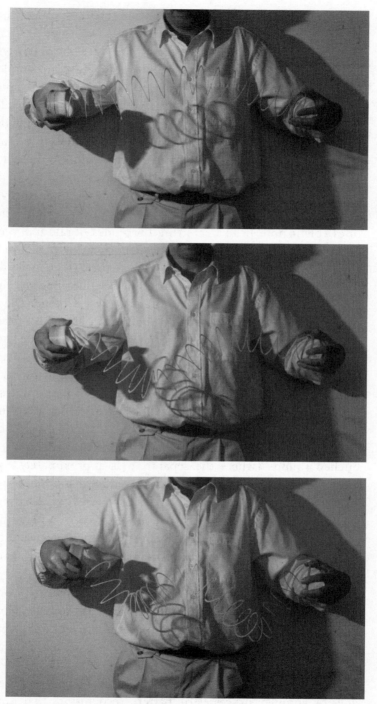

Figure 6.5 The first three modes of vibration of a stretched string visualised using a 'slinky spring'.

of this mode is the same as the repetition rate of the travelling pulses as described by Mersenne's law. If oscillated at two, three or four times the frequency of the first mode, the spring hops into one of its higher modes of vibration, each of which involves progressively more complex motion. In the higher modes, it is amusing to see the contrary motion of the different parts of the spring and the points on the spring, called nodes, which do not move. Real strings support a large number of higher modes.

In the piano, the string is now free to vibrate on its own, but the effect of the hammer blow is to excite combinations of the modes of the string. The free vibrations of the string occur at the resonance frequencies of the string modes. The soundboard is thus driven simultaneously at each of the mode frequencies of the string. It is this mix of sounds which constitutes a piano note. In an ideal string, the modes vibrate at *integer multiples* of the fundamental and generate *harmonic* frequencies.[4] Played individually as a sequence, sounds corresponding to these frequencies would form the harmonic series (Ex. 6.1). Harmonic relationships are highly desirable, because under these circumstances the ear blends the individual components to give the perception of just one note, with a clearly defined pitch. In real strings, the mode frequencies are never quite harmonically related, and it is for this reason that the frequency components making up the final sound are usually referred to as *partials*. The string partials can be seen as equally spaced peaks in the analyses of piano notes shown in Fig. 6.6. These graphs, which show the acoustical *spectra* of the sounds, show what frequency components are present and how they evolve with time. Note that the partials have an increased separation in higher-pitched sounds (where the separation is approximately equal to the fundamental frequency f). The partials reduce in amplitude as time progresses. They decay mainly through friction losses but also partly through useful radiation of sound. The overall duration of a piano note can be several seconds (Fig. 6.4b), but is shorter in the treble than the bass. In fact, notes in the top octave are so short-lived that these strings are not even equipped with dampers.

The perception of musical sounds is a truly remarkable process, particularly when we consider that no two pianos produce identical waveforms and that the tone of a piano changes from note to note. Sound waves impinging on the ear are converted to a stream of nerve impulses which are sent from the inner ear (the cochlea) to the brain.[5] The brain has a remarkable capacity for analysing these nerve impulses, which it does by complex processes of 'pattern recognition', that is, comparing current stimuli with a large array of similar patterns it has previously analysed. Recognition is, therefore, based on prior experience, and this is why training helps to increase aural acuity. Pitch is determined from

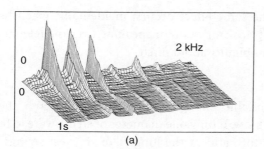

(a)

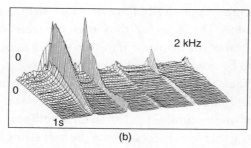

(b)

Figure 6.6 Sound spectra of two piano notes, in which the decaying radiated string partials can readily be seen. The horizontal axes show the frequencies of the partials, the vertical axes show their intensities, and the axes towards the reader show the progression of time; (a) c^1, and (b) g^1, with fundamental frequencies 262 Hz and 392 Hz respectively.

Ex. 6.1 The first eight harmonics of a harmonic series based on C. The approximate frequency associated with each note is shown below the stave.

short-term aspects of the waveform (Fig. 6.4a) and is strongly related to the repetition rate of the sound waveform. The precise shape of the waveform is governed by the relative strengths of the various partials making up the sound, and it is often stated that this spectrum of the sound determines its tone quality or *timbre*. This is an oversimplification, however. The shape of the waveform changes constantly throughout the duration of the sound, and it is better to say that the timbre is determined by the relative frequencies, strengths and evolution and decay rates of the partials. The ear is also very sensitive to the starting transient of the sound, which includes mechanical noise from the keys and case, as well as the long-term envelope of the sound (Fig. 6.4b).

One aspect of piano tone is worth highlighting here. The first few partials of the lowest bass strings are usually poorly represented in the sounds radiated by pianos (particularly from small pianos). It might be imagined that the absence of the fundamental would cause the pitch to rise by an octave. However, the missing fundamental does not alter the basic repetition rate of the sound wave, so we still hear the same pitch, albeit with a different tone. The same effect occurs, incidentally, when listening to music on a small transistor radio or speaking over the telephone, where again there is no ambiguity about pitch.

Inharmonicity

In arriving at a suitable *scaling* for the strings of a piano, the designer applies Mersenne's law. If only one diameter of string were to be used at a constant tension, the ratio of the longest to shortest strings would be about 150:1, requiring impractically long or short strings at the two extremes of the range. The designer thus uses progressively heavier strings towards the bass of the instrument to keep them a sensible length. If solid wire were to be used for the lowest strings they would become rather stiff, and stiffness introduces *inharmonicity* of the string partials, that is, the resonance frequencies of the string modes deviate from their ideal harmonic (or whole-number) relationships. Stiffness makes the higher modes get progressively sharper. Hence the bass strings are always overwound making them more flexible, but nevertheless they suffer rather badly from inharmonicity. Short strings also suffer the same predicament because their diameters are relatively large in relation to their length. Inharmonicity can also be introduced by imperfections in the strings, including rust on plain strings and dirt in the windings of bass strings, or by too great a compliance at the bridge. Inharmonicity is a double-edged sword. Slight inharmonicity ensures that the bridge-driving cycle never quite repeats itself, giving a pleasant 'living' quality to the sound, rather like vibrato in the voice or in a violin. Too much inharmonicity, however, produces a 'bell-like' quality in the sound and can lead to severe intonation difficulties. Piano making seems to have evolved empirically to find acceptable solutions to this problem.

Another source of inharmonic partials is the *longitudinal* modes of the strings. The modes of vibration so far considered involve transverse (sideways) displacements of the string. They are the dominant source of energy. However, the hammer blow can also excite disturbances which involve localised compressions and expansions of the string elements along the length of the string, hence the name 'longitudinal' modes. These usually occur at about ten times the frequencies of equivalent transverse modes. If they were exactly ten times, or some other whole number ratio, that would be fine – the longitudinal modes would then 'harmonise' with the transverse string partials. Unfortunately, they are more often at irrational ratios and their presence has a detrimental effect on the perceived tone quality. The longitudinal modes cannot be tuned, except with great difficulty, at the design stage of the piano. Again, natural evolution of piano making has generated some designs which are more acceptable than others.

Hammer–string interaction

The design and construction of the hammers and the point at which they strike the strings play a crucial role in determining the final sound quality of a piano. The hammers are made from one or two layers of wool felt which are greatly compressed and stretched over a wooden former. Hammer sizes and weights are graded, varying from about 11 g in the bass to 4 g in the treble. The treble hammers are also harder than their bass counterparts. Being compliant, the hammer covering is distorted as it strikes the string and actually remains in contact for a considerable time (one to four milliseconds). For mid-range notes, the contact time can be a sizeable fraction of the pulse cycle time, but in the upper range, the contact time exceeds the pulse cycle time and the hammer then interacts with the pulses travelling on the string and actively starts to alter their shape. Expressed alternatively in the language of modes of vibration, the striking position, the hardness of the hammer and the contact time govern the initial amplitudes of the string partials and thus strongly influence the sound quality. Felt is an interesting material in that it is increasingly more difficult to compress as the applied force increases (this is known as 'non-linear stiffness') and it is only recently that the physics of the string–hammer interaction has been properly understood.[6] Non-linear stiffness also means that the relative intensities of the radiated string partials depend on the striking force. A forceful key-stroke creates a perceptually louder sound partly because it increases the general level of the partials but also because it increases the high-frequency content more rapidly, creating a 'brighter' and more prominent sound.

In most modern pianos the hammer strikes the string about one eighth or ninth of the way along the string. Such a position appears to give a reasonable compromise between relative strengths of low and high partials. At the top end of the range, the hammers move even closer to the string termination, the best striking position often being determined by trial and error. The hardness of the hammers needs careful adjustment if the tone quality is to be even across the playing range. Good pianos will be 'voiced' individually. The hammers are deliberately left on the hard side during manufacture. The piano technician can then soften the felt where required by pricking it to obtain an even tone.[7] Older pianos, which have seen considerable service, might benefit from re-voicing because the hammers tend to harden after repeated use.

Double and triple stringing

Double stringing was common in early keyboard instruments and the practice has continued in the piano. Presumably, the initial intention had been to double the bridge-driving force for each note to produce a louder instrument. This it does, but double and triple stringing also introduces other features of the decay profile known as 'prompt' and 'aftersound'.

The envelope of the sound shown in Fig. 6.4b displays what is called a 'dual decay'. The sound decays rapidly in the initial part of the note, then slows to a much longer-lived aftersound. The net perceived effect is a long, loud sound – the vibrations of a single string would decay much faster. Dual decays come about as a result of different phases of the movements of the strings. For the sake of discussion, it is easiest to consider two strings only. These two strings have pairs of coupled modes, one in which both strings move in the same direction, and one in which they move contrary to each other. The first regime creates a strong bridge-driving force that dissipates energy quickly. The second regime creates a much smaller bridge-driving force that is consequently quieter but much longer lived.[8] Careful tuning of the double- and triple-strung notes allows subtle gradation of the prompt and aftersound and is an important aspect of preparing a piano for a concert performance. If one string is effectively removed, as happens when the *una corda* pedal is in use, the relative amounts of prompt and aftersound change. Thus, the *una corda* pedal is much more than a *soft* pedal.

Structural vibrations

Although the vibrating strings are the source of energy in the piano, it is the soundboard that actually converts this energy into sound. The main requirements of the soundboard are that it should be lightweight but at the same time stiff enough to support the sizeable static forces of the strings. There are few materials which satisfy this stringent stiffness-to-mass criterion. The traditional material is one of a number of European spruces (such as *picea excelsa* or *picea abies*) or, particularly in North America, sitka spruce (*picea sitchensis*). The wood is chosen carefully for straight, even growth, and ideally, though rarely, it is split from the log. Splitting ensures that the wood fibres run parallel to the surface of the board and that the grain lines (the annual growth rings) run perpendicularly through the thickness of the board, both of which ensure maximum stiffness. The soundboard more or less fills the entire case of the piano, and so it has to be made by gluing several boards edge to edge. The soundboard of a modern piano usually has a graded thickness of between 6 and 10 mm and is stiffened on the underside by fairly substantial spruce bars (ribs) running across the board. The hardwood bridge also adds additional stiffness. The soundboard is fixed around the edges to a wooden frame, restraining the motion at its perimeter.

Like the strings, the soundboard has modes of vibration. They are more complex, however, because the bending waves are now travelling across a two-dimensional surface rather than a one-dimensional string, and the resonance frequencies of the modes no longer form a simple series. The lowest mode involves the whole central area of the board moving up and down. The resonance frequency of this mode depends on the size of the piano, but might be as low as 50 Hz on a large grand. At progressively higher frequencies, the soundboard splits up into smaller and smaller vibrating patches, each separated from its neighbour by nodal lines, just like the string. Compared with the string, however, the soundboard modes are rather passive and, apart from contributing small knocking noises at the start of each note, they are basically the servants of the strings.

The ideal sound radiator is a structure which induces volume changes in the surrounding air. The problem in the piano is that the soundboard is open on both sides. Thus, as the soundboard moves upwards compressing the air on the upper side, the underside of the soundboard is busy rarefying the air below it. This leads to poor radiation at low frequencies, when the air literally has time to nip around the edges of the board to relieve the pressure differences on either side rather than generating substantial sound waves. Large soundboards help to minimise this problem. This 'acoustical short-circuiting' is also a problem at higher frequencies when the soundboard has split up into small vibrating patches. The favoured region for sound radiation tends to fall in the range 200–2000 Hz. Smaller pianos will have a higher cut-off at the lower end of the range and the reduced radiation at low frequencies imparts a 'thinner' tone in the bass.

The case of the piano has surprising little effect on the sound radiation, though the high frequencies, which have very directional radiation characteristics, are certainly affected by the opening of the lid.[9] Different veneers or lacquers on the case have no effect on the sound and are purely cosmetic. Lacquers applied to the soundboard are essential, however, in that they help stabilise the wood against movements which occur as a result of humidity changes. There is considerable movement across the width of the board, and a common problem in an older piano might be cracks appearing along the grain. They usually have little effect on the sound, as long as the parts do not rattle.

Although the action incorporates lots of leather and felt on its working surfaces, the keys, action and case are responsible for generating a considerable amount of mechanical noise in the initial part of a piano note. This is particularly noticeable when playing at the top end of the range, when the noise components are not masked by the string partials. Rather than simply being an irritation, these knocking noises are an integral part of the piano sound, and it is interesting to note that synthesised piano sounds lacking these elements are considered unsatisfactory. Some manufacturers are even reputed to go to the trouble of 'tuning' their keywork.

Temperaments and tuning

One significant drawback with keyboard instruments is that the player has no control over the intonation of the instrument. Thus, to facilitate playing in any key, the piano is nominally tuned to a compromise scale called the 'equal-tempered' scale. However, as we will see, practical tuning deviates somewhat from the theory.

As well as establishing a basic pitch (usually to concert A, 440 Hz), 'tuning' is basically concerned with ensuring good intonation of intervals. Consonance of intervals is clearly subjective, but it does to some extent have a physical origin. Consider playing two notes with strictly harmonic partials (Ex. 6.1). If the notes are in unison, the harmonics of each note will align and blend perfectly. When the notes are an octave apart, with a frequency ratio of 2:1, the even-numbered harmonics of the lower tone will again coincide with the harmonics of the upper note and blend perfectly. The fifth involves a frequency ratio of 3:2 of the fundamentals, and less alignment is now found. A specific example may illustrate the point. Take two fundamentals a fifth apart at 200 Hz and 300 Hz. The first note has harmonics at 200, 400, 600, 800 Hz ..., and the second at 300, 600, 900, 1200 Hz ... There is alignment here between the third harmonic of the lower tone and the second harmonic of the upper tone (and other pairs if the sequences were continued), but others 'clash' somewhat to produce a less harmonious sound. As we move from fifth to fourth to third and so on, the amount of harmonic alignment deteriorates and the degree of consonance diminishes. In intervals such as the semitone, the harmonics are so badly aligned that pairs of harmonics start to *beat* with each other producing subjective 'roughness' in the sound.

Singers and violinists and other performers who have complete control of the pitch of their instruments tune intervals such as fifths and fourths to obtain harmonic alignment (or at least attempt to do so).[10] It turns out that it is undesirable to do the same in the piano, and this point is best illustrated by means of the 'circle of fifths'. On a piano keyboard, seven octaves is equivalent to twelve fifths. According to 'harmonic' theory, however, seven octaves is a frequency ratio of 2:1 to the power seven — that is, 128:1 — whilst twelve fifths is a frequency ratio of 3:2 to the power twelve, about 129.75:1. The musical consequence of this mathematical diversion is that the circle of fifths ends up being about a quarter of a semitone sharp. The outcome is that fifths must be deliberately tuned slightly flat if we demand enharmonic equivalence. The same arguments can be applied to fourths, thirds and so on, with the net result that the only solution is to divide the octave into twelve equal parts, that is, equal temperament, and accept that some notes will be a little sharp or flat from their 'optimum'. The frequency ratio of each semitone interval then becomes the twelfth root of two, or 1.05946:1, a ratio that seems completely at odds with the simple whole-number theory found in the harmonic series.

Tuning a piano to an equal-tempered scale is a skilled operation. It basically involves deliberate mis-tuning. The degree of mis-tuning is carefully controlled by counting beat rates of the 'warbling' which is produced by the almost coincident harmonics. Inevitably, the process is not so simple, or electronic tuning aids would by now have replaced the tuner.[11] In fact, tuning turns out to be even more complicated than this, primarily because of inharmonicity.

Inharmonicity was discussed earlier, and the point was made that higher partials are not strictly harmonic. Which pairs of partials, then, should the tuner use to count beat rates? There is, of course, no straight answer, except to say that the tuner uses his or her judgement. Experiments have shown that tuners *stretch* the two extremes of the scale, making octaves (and all the notes in between) rather wider than expected. Fundamental frequencies of notes at the two extremes of the piano range are about a quarter of a semitone sharp (in the high range) or flat (in the low range) of the equal-tempered ideal. The amount of stretching required for good intonation is less in a piano with long strings.

Pianos and performance

The concert grand piano is an imposing instrument in every respect, and there can be few pianists who secretly would not like to possess one. There are several acoustical advantages to building large instruments. The longer bass strings are capable of producing a bigger driving force at the bridge and they also exhibit less inharmonicity. The large soundboard radiates more efficiently, particularly at low frequencies, giving a fuller tone and offers a wider dynamic range. Concert grands are usually sited in a more desirable acoustical environment – the concert hall – and maintained by skilled technicians to operate at the peak of their performance. In contrast, most domestic pianos are built to a rather smaller scale, have to be content with their annual tuning and suffer from poor room acoustics.

Piano performance, however, is not so much about the instrument as the performer. The piano, of course, must function correctly. The piano action must be very carefully *regulated* so that the keys operate the hammers in a smooth progression from bass to treble with an even *key weight*. Regulation also controls the timings of key-strokes and free-flights of the hammers. There is usually a delay of about thirty milli-seconds between striking the key and the hammer hitting the string, but again, this must be evenly set throughout the range for critical performance. At the end of the day, the only real control that the player has over sound production on the piano is the final velocity of the hammer as it leaves the key mechanism. It seems incredible that players perform so musically with such a simple, single control parameter.

Oddly, musicianship is not so much about playing the right note at the right time, but rather to do with deliberate mis-timing of notes. Individual notes might be played out of tempo or at a different dynamic from their neighbours to bring out a melody or to signify the note's position within a phrase. Music psychologists have established various 'rules' which predict with surprising accuracy the timings and dynamics used during musical performance.[12]

To suggest that the only control a player has over the sound quality is the hammer velocity implies that piano 'touch' is unimportant. Undoubtedly, piano touch has more to do with the player maintaining the right frame of mind during a performance than anything physical. However, recent research looking at the resonant properties of the hammers themselves casts new light on this long-standing debate.[13] Hammer shanks are not rigid and have modes of vibration. These modes can be excited in different ways depending on the acceleration of the key mechanism. The shank vibrations can be used to increase or decrease the critical timings between key-stroke and hammer-strike to introduce subtle nuances in the performance. Different piano touch can also affect the knocking noises created during the starting transient. It looks as if piano touch is a real phenomenon.

Finally, we must reflect on the future of the piano. There have been no significant technological improvements in the piano for the last hundred years, though our concept of desirable piano tone has changed somewhat during that period to reflect changing musical tastes and as a result of new trends in the design of concert halls. The piano is, no doubt, here to stay for some time – the wealth of popular music written for this instrument will ensure that. But times are changing. In recent years the piano has lost much ground to electronic keyboards. For the more casual keyboard player, these instruments have many advantages, such as reduced capital cost, low maintenance and a variety of 'feature' sounds. Some of the more recent synthesisers use computer technology and sampled sounds to create very 'authentic' piano tones. None of these instruments, however, is capable of being played with the wide range of expression inherent in the traditional piano.

One new development is worthy of note, however. Yamaha's Disklavier is a conventional piano which incorporates velocity sensors and electro-mechanical actuators under each key. Electronics inside the instrument can detect the player's key-strokes and subsequently reproduce a performance with great fidelity. However, it can also be used more creatively. Computer control allows feedback during live performance to provide instant reproductions or inversions of note sequences with which the player can interact, and the instrument offers new opportunities in avant-garde compositions. Whilst this may seem a world apart from Cristofori's original conception, it shows that there is still active interest in the future of this wonderful instrument.

PART TWO

Repertory

7 Repertory and canon

DOROTHY DE VAL AND CYRIL EHRLICH

In 1972 a well-known pianist confided to an interviewer that his favourite composer was Orlando Gibbons (1583–1625). In a later interview he declared that he 'had doubts about Beethoven' and that he didn't think Chopin was 'a very good composer'; in fact the whole core of the piano-recital repertory was 'a colossal waste of time'.[1]

Such heretical statements could come only from Glenn Gould, whose groundbreaking performances of J. S. Bach (and indeed of Orlando Gibbons) demonstrate a profound understanding and love of contrapuntal writing. Gould dismissed nineteenth-century music purely on the grounds that Romantic composers treated the piano as a 'homophonic instrument'. Leaving aside the breathtaking inaccuracy of that statement, it presumably achieved its main purpose to challenge complacent notions about piano repertory and canon.[2]

Repertory

What are these notions? Ask any pianist about his or her 'repertoire' and out will come a list of works by composers from J. S. Bach to Bartók – that is, if your pianist is at all interested in his or her own century; many will not venture much beyond Brahms. Beethoven will perhaps be predominant, then Mozart and Schubert, some Haydn, Chopin, Schumann, Brahms, Liszt and possibly some Mendelssohn. Choice of repertory is in part influenced by examination requirements, from elementary to diploma level; it is what is taught in our conservatories, whose syllabuses reflect and reinforce prevailing custom. On the other hand, the diversity of the recording industry, particularly since the arrival of CDs, means that we now have more choice of what to listen to than ever before. All works by famous composers and many by obscure ones are available, many of them rare on concert programmes and examination syllabuses. Most concert repertory reflects a lowest common denominator of prevailing taste; programmes of familiar music occasionally spiked with something a bit *recherché*. At the core of repertory is 'what is played'.

This core is drawn largely from the nineteenth century, when the construction of pianos was developing and there was a burgeoning

market for the instrument and its music. Yet what *is* played differs substantially from what *was* played. The nineteenth-century *kleinmeister* had
to fulfil the public demand for easy 'familiar' music to be played at home.
Not surprisingly most of this was ephemeral, but some works from this
time remained popular throughout the century. Such works had to be
both effective and reasonably easy to play; examples include the minuet
from Beethoven's Sonatina Op. 49 No. 2, Felix Mendelssohn's (1809–47)
Lieder ohne Worte ('Songs without words') Op. 62 No. 6 ('Spring song'),
simplified versions of Liszt's Hungarian Rhapsody No. 2 and Grieg's 'To
spring'. This sort of repertory was part of the 'piano culture' which had
developed by the second half of the nineteenth century, when most
middle-class families owned a piano and people learned to play for their
own domestic entertainment. A wider, more sophisticated and difficult
repertory was played by concert performers, who in turn encouraged
their pupils to play it as well; some important figures taught at conservatories and privately, notably Moscheles and Mendelssohn at Leipzig,
Kalkbrenner at Paris, Leschetizky at St Petersburg and later Vienna, and
Clara Schumann at Frankfurt. Famous pianists such as Chopin, Liszt and
Paderewski had a number of private pupils. While some of the repertory
played by these performers is still programmed today – notably the
Beethoven sonatas – much of it is no longer known; for example, who
now marvels over the difficulties of Joseph Wölfl's 'Ne plus ultra' Sonata,
once a favourite of the concert pianist Arabella Goddard?

Core repertory

Out of the repertory extending from the early sonatas of Beethoven and
his contemporaries to the early twentieth century, 'what has stayed' can be
seen as a repertorial core. 'Canonic', exemplary status may overlap but it is
different and will be considered below. Some pieces remained popular for
a time but did not last out the century: Mendelssohn's staple *Lieder ohne
Worte* co-existed for a time with the piano works of Weber, but the latter
did not last much past mid century, except for *Aufforderung zum Tanze*
('Invitation to the dance') Op. 65. Perennial favourites throughout the
'long nineteenth century' included a few of Chopin's waltzes and polonaises and the funeral march from his Sonata Op. 35, the third of Liszt's
Liebestraum pieces, either in its original form or in simplified versions.
Towards the end of the century there was a constant flow of entertaining
ephemera such as Paderewski's famous Minuet in G, Rubinstein's Melody
in F, Grieg's 'To spring' and Christian Sinding's (1856–1941) 'Rustle of
spring', which became regular items in anthologies and remained popular

into the twentieth century, or at least until the 'piano culture' went into decline.

The nineteenth-century canon

Even in the early nineteenth century, before the deluge of ephemeral repertory, there was a core of established keyboard works, many of them not originally conceived for the piano, which were considered in some sense canonic or exemplary. For example, J. S. Bach's *Das wohltemperirte Clavier* ('Well-tempered clavier') was known through manuscript copies until its publication by Imbault, Simrock and others around 1800; an analytical edition of the first book appeared in London in 1810. Thereafter various editions appeared in all the major cities of Europe. Selected sonatas of Domenico Scarlatti had been published in London as early as 1739, chiefly through the efforts of the composer Thomas Roseingrave (1688–1766). Between that date and 1880 the 'lessons' appeared in England in several editions, most notably that of Clementi, who published sonatas 'selected from an elegant collection of manuscripts in his possession' in *c.*1791. Scarlatti's music was also popular in Vienna and in 1839 Czerny published an edition of 200 sonatas.

Among works regarded as canonic, much Beethoven and some Haydn and Mozart soon became established, though only a few works were frequently played. Moreover there was a great deal of functional diversity: Beethoven's Op. 49 sonatinas and the 'Diabelli' Variations were both regarded as exemplary, but for different reasons. The demand for easy pieces for young pianists was great. Within this repertory certain works, such as the Beethoven sonatinas, Mozart's 'Sonata facile' K545 and Clementi's famous Op. 36 set, stood out as exemplary in both musical and pedagogical terms alongside more difficult works, composed with a different purpose.

Works of Beethoven and his contemporaries

Beethoven is unusual in that a very high proportion of his works entered the repertory almost from their date of composition, and remained firmly entrenched throughout the entire century. The piano sonatas had canonic status and were staple items of both concert hall and drawing-room, though some were more popular than others: Moscheles's performance of Op. 106 (the 'Hammerklavier') in London, 1839, woke up critics to the difficulty and sublimity of a work which continued to be rarely performed. Other composers became known more for specific works, either because of their popularity in the concert hall or because of their accessibility to amateurs. Impromptus from Schubert's Op. 90 (D899) and selected *Moments musicaux* Op. 94 (D780) joined Mendelssohn's *Lieder ohne Worte* as drawing-room favourites. But Schubert's sonatas remained outside the canon throughout the century, although a number of them were played at the Monday Popular Concerts in London between 1862 and 1890, with the B♭ Sonata (D960) performed seven times between 1863 and 1882. In the same series, Mendelssohn was well represented, with the most popular works being the *Rondo capriccioso* Op. 14, the prelude and fugue in E minor from Op. 35 and the *Variations sérieuses* Op. 54. Writing in 1880, the pianist–conductor Hans von Bülow wrote of the *Rondo capriccioso* as a 'beloved, ubiquitous possession of the educated dilettante', a favourite of piano teachers, and an enduring, well-crafted piece which had held its place in the repertory despite Mendelssohn's fluctuating popularity during the nineteenth century.[3]

More than any other instrument, the piano catered for both amateur and professional, as much an instrument for the drawing room as for the concert hall. From its earliest days the square piano or *Tafelklavier* became the favourite instrument of musical amateurs, and composers such as J. C. Bach wrote copiously for it. Both Haydn and Mozart wrote piano sonatas for their pupils; in London, where the market was more developed than in Vienna, composers such as Clementi and Dussek wrote a prodigious amount for amateur pianists. Many of their works were 'accompanied sonatas', works primarily for the piano with an easy accompaniment for violin or flute. This genre faded early in the nineteenth century, to be supplanted by the more popular variations and capriccios.

In addition to writing easy music for amateurs to play, Clementi and his younger contemporary Johann Baptist Cramer also wrote studies for the improvement of technique. Cramer's *Studio* (in two parts, published in 1804 and 1810 respectively) and Clementi's *Gradus ad Parnassum* (in three parts, published in 1817, 1819 and 1826 respectively) became models which Chopin turned into a concert genre. They also inspired a host of similar sets of studies by lesser composers such as Steibelt, Moscheles and Stephen Heller (1813–88), which remained popular throughout the century.[4] From early on in the piano's history amateurs were of course keen to play piano arrangements of all sorts of music they heard publicly performed; the composer Joseph Mazzinghi (1765–1844) produced arrangements of various Handel oratorios in the early nineteenth century, and Clementi's piano–vocal score of Joseph Haydn's (1732–1809) *The creation* was published in 1800. Even pieces originally written for the piano were simplified for amateurs, the most famous example being Schubert's Impromptu in G♭ (Op. 90 No. 3, D899) transposed to G major for flat-phobic pianists, and its time signature converted to four crotchets per bar, earning it the sobriquet 'La tranquillité' (Exx. 7.1a and 7.1b).[5] The art of arranging reached heights beyond the grasp of most amateurs with Liszt's many transcriptions of vocal and orchestral repertory, including Schubert songs, Beethoven symphonies and Berlioz's *Symphonie fantastique*. The operatic medleys of the 1830s and 1840s provided opportunities for bravura display by Liszt, his rival Thalberg and other virtuoso contemporaries.

Concert music

The seeds of the nineteenth-century repertory were already sown by 1820, but if Beethoven's status was never in doubt, the reputations of some contemporaries were more vulnerable. Programmes at the Leipzig Gewandhaus in the first half of the century included concertos by Dussek, Kalkbrenner, Moscheles and Hummel which, with the exception of Hummel's Concerto in B minor and Moscheles's in G minor, disappeared from programmes after the mid 1830s.[6] The Philharmonic programmes reveal a similar pattern: a Moscheles concerto was last played in 1842, and one by Hummel in 1862.[7] The popularity of Moscheles's works may have been due in part to his own virtuoso performances of them. Unlike Beethoven, Moscheles and Hummel continued to play their own works, a convention that persisted throughout the period.

Music publishing

The amateur pianist soon had a fairly wide choice of music to play at home. An 1820 catalogue of the Parisian publisher Sieber is fairly typical: players were offered sonatas of Beethoven up to 'op. 42' (*sic*); sonatas by Clementi, Cramer, Dussek, Hummel, Kalkbrenner, Koželuch and Steibelt jostled for places next to works by Haydn and Mozart. 'Musique facile', mostly by London composers, plus a host of variations by a variety of composers, were offered to tempt the less proficient player.

By 1830 piano repertory had taken a more virtuoso turn. The London publisher Goulding and d'Almaine now offered music with drawing-room dazzle by popular pianists of the day such as Herz, Hünten, Kalkbrenner and the young Carl Czerny (Fig. 7.1). A more comprehensive catalogue published by the Viennese publisher Artaria in 1837 contrasts

Ex. 7.1a Schubert, Impromptu Op. 90 No. 3 (Bärenreiter, 1984).

with Goulding's in its mixture of old and new: there is a small selection of sonatas by Haydn and Mozart, all of Beethoven's sonatas and a fair number by Clementi, Cramer and Dussek. Mozart's variations take priority over his sonatas, perhaps suggesting that the sonata was considered obsolete and had been supplanted by lighter genres. The overall impression is of a catalogue that attempts to consolidate past repertory alongside the new pieces by Herz, Kalkbrenner and Moscheles. Separate sections offered popular dance music and operatic overtures arranged for piano. A contemporary catalogue of works published by Haslinger, also of Vienna, offers a similar array, but includes some works of Schubert (again the Op. 90 Impromptus) and the virtuosos Thalberg and Pixis as well. There is but a small selection of Mozart's sonatas, and only the better-known (and by this time quasi-canonic) works by Clementi (the Op. 36 Sonatinas, the *Gradus*), Dussek (sonatas 'Le retour' and 'L'invocation') and Cramer's studies. Beethoven dominates with the complete sonatas, the Op. 33 Bagatelles and 'Andante favori' (WoO 57), as well as with concertos and

Ex. 7.1b Schubert, Impromptu Op. 90 No. 3 (Schloesser, 1890).

arrangements of the symphonies. The catalogue reflects the excitement of
the 1830s, with established older favourites and new virtuoso pieces.

A trawl through publishers' catalogues up to 1850 reveals similar patterns. There is always a selection of popular dance music for amateurs to
play, usually by composers now forgotten. D'Almaine & Co.'s 1840 catalogue was largely devoted to rondos by Herz and Kiallmark, each given a
poetic title. The London publisher Wessel continued the convention of
giving salon music poetic titles, subjecting even Chopin to such titles as
'Le banquet infernal' (Scherzo Op. 20), 'La gracieuse' (Ballade Op. 38) and
'Les plaintives' (Nocturnes Op. 27).

Keyboard tutors

The profusion of keyboard tutors from the late eighteenth century
onwards provided a selection of music, though much of this was chosen

PUBLISHED BY

GOULDING AND D'ALMAINE, 20, SOHO SQUARE.

	s	d
Adams' Mélange, from Auber's 'Le Philtre,' or the Village Coquette	3	0
Abel's Rondo on a Theme from 'La Gazza Ladra'	3	0
——— Brilliant Rondo, Op. 2	3	0
Burrowes' Fantasia, with Airs from 'Mosè in Egitto'	3	0
——— Ditto 'La Gazza Ladra'	3	0
——— Ditto 'La Donna del Lago'	3	0
——— Select Airs from Spohr's 'Azor and Zemira,' 2 books, each	4	0
——— Ditto from Rossini's 'Guillaume Tell,' 4 books, each	4	0
——— Overture to ditto Fl. Accomp.	3	6
——— Select Airs from Auber's 'Masaniello,' 4 books, each	4	0
——— Overture to ditto ditto Fl. Accomp.	3	6
——— Variations on the Air Tyrolien from 'Guillaume Tell'	2	6
——— Les Bijoux, Three Waltzes	2	6
Chaulieu's Fantasia on 'Ma Nacelle'	4	0
——— Ditto on Madame Stockhausen's Airs	4	0
——— Ditto on Airs in 'Les Deux Nuits'	3	0
——— Variations on a Chorus in ditto	3	6
——— Ditto on a March in 'Guillaume Tell'	3	0
——— Ditto on Bishop's Tyrolien Quintett	3	0
——— Rondo Brilliant, on a Ballad from 'Zampa'	3	6
——— Brilliant Variations, on a Barcarolle from ditto	3	6
——— Le Ballet, a Divertimento	3	0
——— Souvenir du Grand Prix, ou le Voyage à Dieppe	3	0
——— Rondo, on an Air from 'Le Philtre,' or the Love Charm	4	0
——— Divertimento from 'L'Orgie'	3	0
Czerny's Variations on the Grenadier's March	4	0
——— Fantasia on Themes from Mozart, Haydn, &c.	4	0
——— Three Familiar Rondos, Opera 158, Book I	3	6

These Rondos have been written at the express desire of the Publishers, to follow the Instruction Book. Book 2 is for 4 hands.

	s	d
——— Rondeau de Chasse Op. 217	3	0
——— Variations Brillantes on a 'Pas de trois' Op. 219	3	0
——— Variations on the Tyrolien in 'Guillaume Tell,' Op. 220	3	0
Favre, Marseillois Hymn	2	6
——— La Parisienne	1	6
Harris (G. F.) Mélange on Airs from 'Guillaume Tell'	2	6
Herz's Variations on an Air by T. Labarre	4	0
——— Le Fête Pastorale, Grand Fantasia	5	0
——— Polonaise Brillante	4	0
——— Brilliant Variations on a Chorus from 'Euryanthe'	5	0
——— Trois Rondeaux Caracteristiques each	3	0
No. 1. A la Francaise		
2. A l'Anglaise		
3. A l'Allemande		
——— Variations de Concert on the March from 'Guillaume Tell'	5	0
——— Original Theme with Variations	5	0
——— Grand Trio for Pianoforte, Violin, and Violoncello	10	6
——— Ditto as a Solo for the Pianoforte	4	0
——— Les Elégantes 1st set of Contredanses Variées	5	0
——— Les Coquettes 2nd set	5	0
——— La Mode 3rd set	4	0
——— Brilliant Variations from 'La Neige'	5	0
——— Ditto on 'Le petit Tambour'	4	0
——— Ditto on 'Non piu mesta'	4	0
——— Ditto on a Swiss Air	4	0
——— Ditto on 'Nel Selenzio'	3	6
——— Ditto on an Air from 'La Violette'	4	0
——— Ditto on 'La Parisienne'	4	0
——— First Divertimento	3	0
——— Second ditto	2	6
——— Capriccio	3	0
——— Brilliant Rondo, dedicated to Moscheles	5	0
——— Variations and Rondo on a favorite Air	4	0
——— Rondoletto	3	6
——— Rondo on the Barcarolle from 'Marie'	3	0
——— Variations on a Tyrolese Air	3	0
——— Ditto German Air	3	0
——— Ditto Venetian Air	3	0
——— Ditto 'Aurora che sorgerai'	4	0
——— Ditto Saxon Air	3	0
——— Ditto Tyrolese Air	3	6
——— Allegro and easy Variations	2	6
——— Rondo Capriccio on the Barcarolle from 'Masaniello'	3	6
——— Fantasia on a Trio, by Carafa "Notre Dame du Mont Carmel"	5	0
——— Rondo Cossacca	3	6
——— Waltz Rondino	2	0
——— Rondo on Boieldieu's Carillon from 'Les Deux Nuits'	3	0
——— Polacca introducing 'Dormez donc, mes chères amours'	3	0
——— Three Notturnos, La Dolcezza, La Semplicita, and La Melanchonia	4	0
——— Trois Airs de Ballet, from 'Mosè in Egitto' each	3	0
——— Ditto from 'Masaniello' each	3	0
——— Six Airs de Ballet, from 'Guillaume Tell' each	3	0
No. 1. La Valse Suisse No. 4. La Valse Hongroise		
2. La Contredanse 5. Le Pas d'Archers		
3. La Tyrolienne 6. La Polonoise		
——— Russian Airs, Pianoforte and Flute	5	0
——— Exercises and Studies fingered; being a Series of admirable Lessons to form the hand of the Pupil	4	0
——— Twenty-four Grand Studies	10	6
Holder's Swiss Toy Girl	3	0
Hummel's (J. N.) Capriccio	3	0
——— La Bella Capricciosa	3	6
Hunten's Rondoletto	3	0
——— Deux Airs Tyroliens, avec Variations each	3	0
——— Quatre Rondeaux	3	0
——— Brilliant Fantasia Op. 48	5	0
——— Rondeau Brillante No. 1	3	0
——— Rondeau Militaire No. 2	3	0
Kalkbrenner's Variations, 'Will you come to the Bower'	3	0
——— Ditto, 'Rule Britannia'	3	0
——— Ditto, 'Tu vedrai la Sventurata'	3	0
——— Fantasia, 'Les Charmes de Berlin'	3	0
——— Capriccio, with 'Bid me Discourse'	2	6
——— 'La Mélancholie et la Gaité,' Romance et Rondeau Brillante	3	0
——— Rondino Brillante, Opera 101	4	0

	s	d
Karr's Fantasia on Auber's 'Le Philtre,' or 'Love Charm'	3	0
Kiallmark's La Fleurette, Air Allemand Rondino	2	6
——— Dance of the Witches Rondo	3	0
——— Air Marziale Rondo	3	0
——— Adèle,—Petite Divertissement	3	0
——— Lisette—Petite Recréation	3	0
——— Mélange Ecossais	3	0
——— Variations on 'Weber's last Waltz'	3	0
——— Ditto on 'Strike for Tyrol and Liberty'	3	0
——— Ditto on 'Isle of Beauty'	3	0
——— Ditto on 'O merry row the bonnie bark'	3	0
——— Les petits Delassements, Nos. 1 to 6 each	3	0
——— Divertimento, with 'Red Cross Knight'	3	0
——— Ditto from 'Masaniello' each	3	0
Kuhlau's Trois Airs Variés	3	0
——— Trois Rondeaux, sur des motifs favoris des Noces de Figaro de Mozart	2	6
No. 1. Cavatine du Pirate		
2. Mélodie Autrichienne		
3. Theme de J. N. Hummel		
Latour's Auber's Overture, 'Le Philtre,' or 'The Love Charm' Flute Ac.	3	6
——— Select Airs from ditto	3	0
Macdonald's Snuff-box Waltzes Sets 1 to 4, each	1	0
Manning's L'Abeille, with Popular Airs Nos. 1 to 6, each	2	6
——— Les Fleurs du Jardin, ditto Nos. 1 to 6, each	2	0
Mazzinghi's Reminiscences of various Authors Nos. 1 to 3, each	2	6
——— The Rose shall cease to blow	2	6
——— Airs in 'Cinderella,' (Flute ad lib.) 6 books, each	4	0
——— Rondo on 'Non piu mesta'	2	0
Merriott's (J.) 'Oh, no, we never mention her,' Variations	2	6
——— Second Band March	2	0
——— 'She never blamed him,' Variations	2	6
——— 'Jock o'Hazledean,' ditto	2	6
Meves' 'Ah, tu non sai'	2	6
——— 'Elena! Oh, tu ch'io'	2	6
Moscheles' Three Brilliant Rondos, Opera 67 each	3	0
——— Airs in Beethoven's Fidelio 2 books, each	5	0
Moralt's Divertimento, 'The Dahlia'	3	0
Rawlings' Fantasia from Spohr's 'Azor and Zemira'	3	0
——— Patriotic Divertimento, with Spanish Airs	2	6
——— King William IV. March	2	0
——— Rondo on 'The Tartar Drum'	2	6
——— Ditto 'They mourn me dead'	2	0
——— Ditto 'Lilla's a Lady'	2	6
——— Variations on 'It is not on the Battle Field'	3	0
——— Ditto 'Oh, no, we never mention her'	3	0
——— Divertimento,—Windsor Forest, (Flute ad lib.)	3	0
——— Il Liuto—Divertimento, with 'O twine a wreath'	3	0
——— L'Elégante à la Sontag	4	0
Ries's Rondo on a Danish Air	3	0
——— Ditto German Air	3	0
——— Bacchanale and Rondo	5	0
——— Rondo, 'As it fell upon a day'	3	0
Valentine's 'Flowers of Harmony,' Nos. 1 to 6, each	2	6
——— 'Musical Mirror' ditto	2	6
——— 'Sacred Melodies' ditto	2	6
——— Aria alla Scozzese	2	0
——— Aria alla Francese	2	0
——— Aria all' Espagnol	1	6
——— Tyrolienne from 'William Tell'	1	0
——— Divertimento, with 'The King, God bless him'	2	6
——— 'Giovinetto Cavalier,' Variations	3	6
——— 'Mynheer Vandunck,' ditto	2	6
——— 'Chough and Crow,' ditto	2	6
——— 'My lodging is on the cold Ground,' ditto	2	6

DUETS FOR THE PIANO-FORTE.

	s	d
Bruguìre—Gems of Handel, Nos. 1 to 6	3	0
Burrowes' Airs in Rossini's 'Il Barbiere di Siviglia,' 4 books each	4	0
——— Ditto 'Otello' 3 books	4	0
——— Ditto 'Guillaume Tell' 4 books	5	0
——— Ditto Auber's 'Masaniello' 4 books	4	6
——— Ditto Spohr's 'Azor and Zemira' 2 books	4	0
——— Overture 'Guillaume Tell'	4	0
Czerney's Familiar Rondos, Opera 158, book 2	4	0
Favre, Marseillois Hymn	2	6
——— La Parisienne	2	0
Herz's Variations on 'Au clair de la lune'	4	0
——— 'Les Elégantes,' 1st Set Quadrilles	5	0
——— 'Les Coquettes,' 2nd ditto	5	0
——— 'La Mode,' 3rd ditto	5	0
——— Gallopade Variée	2	6
——— Brilliant Variations on a March in Rossini's 'Guillaume Tell'	5	0
Hunten's Variations Militaires on 'Marseillois Hymn'	5	0
——— Polacca on 'Dormez donc, &c.' by Henri Herz	5	0
——— Variations on a March from 'Guillaume Tell'	5	0
——— Ditto on an Air from 'Les Deux Nuits'	4	0
Kuhlau's Air Autrichien	4	0
——— Air Militaire Anglais	4	0
——— Galopade Hongraise	4	0
Mazzinghi's 'Heavens are telling,' Creation	4	0
——— Airs in 'Cinderella' 5 books, each	5	0
——— Overture, 'Cinderella'	4	6
——— Ditto 'Sargino'	4	6
——— Arrangement of 'Non piu mesta'	4	0
Ries's Variations on a March in 'Aline'	4	0
——— Ditto Rhinish Carnival Air	3	6
Saffery's 'When thy bosom heaves the sigh'	2	6
Syke's (C. T.) Admired Serenade, 'Isabel'	3	0
——— Bishop's Popular Airs, 'Home,' and 'Should he upbraid'	3	0
——— Pas seul, from 'Love in a Tub'	3	0
——— Ditto, 'Caractacus'	2	0
——— 'Bid me discourse'	3	0
——— 'As it fell upon a Day'	3	0
——— Overture to 'Tancredi'	3	0

PIANO-FORTES FOR SALE OR HIRE.

Instruments Tuned and Repaired

Figure 7.1 Extract from a catalogue by Goulding and D'Almaine, London, c.1830.

primarily for didactic purposes and does not *per se* represent a repertory, still less a canon. Clementi's selection of 'lessons' for his *Introduction to the art of playing on the pianoforte* (1801) by such diverse composers as Bach, Handel, Scarlatti, Couperin and Rameau, in addition to his contemporaries Haydn, Pleyel and Beethoven, reflects his eclecticism as a collector more than any wish to create a canon. It is above all, in Plantinga's words, 'a splendid anthology of easy keyboard music'.[8] Another early influential tutor which included an anthology of pieces was Louis Adam's *Méthode de piano du Conservatoire* (officially adopted by the Paris Conservatoire in 1804, published in 1805) which included a more substantial anthology, with fugues by Bach and Handel, a Scarlatti sonata (Kp113), some pieces by C. P. E. Bach (from the *Probestücke* appended to his treatise on keyboard playing), the first movement of Mozart's Sonata in A minor K310, the outer movements of the Sonata in A K331 (the rondo 'alla Turca' was evidently already a favourite), and the French-overture style *Fragment einer Suite*, K399. There is some virtuoso Clementi, with the toccata from Op. 11, and two movements from the Sonata Op. 12 No. 2. A later edition of the treatise, co-authored by Ludwig Wenzel Lachnith, included Haydn's Sonata in D (HobXVI:51), the scherzo from Beethoven's Op. 2 No. 2, Mozart's K545 Sonata complete, plus various pieces by Koželuch, Steibelt, Dussek and Cramer. The inclusion of arrangements of symphonic works alongside piano pieces reflects the public's appetite for a wide repertory rather than for the canon. Though the collection was selective, the purpose was to educate and broaden rather than to prescribe.

It was left to the indefatigable Carl Czerny to consolidate repertorial gains with his *Verzeichnis der besten und brauchbarsten Werke allen bekannten Tonsetzer für das Pianoforte*, which was published as part 4 of his *Vollständige theoretische–praktische Pianoforteschule* (Vienna, 1838–9; pt 4, 1847). Although published somewhat belatedly as part of a tutor, its very title places it separately from the treatise; it is prescriptive rather than illustrative or didactic. In his list (there is no actual music) Czerny included Mozart's K310, K533/494, the C minor Fantasie and Sonata, K475 and K457, the A minor Rondo K511, the B minor Adagio K540, the Gigue in G, K574 and the 'Je suis Lindor' Variations K354. Several of Clementi's sonatas were listed, including the 'grand' sonatas of Opp. 34 and 40; Dussek and Cramer are well represented with sonatas and some shorter works. There is a selection of Beethoven's sonatas in addition to the variations Opp. 34 and 35, the Op. 33 Bagatelles and the Thirty-two Variations (WoO 80). Hummel's sonatas Opp. 13, 81 and 106 were deemed worthy of mention in addition to the Fantasie Op. 18 and the B minor Rondo Op. 109. Of the Paris virtuosos, Kalkbrenner, Herz and

Steibelt are represented especially by their studies; Moscheles's Op. 70 études receive commendation. There is a smattering of Louis Spohr, Pixis, Joseph Mayseder, Jan Václav Voříšek and George Onslow; Czerny parades his own prolific output without blush. Schubert's D major Sonata Op. 53 (D850) merits inclusion with the Op. 15 'Wanderer' Fantasy, the Impromptus Op. 142 (D935) and the *Moments musicaux*. Mendelssohn's *Lieder ohne Worte* are commended with the *Rondo capriccioso*, the Fantasy on 'The last rose of spring' Op. 15, *Variations sérieuses*, the *Scherzo a capriccio* in F♯ minor, plus the Six Preludes and Fugues Op. 35. Chopin, Liszt and Robert and Clara Schumann are similarly well represented. Also included are Döhler, Henselt, Hiller, Ferdinand Heller, Dreyschock, Theodore Kullak, William Sterndale Bennett and Cipriani Potter.

Until this time it had not seemed necessary to consolidate repertory in this way. Czerny's criterion – to select the 'best and 'most useful' works – is perhaps not equivalent to choosing a canon; historically his selection goes no further back than Mozart's K310 (1778), but the title suggests an attempt to select worthwhile music out of a huge and growing repertory. Alongside works by 'great' composers, Czerny in effect provides a useful *catalogue raisonné* of *kleinmeister* whose works would be less vaunted by the end of the century. Clearly he could have no perspective on his contemporaries: composers such as August Eberhard Müller, Kalkbrenner and Herz were forgotten by the end of the century, though the studies of Steibelt, which are included here along with four sonatas, remained popular for some time.

Anthologies

Anthologies did not exist merely as adjuncts to tutors, but became an important entity in their own right. The criteria for compilation varied from author to author, but a look at a selection of them reveals certain principles at work. Early collections existed mainly to promote a publisher's list; an early example can be found in the inappropriately titled *Répertoire des clavecinistes*, published by Hans Georg Nägeli in seventeen volumes in Zurich between 1803 and 1811. (It is unlikely that anyone would have played this music on the 'clavecin', or harpsichord.) Like many publishers' collections of the time, this included popular repertory by London composers, notably Clementi, and works by Beethoven (Op. 31 Nos. 1 and 2), Václav Tomášek (1774–1850), Christoph Weyse (1774–1842) and Liste, but there is nothing by Mozart or Haydn. Later collections produced independently tended to have a historical perspective and were also more selective, separating a canon from general repertory.

Perhaps the most significant such collection was *Le trésor des pianistes*, compiled by Jacques Hippolyte Aristide Farrenc and his wife Louise (*née* Dumont), which was published in Paris between 1861 and 1872. In twenty-three volumes, this anthology had a historical slant, including works by Byrd, Bull, Gibbons, Merulo, Frescobaldi, Couperin and Rameau. The first eleven volumes deal with 'historical' repertory from William Byrd (1543–1623) to Johann Mattheson (1681–1764); volumes 12 and 13 are devoted to the sonatas of C. P. E. Bach, hardly a popular composer in the 1860s. Beethoven and Clementi are well represented, mostly with sonatas, while a volume is devoted to Hummel's variations. Even with the cutoff date of 1850, there is only one volume devoted to the works of Ries, Weber, Mendelssohn and Chopin, who is here represented by nine nocturnes. In his review of the early volumes, Fétis commented that the hitherto unknown works now made available to the public would become 'le répertoire permanent des pianistes'.[9]

Clearly *Le trésor* had serious aspirations; in the same volume of the *Revue et gazette musicale* in which Fétis's review appears there is a publisher's advertisement for 'Répertoire de musique moderne pour le piano'. Here is an amateur's goldmine, with pieces chosen for their 'playability' and instant effect: Chopin's *Grande valse brilliante* Op. 34 No. 1, Liszt's *Mazeppa*, Mendelssohn's 'Song without words' 'la fileuse' (Op. 67 No. 4, 'The Bees' Wedding') plus a plethora of polkas, études, marches, caprices, serenades and mazurkas by a host of nonentities. This was repertory writ large, if loose and evanescent: the works of Döhler, Kalkbrenner, Rosenhain, Thalberg and most of the others would not last much beyond their publication date but would enjoy instant popularity. Conversely the music of *Le trésor* may not have delighted contemporary Parisian society but it would stand the test of time. Pianists themselves, the Farrencs had consciously tried to establish a historical canon of keyboard works (without differentiating between harpsichord and piano) even when it meant unearthing old and unfamiliar works, and aimed their anthology at the serious pianist–scholar.

The French anthology was complemented by the German *Bibliothek älterer und neuerer Klaviermusik*, compiled by Franz Kroll and published in Berlin between 1869 and 1882. In fifty parts – each contains just one work – the anthology emphasised the early nineteenth-century repertory of Beethoven, Schubert and Weber. In contrast to Czerny's publication, none of the virtuoso pianists is included. Unlike *Le trésor*, there is no harpsichord repertory except pieces by Bach and Handel. Bach is represented by the partitas in B♭ and C minor, the C minor toccata, the two-part inventions, two of the English suites; Handel by four suites and the ever-popular 'Harmonious Blacksmith' variations. There is a good selection of

Mozart sonatas and other pieces, but unlike *Le trésor* nothing by Haydn; Beethoven is well represented with sonatas and two sets of variations (Op. 34 and the 32 Variations). There is a healthy offering of five Schubert sonatas, plus the *Moments musicaux*, the Op. 90 Impromptus (with No. 3 transposed) and the 'Wanderer' Fantasy; Weber is particularly well represented with four sonatas plus the salon favourites *Rondo brillante* Op. 62, *Invitation to the dance*, *Polacca brillante* Op. 72, *Grande polonaise* Op. 21 and the *Konzertstück* Op. 79.

Kroll's *Bibliothek* was an attempt to consolidate repertory from *c.*1730 to 1830, thus taking in well-known keyboard music by Bach and Handel, and established piano repertory. Its narrow chronological span precluded the unashamedly historical approach favoured by the Farrencs, but its very selectivity came close to the creation of a canon of eighteenth- and early nineteenth-century works.

Complete works

Some composers achieved canonic status of a sort when their 'complete works' were published. The complete piano sonatas of Mozart were not published until 1815 by Peters in Leipzig; there was then a hiatus until 1836, when Cipriani Potter began his edition of the complete keyboard works and chamber works with keyboard. Subsequent editions of the sonatas followed in 1862 (London, edited by Charles Hallé) and 1869 (Offenbach/Main, edited by Ernst Pauer). The firm of Breitkopf und Härtel of Leipzig began an edition of all Mozart's works in 1877, at a time when the music of Beethoven, Mendelssohn, Chopin, Schumann and Brahms was mounting in popularity. Earlier in the century (1803–19) they had published thirteen volumes of the works of Clementi; it is, however, incomplete. They also published Dussek's works at about the same time (1813–17). Collecting selections of Beethoven's piano works was attractive to publishers from early on, with Tobias Haslinger of Vienna publishing thirty of the sonatas shortly after the composer's death. The complete piano works, however, were not collected together until mid century, first by the English composer William Sterndale Bennett (1850–66), then by the pianist and pedagogue E. H. Lindsay Sloper (1851–3), Carl Czerny (1852–4) and Charles Hallé (1855–70).[10] The French edition, published by Brandus et Cie, appeared *c.*1860. Liszt began an edition of the complete works in twenty-five volumes in 1857 for Holle of Wolfenbüttel, and Breitkopf und Härtel began publishing the *Gesamtausgabe* in 1862; Holle began on Schubert in about 1867. Breitkopf und Härtel were undoubtedly the leading publishers of 'complete works', with Mendelssohn (1874–7), Chopin (1878–1902), Schumann (1880–93), Schubert (1884–97), Haydn (1907, abandoned after eleven volumes) and Brahms (1926). Publication of the complete works of J. S. Bach began in 1851, and those of Handel in 1858.

Historical recitals

The publication of anthologies coincided with the rise of the 'historical recital' in the 1860s, though Moscheles had pioneered the idea three decades earlier with his musical 'matinées' and 'soirées', in which he played works of J. S. Bach, Handel and Scarlatti, often on the harpsichord.[11] The solo piano recital as we know it today was unfamiliar to nineteenth-century audiences; concerts were by and large miscellaneous affairs lasting several hours, consisting of vocal, chamber and orchestral music. Even Moscheles shared his programmes with others, mainly singers. The pianists might have a solo to play, but would be expected to perform in chamber ensembles as well. It is generally accepted that Liszt gave the first public solo piano 'recital' – the very word was new in this context – in 1840, but the usual practice was for several artists to share the platform.[12] In fact it is possible that the so-called historical recital came about as a means of injecting a variety of styles into a programme made up entirely of piano music, far too monotonous for nineteenth-century audiences.

In 1863 the pianist and historian Ernst Pauer gave six historical performances in London, including music from the early seventeenth century to his own time. Each programme introduced some early keyboard pieces by composers such as Nicola Porpora (1686–1768) and Mattheson. Like the Farrencs, Pauer also included works by Scarlatti, Handel, J. S. Bach and various sons, and the *clavecinistes* François Couperin (1668–1733) and Jean-Philippe Rameau (1683–1764) but played them on the piano. (Pauer began experimenting with harpsichords in the 1870s.) Clementi and some of his contemporaries were also included. The virtuoso pianists of the 1830s were represented alongside Chopin and Schumann, from whose *Kreisleriana* selected numbers appeared in the fourth programme. It is a measure of Pauer's eclectic pianism that he was as at ease with a late Beethoven sonata as with a gondola song by Henselt. Significantly one entire programme was devoted to drawing-room music, an indication at least of current prevalence. The wide span of Pauer's programmes was probably didactic in intent, and the programmes were eventually published with Pauer's comments. He considered, for example, that Stephen Heller was 'healthier and fresher in expression than Chopin'.[13]

The pianist and composer Anton Rubinstein gave a series of seven historical recitals in 1885–6 in various cities. Rubinstein's chronological programmes began with harpsichord music by the English virginalists and the French *clavecinistes*, moving on through J. S. Bach, Handel, C. P. E. Bach, Haydn (F minor Variations) and Mozart (C minor Fantasy K475, the Gigue in G K574 and the rondo 'alla Turca' from the Sonata K331). The second programme was devoted entirely to Beethoven sonatas, including Opp. 101, 109 and 111. The third and fourth programmes featured Schubert (the 'Wanderer' Fantasy plus a selection of *Moments musicaux* and impromptus) and Mendelssohn (*Variations sérieuses*, two capriccios and various *Songs without words*). Schumann was well represented with major works such as *Kreisleriana*, *Carnaval* and the *Etudes symphoniques*. The selection of Liszt's works included the *Consolations* (in E and D♭), two Hungarian rhapsodies, *Au bord d'une source*, transcriptions of Schubert songs and operatic arrangements. The selections from the works of Henselt and Thalberg were in a similar vein. In contrast to Pauer's didactic programmes, Rubinstein's appear to have a distinctly 'canonic' purpose.

Drawing-room music

Pauer's programme devoted specifically to drawing-room music reflects the importance of this genre in the second half of the century. A Peters catalogue of 1900 included a 'salon album' in seventeen volumes, full of works by composers unknown today. As an indication of how wide the repertory had become, it sits comfortably between the entries for Rubinstein and Scarlatti. Peters also advertised a 'pianoforte album', the prototype of similar publications today, with familiar pieces playable by the amateur. A Chopin waltz and some short character pieces by Mendelssohn and Schumann feature alongside works by Kalkbrenner, Field and Dussek; Weber's hardy perennial *Invitation to the dance* finds a place with a *Moment musical* of Schubert. The main list in this same catalogue illustrated contemporary attitudes to repertory and canon. A 'gavotte album' is devoted to the earlier generations with its inclusion of composers such as Corelli, Rameau, Bach, Handel, Gluck and Leclair among others. There were various editions of Bach's inventions, suites and the *Well-tempered clavier*. Haydn and Clementi are well represented, and the complete piano works of Beethoven and Chopin are offered as a matter of course. Even the discredited virtuosos Hünten and Kalkbrenner merit collections of *beliebte* (favourite) or *berühmte* (famous) compositions, as do Chopin, Haydn, Mendelssohn and Mozart. The most popular composer appears to be Grieg, who is extensively published and also appears in a list of *neue Meister* with Jensen, Raff, Rubinstein, Tchaikovsky, Moszkowski, Sinding and Liszt. Brahms is represented only by some of his vocal music and the Hungarian Dances.

In England, a similar compilation of popular music appeared in C. V. Wilkinson's *Well-known piano solos: how to play them with understanding, expression and effect* (1909). Paderewski, the best-known pianist of the day, finds prominent place with various minuets (including the inescapable one in G) and a 'mélodie'. Wilkinson's collection in fact almost amounts to a 'top of the pops' of current amateur piano pieces. There is a nod to earlier repertory by Bach, Handel and Scarlatti, while the favoured Beethoven sonatas are Op. 26, Op. 27 No. 2 ('Moonlight') and Op. 31 No. 3 ('La chasse'). Many of the selections are contemporary: composers such as Sinding, Grieg and Chaminade are well represented. Older pieces, well established in the repertory by this time, are also here: chief among them Mendelssohn's 'Spring song' and character pieces by Schubert, Schumann and Chopin.

E. H. Lindsay Sloper offered a similar collection to Wilkinson's, blending familiar repertory with new pieces in his *Repertory of select pianoforte works*, published posthumously in 1892. The selection is fairly catholic, ranging from a Handel suite to short pieces by Louis Moreau Gottschalk (1829–69), with deference to Haydn and Mozart in between. Perhaps because of the ubiquity of his works, Beethoven is here only by virtue of 'Für Elise', but there is a better representation of later composers such as Schubert (Scherzo in B♭ D593), Chopin (a waltz, the Bolero), Schumann (one of the *Nachtstücke* Op. 23) and some Liszt. Unlike Wilkinson's decidedly popular selection, Sloper's veered towards the quirky and unusual; after all, the *Grand galop chromatique* is not Liszt's best-known work. It is important to remember, though, that as with other compilations of this kind, choice of pieces might also have been influenced by copyright. Sloper's anthology must have had only parochial appeal as even at this late date it retained the outmoded 'English' fingering (where the thumb is indicated by a cross and the first finger by '1') throughout. Nevertheless as a companion to other similar collections it shows an attempt to combine some prevailing popular repertory with lesser-known pieces to whet the appetite of the keen amateur.

Concert series reflected a similar shuffling of works between repertory and canon. In London the highly successful Monday Popular Concerts (1859–98), held in St James's Hall, featured the piano in solo and chamber works. In addition to the expected Beethoven sonatas (Op. 10 No. 3, Op. 26, Op. 27 No. 2, Opp. 28, 53, 57, 81 and 90), Schubert's sonatas were also performed, the most popular being those in G (D894), A (D664) and B♭

(D960). Haydn's string quartets were favoured over his piano works, though some sonatas and the F minor Variations found their way onto a few programmes. Sonatas by Clementi and Dussek were played in the 1860s; the latter's 'Plus ultra' Sonata (also known as 'Le retour à Paris') remained popular in the succeeding decade. The solid favourites of the programmes, however, were Chopin, Mendelssohn and Schumann. Mendelssohn's chamber music remained popular; the Andante and Variations Op. 82, Andante and Rondo capriccioso Op. 14, the E minor Prelude and Fugue Op 35 No. 1, the *Presto scherzando* and the *Variations sérieuses*. Schumann's longer works, such as *Carnaval, Kreisleriana* and the *Etudes symphoniques* were also popular.

Institutions

The establishment of the Associated Board of the Royal Schools of Music in 1889 and the examinations which they set also give valuable indications of the repertory taught both in institutions and by an ever-growing army of private teachers.[14] In 1898 the German writer Oscar Bie declared 'piano playing' to be 'a universal business', running the gamut from amateur to professional. According to Bie, the largest music school in the world was the Guildhall, with 2,700 students, and still expanding. By 1900 London alone boasted some thirty-three 'colleges of music', while most European centres had well-established conservatories, though these catered for far fewer students, and were presumably more selective.[15]

The Associated Board examinations, which began in 1890, with separate sets for schools and privately taught pupils, attempted to set levels of achievement for young pianists at different stages of their progress. The earliest piano examinations were set at only two levels, junior (aged 12–16) and senior (aged over 16); candidates were expected to play three studies and three pieces. At junior level studies by Cramer and Steibelt featured prominently along with inventions and preludes of J. S. Bach. At senior level pupils progressed from Cramer to Clementi's *Gradus*, the second most popular item after Moscheles's Op. 70 studies. Chopin studies were set only twice. Favoured composers of pieces chosen for junior level were Mozart, Beethoven and Mendelssohn; Haydn, Schubert and Schumann feature but once, while the contemporary Scharwenka is listed twice. At senior level selections from Beethoven sonatas proved to be the most popular, while Chopin and Schumann were represented by short pieces. Other composers were Hummel, Weber, Rheinberger and Raff.[16]

Books on the piano and its repertory

Books about the piano and its repertory published from the 1880s onward attempted to classify and consolidate the mass of material available to performers. Clearly there might be regional preferences for certain composers, but most music was widely available through continental and English publishers, and their agents in different countries. Adolf Prosniz's *Handbuch der Clavierliteratur von 1450 bis 1830* (Vienna, 1887) pushed back the frontiers of repertory even further than had other writers, allowing himself a perspective of over five decades on the offerings of his own century. Like Kroll he excluded anything past Weber and Schubert. (A second volume was planned but never appeared.) Prosniz divided the study into two 'epochs', the second one beginning at 1750, which allowed for the sons of Bach and other clavichord or early piano composers. Prosniz provided a 'league table' of composers, arranged in descending order of merit, from the highest order (C. P. E. Bach, Mozart, Haydn, Beethoven, Clementi, Hummel, Weber and Schubert), to the second rung (Dussek, Cramer, Field, Spohr, Kalkbrenner, Czerny and Moscheles) to a long list of 'others with artistic or literary-historical merit'. Prosniz goes on to list the best pieces of selected composers, along with information on editions. Various sonatas of Haydn and Mozart are mentioned; eight of Mozart's concertos are listed as being 'of first rank'. Though subjective, the book provides valuable insight into late-nineteenth-century taste (albeit a particularly German one), and gives an idea of a developing canon and an ordering of an established repertory according to merit.

Oscar Bie's *A history of the pianoforte and pianoforte players* (1898; Eng. trans. 1899), like Prosniz, gives highly subjective opinions on composers and compositions, but extends the boundaries to the author's day. The opinionated Bie pronounces on music and musicians from the Elizabethan virginalists onwards. Discussing music post 1830, he is keen to classify it according to different 'schools' represented by figures such as Hummel, Kalkbrenner, Adam and Czerny. From his late-nineteenth-century vantage point, Bie banishes composers such as Weber and Moscheles to the periphery; Schubert's 'greatest achievement' was his *Moments musicaux*, and Mendelssohn was merely a 'composer for young girls, the elegant romanticist of the drawing-room'. Schumann, Chopin and Liszt are given rather more commendation. Above all, Bie declares that the piano had become 'an essential part of life', bridging the musical lives of amateurs and professionals. It was 'an engine of social and home intercourse' and an integral part of life itself.[17]

Bie's comments applied only to the long nineteenth century. Since then the piano has ceased to be the focus of domestic musical and social entertainment. Who needs to play orchestral arrangements if the orchestra can be brought into the drawing-room? Gould, the heretic pianist, was one of the first to flee the confines of the concert hall in search of liberation in the recording studio which allowed him to play Gibbons and Schoenberg: the same industry still probes into the farthest reaches of the keyboard repertory, unheard and unheard of in conservatory or concert hall. For writers such as Bie and Prosniz the classification of piano repertory was clear-cut. A century later the view is rather different. The end of the piano culture has led to a shift in emphasis and a diversity in musical life unimaginable a century ago. The wonder is not that we have lost a readily identifiable canon, but that so much of it remains.

8 The music of the early pianists (to *c.*1830)

DAVID ROWLAND

Introduction

Many factors shaped the piano music of the late eighteenth and early nineteenth centuries. This was a period of change during which keyboard instruments extended from five to seven octaves, and from the relatively light-framed instruments of the 1760s and 1770s to the much more robust concert pianos of the 1820s (see chapter 2). It was also a period which saw an increasing emphasis on virtuoso performance and technique. At the same time, amateur music making increased rapidly and publishing houses expanded to satisfy the ever-increasing demand for cheaper, popular music. These and other factors led composers to write in certain ways for certain audiences, and if we are to understand the piano music of this period we must first give some attention to the circumstances in which composers worked as well as the settings in which music was performed.

One of the most significant developments of the late eighteenth century was the establishment of the public concert. Concerts for a paying audience had existed prior to this time, but their popularity grew in importance at the end of the eighteenth century to such an extent that composers who might previously have devoted their energies to the service of a rich aristocratic patron now found themselves writing to satisfy the public taste. London was the most important centre for the public concert at the time, with its newly rich mercantile class, and concert promoters such as Johann Christian Bach and Johann Peter Salomon lost no time in engaging a wide variety of musicians for their series of subscription concerts. The programmes were varied and the cast was truly international, as this programme which dates from the period of Haydn's second London visit demonstrates:

Concert at the New Rooms, King's Theatre, May 29th 1795

Part I

Overture, Dr Haydn, under his direction
Concerto, Oboe, Mr. Harrington
Song, Mrs. N. Corri (being her first appearance)
Concerto Piano Forte, Mr. Dussek
The Grand March of Alceste, arranged as a Glee, by Mr. Dussek

Part II

Grand Overture, Haydn
Song, Madame Dussek
Concerto Violin, Mr. Giornovichi
Song, Handel, Mr. Nield
Concerto, Harp, Madame Dussek
Finale.[1]

The solo piano recital was a mid-nineteenth-century invention (see chapters 4 and 7), prior to which pianists took their place alongside many other musicians in a mixed programme. Audiences were often tempted by the appeal of novelty, and concert announcements frequently mention a virtuoso 'newly arrived' in town, or a work 'expressly composed' for the occasion. As a result, pianists (who usually played their own works) composed a regular stream of works appropriate for public performance – often concertos, but sometimes also sonatas (especially in the eighteenth century).

Mixed orchestral concerts were also given in the large aristocratic houses of Europe, at least until the Napoleonic and other wars exhausted the wealth of many families. In these private circles, however, there were also opportunities for smaller-scale soirées at which pianists would perform their latest sonatas, or accompany other instrumentalists. Musicians were also called upon to give lessons to members of wealthy families – especially the daughters, for whom playing the piano was considered a necessary accomplishment. It was for these pupils that so many sonatas of the period were written. Some pupils were evidently extremely gifted, such as Theresa Jansen, for whom Haydn and Clementi composed some of their most difficult sonatas. The majority, however, were less able and required sonatas only of moderate difficulty which often contained rondos on popular themes or some other means of appealing to popular domestic taste.

Composing for publication was relatively new in the late eighteenth century. Prior to this composers had sometimes appealed to subscribers for funds to publish, or they had simply borne the cost of publication themselves, with the result that composers in the first part of the century could normally expect to see only a small part of their output in print. By the end of the eighteenth century, however, a new piano-owning domestic market was opening up to the extent that a composer such as Beethoven had publishers competing with one another for his latest works which were sometimes published simultaneously in two or three countries. Publishing provided a new lucrative source of income.

Publishers were anxious to maximise their profits and it quickly became clear that the works which sold best tended to be the least substantial in terms of musical worth, as Madame Pleyel wrote to her husband: 'We will do far better to print all sorts of small works every day, which require no great advances and on which the return is sure.'[2] As a result, from the 1790s onwards there appeared hundreds of *pot pourris* and other works based on popular themes as well as descriptive pieces such as Steibelt's *Allegorical Overture in Commemoration of the Signal NAVAL VICTORY obtained by ADMIRAL DUNCAN over the Dutch Fleet [on] the 11th of October 1797* (Figs. 8.1 and 8.2), dances and teaching pieces. This repertory is generally of an extremely low quality but its existence signalled a change in emphasis away from the sonatas of the eighteenth century towards works in a newer style, often in a single movement and entitled 'bagatelle', 'impromptu', 'nocturne', 'prelude' and the like.

The solo repertory of the eighteenth century

The eighteenth-century repertory for solo piano is dominated by sonatas, of which thousands were written all over Europe in the second half of the century. The term 'sonata' itself is imprecise: it denotes a work in two or more contrasting movements, but beyond that it is difficult to generalise. The precise format of the sonata as a whole, and the structure and type of individual movements, seem to have been dependent on the decisions of individual composers who were guided to a certain extent by local or national fashions.[3]

Two-movement sonatas were common in the late eighteenth century. J. C. Bach's Op. 5, for example – the first music to be published for the piano in London in 1766 – comprises six sonatas, three of which are in three movements, the other three being in two movements. Many of Clementi's sets of sonatas follow a similar pattern, although on occasion he composed sonatas in four movements. Haydn and Mozart both favoured a three-movement structure, Mozart exclusively so.

Individual movements within sonatas follow no set pattern, although it is relatively uncommon for the first movement to be anything other than a sonata form. Even here there are exceptions, however, such as the first movement of Mozart's Sonata in A major K331 and Haydn's two sonatas in G major HobXVI:39 and 40, all in variation form, or Mozart's K282 (E♭ major), a slow movement. Middle movements offer a wider range. In works of the 1760s and 1770s in particular the minuet and trio proved popular: lyrical slow movements were more common later in the century. It is in final movements where variety is greatest. In earlier works of the period, minuets and trios again proved popular (Haydn and J. C. Bach). A few sonatas have sets of variations (Mozart's K284 in D).

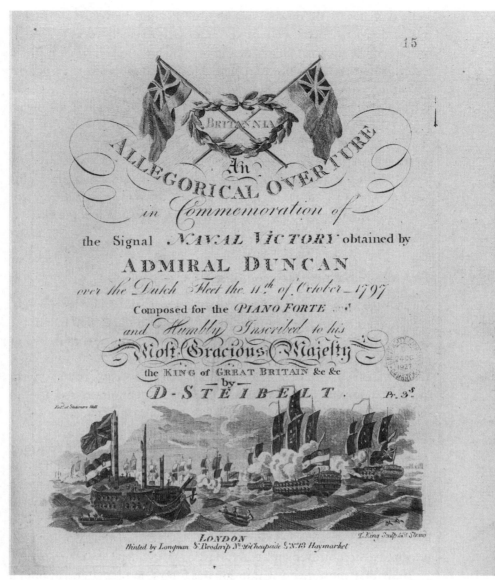

Figure 8.1 Steibelt, *An Allegorical Overture* (1797), title page.

Most commonly, however, composers chose a rondo or a sonata form. Rondos were often lightweight – perhaps based on a popular theme (for example, Dussek's Op. 25 No. 3 on 'Rule Britannia') or a dance – although they were not always so. Some of Mozart's later rondo finales have a substance which is reminiscent of the finales of his later, 'end-weighted' symphonies: the last movement of K533 in F, for example, climaxes in a contrapuntal passage (bars 152ff.) while the finale of K457 in C minor is unrelentingly serious and dramatic.

Figure 8.2 Steibelt, *An Allegorical Overture* (1797), p. 8.

Many aspects of keyboard technique and compositional style can be
traced through keyboard sonatas from the second half of the eighteenth
century. J. C. Bach's sonatas epitomise the *galant* style of the 1760s and
1770s. The *galant* is often associated with Italy, where Bach had lived from
1754 to 1762. It is essentially a melodic style in which the melody often
comprises somewhat fussy figuration and in which the left-hand part frequently fulfils an accompanying role, with Alberti and other figures maintaining movement amidst lengthy passages of slow harmonic rhythm (Ex.

Ex. 8.1 J. C. Bach, Sonata Op. 5 No. 3, bars 1–4.

Ex. 8.2 C. P. E. Bach, 'Prussian' Sonata No. 1, slow movement, bars 1–8

8.1). Two-part texture predominates, the phrasing falls into two- or four-bar patterns with frequent cadences and the structure is clearly delineated. Charles Burney summed up many aspects of the style by commenting that 'Bach seems to have been the first composer who observed the law of *contrast*, as a *principle*.'[4]

Bach's brother Carl Philipp Emanuel espoused an altogether different style which he developed at first on the clavichord, only later including the piano on the title pages of his published sonatas. C. P. E. Bach's *Empfindsamerstil* was avowedly expressive and he uses every element in his music to move or surprise the listener. Melodies often lack the easy flow of the *galant* style, with sudden changes of direction, or expressive pauses – recitative style is sometimes adopted (Ex. 8.2). The harmony likewise has a tendency to unpredictability with frequent excursions into distantly related keys. The texture is often thicker than the simple two-part writing of the *galant*, and makes greater use of the bass of the keyboard.

C. P. E. Bach was greatly revered in parts of Germany and Austria and many elements of his style passed into the music of his contemporaries and successors. Haydn expressed admiration for his style and many of the characteristics described above can be found in his sonatas (many of them evidently written for the clavichord), albeit in a less eccentric form. Haydn's sonatas also exemplify a trend which can perhaps be observed more clearly in his symphonies – a tendency towards motivic economy. This is expressed in a number of ways, one of the most striking of which is Haydn's frequent use of the same material for the beginning of both the first and second subject groups in his first movements. His development sections also demonstrate an ability to construct lengthy passages of music from a minimum of musical material. This degree of motivic economy can also be found in Clementi's sonatas, although it is a feature which is often overlooked in favour of one of the more immediately striking features of Clementi's works – their virtuosity. Virtuosity is apparent most obviously in Clementi's Op. 2 sonatas, especially No. 2 in C major, the 'celebrated octave lesson' (performed at first by Clementi on the harpsichord). Here, passages in thirds, sixths and octaves are more prominent than lyrical expression – a criticism voiced by Mozart who referred to Clementi after the two performed in a contest together in 1781 as 'a mere *mechanicus*'.[5]

Despite the shortcomings of some of Clementi's sonatas his adventurousness in exploiting new textures was a significant development which other members of the London School continued. Both Dussek and Cramer, in their 'professional' sonatas (rather than those written for their aristocratic pupils), use the most up-to-date textures, such as the extended left-hand accompanying figures so common in their works from the mid 1790s onwards (see below). The impact of these developments can also be seen on Haydn's last three sonatas, composed during his second London visit, and some of Beethoven's sonatas in which he borrows textures and ideas from sonatas by members of the London School.[6]

Aside from these developments, Mozart's piano sonatas occupy a unique place. In terms of style they resemble most closely the works of J. C. Bach, whose music Mozart admired and on occasion arranged for his own purposes.[7] Mozart's earliest sonatas, written in Munich in 1775, resemble J. C. Bach's in their light, *galant* textures and in their abundance of melodic material. The lyricism and poignancy of some of their slow movements, however, point towards the fully developed middle movements of the much more ambitious sonatas of his Vienna years. Some of these – the Sonata in F K533, for example – have slow movements in fully fledged sonata forms, with both sections repeated and extensive development sections. The sources of Mozart's sonatas also reveal something of his performance style. In those works that were carefully prepared for publication, such as K332, dynamic and articulation markings abound, and in the first edition of the slow movement of this sonata the return of

the first nineteen bars of the movement (bars 21–39) is heavily embell-
ished. This, presumably, represents the sort of performance that Mozart
would have given of parallel passages in less meticulously prepared works,
for example, the recapitulation of the slow movement of the Sonata in G
K283.

Works other than sonatas occupy a much smaller part of the eighteenth-century repertory. Among these other pieces, however, is a
significant group based on improvisatory styles. Improvisation was an
important element of performance and pianists were often called upon to
demonstrate their prowess. On the occasion of Mozart's and Clementi's
pianistic 'dual' in 1781, for example, both men improvised: 'After we had
stood on ceremony long enough, the Emperor declared that Clementi
ought to begin. "La Santa Chiesa Cattolica", he said, Clementi being a
Roman. He improvised and then played a sonata. The Emperor then
turned to me: "Allons, fire away." I improvised and played variations . . .'[8]
An account of one of Dussek's concerts in London in the 1790s also
describes how he, 'now seated, tried his instrument in a prelude' before
playing a concerto.[9] Biographies of Beethoven contain numerous
accounts of his improvisations.

It is of course impossible to discover what these pianists improvised,
but it may have been similar to the style of works in comparatively free
forms. Most obviously, there are the fantasias. Mozart wrote a handful,
ranging from the relatively early Fantasia in C K395 (1777), which is little
more than a sequence of various sorts of keyboard figuration, to the C
minor Fantasia K475 which takes almost ten minutes to play and has six
main sections, each depending on its own characteristic motivic or
melodic material. Other composers wrote similar works under different
headings: Clementi preferred to use the title 'capriccio'. Haydn seems to
have used both the title 'capriccio' and 'fantasia' when referring to one of
his most eccentric works, the Fantasia in C major HobXVII/4, which is in
fact a rondo, but which includes all kinds of novel effects, such as a pause
over a bass octave 'till one can no longer hear the sound', and octave glissandi in the right-hand part at the end of the work. Still under the heading
'improvised styles' should be mentioned preludes, which pianists often
used to introduce more substantial works, or to connect two works in
different keys. They were generally rather insubstantial works. Clementi's
Musical characteristics contains a number of preludes in the styles of
various composers.

Composers used popular contemporary melodies in a variety of ways
in the late eighteenth century. In London, it was fashionable to publish
rondos on the latest popular melodies. Such works were less common in
southern Germany and Austria, especially with Mozart: his rondos are

substantial and inventive works, and in the case of the A minor Rondo K511, one of the most serious works that he wrote for piano. In Vienna and in other parts of Europe many of the popular melodies of the day formed the basis for sets of variations. Mozart wrote more than a dozen sets of variations throughout his career, of which about half were based on popular operatic melodies. The others were based on songs or themes from instrumental works by other composers. Only two (K54 and K573) have unidentified themes: they may be original. When Beethoven arrived in Vienna in 1792 he had already composed four sets of variations for solo keyboard: eight more sets were to follow before the end of the century and seven more after that, of which the C minor (WoO 80) and 'Diabelli' variations are the best known.

Sonatas by Beethoven, Schubert and their contemporaries

Despite the declining popularity of sonatas at the end of the eighteenth century, many continued to be written by well-known figures such as Beethoven and Schubert, as well as numerous less significant figures such as Johann Nepomuk Hummel, Ferdinand Ries, Carl Czerny and others. Of those by lesser composers, many sonatas were written for the popular market, as evidenced in their rondo finales based on operatic themes and songs, or the accompanying (optional) violin, flute and cello parts which are seldom of any thematic significance. Beethoven's and Schubert's sonatas, however, show little evidence of appealing to amateur taste: there are few, if any, populist elements in their sonatas, and many of these works are written in such a way that only a professional technique can do them justice.

Neither Beethoven nor Schubert seems to have written his sonatas for the concert platform: very few public performances of these works are recorded in the composer's lifetime. Beethoven's sonatas were generally dedicated to his aristocratic patrons, who either played the pieces themselves or hosted soirées at which the composer performed them. All of them (with the exception of two early works) were published during his lifetime, usually within a year or two of composition, and most were performed frequently throughout the nineteenth century. Indeed, many nineteenth-century writers 'interpreted' Beethoven's sonatas, adding titles to them such as 'Appassionata' (Op. 57). Schubert's sonatas were probably written for the close circle of his friends, who gathered in the evenings to sing Schubert's songs and to hear his instrumental works performed. Only three out of the fourteen were published in his lifetime and, despite the championship of figures such as Schumann, the sonatas only gradually gained acceptance among pianists.

Beethoven wrote thirty-two sonatas with opus numbers: four additional complete early sonatas exist as well as one with just two movements (WoO 50) and there are two spurious sonatinas. Beginning with Op. 2 (composed 1793–5, published 1796), the order in which the sonatas were composed follows the order of opus numbers, with the exception of Op. 49 Nos. 1 and 2, both works of slight dimensions, which were composed in the mid 1790s, but not published until 1805. There was a steady stream of sonatas up to Op. 57 (composed 1804–5, published 1807) after which Beethoven left off composing sonatas for four years. In 1809 Clementi, in his capacity as a music publisher, managed to elicit from Beethoven the two sonatas Opp. 78 and 79. Around the same time Op. 81 ('Das Lebewohl') was written on the occasion of the departure from and return to Vienna of Archduke Rudolph, Beethoven's patron. Another gap followed, after which Op. 90 was written in 1814. The last five sonatas were composed in the years 1816–22.

Beethoven's sonatas illustrate his changing circumstances and the development of his compositional style throughout his Vienna years – from 1792 to his death in 1827. Op. 2, dedicated to his teacher Haydn, marks his arrival as both composer and performer. The first movements contain much carefully crafted motivic working and some harmonic surprise, such as the elements of dominant minor harmony in the second subject-group of each sonata's exposition. All three sonatas are substantial works, with scherzos and trios in addition to the usual three movements, and there is a strong element of virtuoso display, especially in No. 3. Having established himself as a pianist and composer, Beethoven's subsequent sonatas demonstrate his constant inclination to innovate: the slow introduction of Op. 13 (which returns in the middle of the movement), the first-movement variations and funeral march of Op. 26 are evidence of this, although all of these particular elements can be found in earlier sonatas by other composers. It is less easy to find a precedent for the two sonatas Op. 27, both of which were termed 'Sonata quasi una Fantasia' and both of which are unconventional in a variety of ways. Beethoven was persuaded to remove the original slow movement of Op. 53, which would have made an already hugely expanded work still bigger – the slow movement was later published as the 'Andante favori' in F – and the individuality of this and subsequent sonatas is stressed by the publication of each one with its own opus number. Much has been written about the last five sonatas, with their 'spiritual' qualities, trills, fugal passages and enormous range of expression. Their unique formal and stylistic elements posed huge dilemmas for those who followed. Some composers ignored the challenge altogether, choosing instead to follow a more conventional model while others looked for equally inventive solutions to the sonata problem.

Despite the neglect suffered by Schubert as an instrumental composer both during and after his lifetime, his sonatas are arguably just as revolutionary as Beethoven's. This is so in a number of ways, though more in terms of the internal stylistic elements of individual movements than in overall construction. That Schubert had initial difficulties with the composition of sonatas is evidenced in a number of works dating from 1815–19. During this time, Schubert left unfinished almost twice as many sonatas as he completed. It is impossible to be certain of the reasons for this. However, judging from the available evidence it appears that in order to write first movements of adequate length Schubert at first tended towards too much repetition of thematic material. In order to counter this problem, and to tighten the structure, he then proceeded to experiment with shorter first movements in two unfinished sonatas, those in A♭ (D557) and E minor (D566). The expositions of these two works are 39 and 37 bars long respectively, compared with expositions of 53, 65, 86 and 104 bars in earlier works. Schubert's final solution was arguably much more radical than Beethoven's occasional use of unconventional keys in his expositions: Schubert tends, in later works, to allow his melodic material to unfold and develop through a wide variety of keys. In the B major Sonata D575 (1817), for example, the exposition passes from B major to G major and E major before finally settling in the dominant F♯ major, and in the expositions of later sonatas it is common procedure for Schubert to use a number of keys other than the tonic and dominant (or relative major). This feature and other factors contribute to the 'heavenly length' on which Schumann commented in Schubert's sonatas.

In addition to Beethoven and Schubert, Weber deserves to be mentioned as a composer who treated the sonata with a greater degree of seriousness than many of his contemporaries. His four solo sonatas, published in Berlin in the years 1812–23, favour the four-movement plan and have the appearance of works for public performance. They use the most up-to-date piano figuration of their day – one factor which is absent in much of Beethoven's and Schubert's writing – and exploit the full range of the piano of six and a half octaves.

New styles and forms of the nineteenth century

The development of new keyboard textures by members of the London School and others at the end of the eighteenth century as well as the growing popular market for piano music, were two important factors which caused a change in emphasis away from the sonata to new types of work for piano solo and a greater emphasis on some older forms. One

Ex. 8.3 Field, Nocturne No. 1, bars 1–2.

important figure in this process was John Field, one of Clementi's pupils, who settled in Russia in the early years of the nineteenth century. Field's sonatas do not bear comparison with Beethoven's or Schubert's, but his nocturnes, the first of which was published in 1812, could be said to be some of the earliest truly Romantic music for piano. They are single-movement works which are formally simple, and in which the interest lies in decorated melody and piano texture. Many of these works are based upon keyboard figuration which was developed in the 1790s, namely an 'um-pah' left-hand part, which relies on the sustaining pedal for its success, with a decorated melody for the right hand (Ex. 8.3). This 'nocturne style' was taken up by a number of composers, most notably Chopin.

Another Clementi pupil, Johann Baptist Cramer, published the first piano études in 1804. These are quite unlike the numerous pieces for beginners found in eighteenth-century didactic literature: rather, they are works which are worthy of public performance in which Cramer drew together many of the more taxing techniques of the time. Many sets of études followed Cramer's examples, leading to the concert studies by major nineteenth-century concert virtuosos such as Liszt and Chopin.

Alongside nocturnes and études, a large number of other single-movement works appeared under a bewildering variety of titles. Beethoven wrote about twenty-five bagatelles (literally 'trifles'), beginning with Op. 33 (published 1803). Schubert wrote small-scale works under headings such as *Moments musicaux* and 'impromptu', while other composers used titles as unimaginative as 'pièce' or as exotic as 'éclogue' (Tomášek's Op. 35 of 1807). Dances were popular too, especially waltzes, polonaises and écossaises. Most of these works were composed for the domestic market and are therefore technically undemanding and formally simple, although some, such as Weber's *Grand polonaise* and *Polacca brillante*, would test an amateur technique.

Musically, much of this repertory is interesting only insofar as it led to some of the more enduring works by the next generation of pianists. Occasionally, however, one comes across works of much greater significance other than sonatas. Schubert's 'Wanderer' Fantasy falls into this category because it is one of the first large-scale, multi-section works whose structure is based upon the development of a theme. It is in four sections which correspond to the four movements of a sonata. The first section, in C major, begins with an idea which comprises little more than a rhythm and the interval of a semitone. What would normally be termed a second subject-group (in E major) adds to the opening rhythm a melodic tail, which itself becomes the main melodic material of a third section in E♭. The first section concludes without a recapitulation and subsequent sections use and develop the melodic material which has already been presented. In its time, it was a radical approach to large-scale composition and bears a striking resemblance to aspects of Liszt's much later Sonata in B minor. (Liszt arranged Schubert's 'Wanderer' Fantasy for piano and orchestra.)

Concertos

Whilst a detailed discussion of concertos lies outside the scope of this volume it would give a false impression, especially of the eighteenth-century repertory, to ignore them altogether. Simple statistics illustrate the importance of concertos to a number of composers: J. C. Bach and Mozart each wrote about twenty-five – more than the number of solo sonatas by each composer – and C. P. E. Bach wrote fifty. Not all of these were for piano. Several were composed for harpsichord and a few for organ, and most of them are capable of performance on more than one keyboard instrument; but as we discussed in chapter 2, keyboard players appear to have been accustomed to performing on one or other instrument as the occasion demanded.

Some concertos in the eighteenth century may have been written for publication but most were composed for specific performances, either by the composers themselves or by other keyboard players. The majority of Mozart's were written for himself, some of them at great speed for impending performance. This is particularly the case with some of his virtuoso concertos from the mid 1780s, composed for some subscription concerts which Mozart himself organised, at a time when he was at the peak of his performing powers. Mozart's father arrived in Vienna on 16 February 1785, the date of the first performance of K466 in D minor, and reported in a letter to his daughter: 'we had a new and very fine concerto by Wolfgang, which the copyist was still copying when we arrived, and the rondo of which your brother did not even have time to play through, as he had to supervise the copying'.[10] Less than a month later, on 9 March,

Mozart entered into his catalogue of compositions a new concerto, K467 in C, which was premiered on the following day amidst a heavy schedule of 'teaching music, composing and so forth'.[11] It is no wonder that the piano parts of these concertos contain a number of abbreviations, and that the cadenzas were improvised at the concerts. Concertos written for other performers were more carefully notated, however, to the extent that some works (such as K246) have as many as three different cadenzas for some movements, composed for performance on different occasions.

The eighteenth-century concept of the concerto is one of partnership between soloist and orchestra which is expressed in a number of ways. Earlier concertos by J. C. and C. P. E. Bach, some of which are in just two movements and take about ten minutes to play, are more like chamber works with only string parts in the 'orchestra' (sometimes omitting the viola): any thought of a dramatic opposition of forces on the concert platform is far removed from these pieces. In all eighteenth-century concertos the soloist plays more or less throughout, performing a continuo role in the orchestral tuttis, stressing again the sense of unity between keyboard and orchestra. Partnership is also expressed in the use of thematic material. In many of Mozart's concertos, for example, the keyboard enters after some considerable time with the same music as the beginning of the orchestral tutti, and thereafter themes and motifs are passed freely between them.

A number of eighteenth-century characteristics passed into Beethoven's concertos, such as the use of the piano as a continuo instrument.[12] Nevertheless, with Beethoven and his contemporaries the concerto was to become much grander than its eighteenth-century counterpart and few composers wrote more than a handful each. The scale of concertos increased alongside symphonic works and the orchestral forces grew accordingly. By this time the power of the piano had increased sufficiently to compete with the orchestra and a polarity between soloist and orchestra began to emerge. In the Andante con moto of Beethoven's Fourth Piano Concerto (first performed in 1808), for example, the piano has markedly different thematic material from the strings, and during the course of the short movement the piano becomes increasingly dominant. In Beethoven's last concerto the piano begins with a dramatic flourish following a single orchestral chord, as if to emphasise the piano's dominance at the outset. This, rather than the eighteenth-century model, was followed by subsequent composers of concertos.

Duets

Keyboard duets were written before the eighteenth century and there is also a small repertory from the period 1700–60. However, from the 1760s onwards there was a rapid expansion of duet composition, almost all of it for the domestic market. 'Domestic market' in this context has a variety of meanings. Many of Mozart's duets, for example, were written for him and his sister to play as children and adolescents on their European tours of the 1760s and 1770s. Other duets of the period such as Haydn's *Il maestro e lo scolare* were written as teaching pieces. Another group of works, increasingly popular after about 1790, consisted of arrangements for piano duet of symphonies and other large-scale works for home performance. All of these types of duet were commonly published for four hands on a single keyboard: duets for two performers at two instruments occasionally appeared, but these were comparatively rare.

Leopold Mozart claimed that Wolfgang's Sonata in D K19d was the first work of its kind. He may have been correct, but by the end of the next decade several more sonatas for duet on one keyboard had appeared, such as Burney's four sonatas of 1777, J. C. Bach's sonatas – included in Opp. 15 and 18 (1778 and 1781) – and Clementi's Op. 3 (1779). Many more followed by these and other composers, notably in London. Many of the works are technically undemanding, but sometimes one comes across a really substantial work, such as Mozart's F major sonata K497, or his Sonata in D K448 for two pianos.

Most duets of the eighteenth century are sonatas, although there are a few sets of variations. By the end of the century, however, transcriptions for symphonies began to appear. Haydn's were the first, being published in London in the closing years of the century, but Mozart's and Beethoven's symphonies followed. The composers themselves had little interest in arranging their own works in this way, but seem to have been content to see others do so. Czerny, for example, who always had an eye for a commercial publishing success, arranged Beethoven's symphonies as well as some of his choral works, along with some of Mozart's symphonies. Beethoven seems to have had little interest in piano duets. An early sonata, Op. 6, and two sets of variations are all that he wrote before 1800. After that, a set of marches Op. 45 appeared in 1804, marking the beginning of a trend in the nineteenth century for small-scale works of this kind, particularly dances. Beethoven's only other duet was an arrangement of the *Grosse Fuge* Op. 133. Compared with Beethoven's slight duet output Schubert's is extremely rich. Inevitably, there are many marches, dances and variations which were composed for the amateur market, many of which were published in the mid 1820s, but there are also works of real substance such as the 'Grand duo' Sonata in C D812 and the F minor Fantasia D940, both of which were published posthumously, and both of which stand comparison with any of the solo repertory by any of Schubert's early nineteenth-century contemporaries.

9 Piano music for concert hall and salon *c.*1830–1900

J. BARRIE JONES

Salon and concert hall

Britain was an early pioneer in the development of public concerts: they were well established throughout the country by *c.*1750. In France, concerts were equally popular but, as in other aspects of French life and culture, were centred mainly on the capital to a greater extent than were their British counterparts. Public concerts were less in evidence in Germany and Austria until the early nineteenth century, though by then the citizens of Frankfurt, Leipzig, Berlin and Vienna were able to participate in a relatively thriving concert environment.

The salon is less easy to describe than a public concert. There had been a long tradition of intellectual gatherings of connoisseurs and aristocrats, but today 'salon' usually refers to 'a part-intellectual and part-social gathering in a domestic (aristocratic or bourgeois) setting: a peculiarly nineteenth-century phenomenon principally found in the larger European capitals'.[1] This is fine as far as it goes, though it is hardly comprehensive, since an all-embracing definition is far from easy. (It is therefore curious that most music dictionaries, including *The New Grove*, make no attempt to define 'salon'.) When Amy Fay,[2] the American piano student from Boston, studied with Liszt in Weimar during the 1870s, the salon in which she was invited to perform from time to time was a large room in the ducal palace. These essentially private functions were attended by highly intelligent and articulate, frequently titled, persons: here the depreciatory overtones sometimes suggested by 'salon' are inappropriate. The same is equally true of many of the Parisian salons throughout the nineteenth century. The new 'difficult' music of Fauré, for instance, was usually appreciated there, less so in the concert halls. Indeed Fauré probably intended most of his piano music and *mélodies* for the salon and his chamber works for large halls: the character itself of the music makes this evident. Fifty years earlier Chopin's music had exhibited a similar dichotomy. The waltzes, nocturnes and many of the mazurkas are clearly salon music (in the best sense). The sonatas, ballades, scherzos and polonaises, though played by Chopin and others in the salon, seem more obviously concert music, appropriate for large halls. As is well known, Chopin's concert appearances were rare and undertaken with reluctance;

critics, while admiring his technical dexterity, frequently remarked on the quietness of his playing in respect of the size of the hall. The finesse and subtlety of Chopin's performances were shown to best advantage in the salon. Those were relatively private affairs where the nobility, literati, artists, musicians and cognoscenti intermingled at will, though incidentally, this was much less true of the London salons at this period.

It is a small but significant step from the virtually private salon to the absolutely private domestic dwelling: the essentially bourgeois home of the new wealthy middle class. The piano was an indispensable fixture in such homes, representing as it did both wealth and culture. The young ladies (almost never gentlemen) of the household required an appropriate repertory: hence the rise of domestic music. Appropriately graded examples (Schumann's *Album für die Jugend*), pieces both reflective and virtuoso (Mendelssohn's *Lieder ohne Worte*, 'Songs without Words'), an enormous number of transcriptions, from the easy to the almost impossible, many of these became the pinnacle of an amateur's musical ambition.

Felix Mendelssohn

Mendelssohn played a leading role in the formation and development of a nineteenth-century piano style. For all his indebtedness to keyboard figurations ultimately deriving from Hummel and Weber, Mendelssohn's best piano works exemplify a number of features sometimes associated with more innovative composers. As Hutcheson observed,[3] Mendelssohn's substitution of the double broken octaves as found in the first movement of Beethoven's Sonata Op. 2 No. 3 by the more practical and brilliant alternating octaves, as at the end of the *Rondo capriccioso* Op. 14 (Exx. 9.1, 9.2), proved a major and universally followed innovation. 'Three-handed' writing (a centrally placed melody with accompanimental figurations above and below it), a technique attributed to Francesco Pollini around 1812 though associated particularly with Thalberg (see Ex. 4.1), is seen in a rudimentary form as early as 1826 in the second subject of the finale of Mendelssohn's Sonata in E Op. 6. Three-hand writing is an essential feature in many of the Songs without Words, since the technique springs from the imitation of the human voice by a tune often placed around middle c, the area where a cantabile melody carries best. The fairy-like scherzos that, in the piano pieces, make considerable use of wrist staccato, though foreshadowed in Weber's *Momento capriccioso* Op. 12, were raised by Mendelssohn to a peak of artistic perfection in orchestral, chamber and piano music. A piece such as the Song without Words Op. 67 No. 4 is technically more difficult to play now than

Ex. 9.1 Mendelssohn, *Rondo capriccioso* Op. 14, bar 227.

Ex. 9.2 Beethoven, Sonata Op. 2 No. 3, bar 252.

it was on the lighter action of the pianos of Mendelssohn's time. This apart, all of Mendelssohn's technical innovations are achieved without undue strain on the performer's abilities: the composer was able to fashion his piano-writing to suit either amateurs or concert virtuosos (often himself).

The forty-eight Songs without Words represent Mendelssohn's principal contribution to the domestic music repertory. Usually in ternary form, the composer almost always reworks the final section, unlike Grieg whose ABA structures in the Lyric Pieces generally present a straight repetition of A the second time round. The most saccharine of these pieces (Nos. 9, 30, 40 and 44 for example) are invariably more inventive than the pale imitations of them by later composers. The best are still worthy of the concert platform, as Liszt and Clara Schumann had demonstrated in the nineteenth century. The celebrated *Rondo capriccioso*, 'the coping-stone of every English maiden's pianistic culture',[4] belongs to the same category.

Amongst Mendelssohn's most inventive and substantial concert works are the Six Preludes and Fugues Op. 35. The composer's interest in the past was pronounced, and this baroque structure becomes in his hands a modern genre, strikingly appropriate for the concert hall. The introduction of an original chorale as the bold culmination of the E minor prelude and fugue is strikingly new and may have been in César Franck's (1822–90) mind when, fifty years later, he wrote his Prelude, Chorale and Fugue. The *Variations sérieuses* Op. 54, whose title was a protest against the early nineteenth-century trivialisation of one of the oldest instrumental structures, makes a ready appeal to both performer and audience.

In assessing Mendelssohn's work, one should remember that – most unromantically – he wrote composition exercises in addition to real music: everything published after Op. 73 was posthumous, and never intended for publication unless revision was envisaged. (The 'Italian' Symphony and the last two books of Songs without Words fall into this category.) The infrequency with which Mendelssohn's piano works are heard in the concert hall is in no way indicative of their overall merit.

Robert Schumann

Schumann, by temperament Mendelssohn's opposite, is one of the three most enduring romantic piano writers: the others are Chopin and Liszt. Schumann had originally intended to become a virtuoso pianist; his very earliest compositions (either unpublished or later reworked) show some influence of Moscheles and Hummel. Nevertheless, Schumann soon developed a style of startling originality wherein any virtuosity is put to the service of the musical thought. He avoided empty scales and arpeggios, and tended to avoid extended passages employing the extreme limits of the instrument. Textural variety, harmonic originality and a supreme gift for melody compensate for a certain reluctance to use the keyboard in an overtly colouristic manner. Schumann's larger works avoid obvious virtuoso effects, though they display some flamboyance and were intended for concert use. His short pieces, sometimes a page or less, were frequently assembled into collections of varying length. These collections often display an *innig* (that is, intimate but with an ardent warmth), highly poetic quality, comparable with Heine's lyric poetry, although the musical influence stemmed from Beethoven's *An die ferne Geliebte* and the slower-moving areas of the late sonatas.[5] Much of Schumann's piano music dates from the 1830s.

Schumann may have had the idea of assembling a collection of short movements into a composite work from similar publications by Hummel and Schubert. Schumann's pieces, sometimes known as 'piano cycles', and almost all of which were inspired by the pianist Clara Wieck, often represent the composer at his most esoteric. In fact they were played only in the salons of Leipzig and other German cities, and were virtually unplayed in concert halls until after Schumann's death. The earliest set of pieces is *Papillons* Op. 2. This prototype of the composer's later assemblages is strikingly original and inventive. The twelve movements originally bore titles taken from Jean-Paul Richter's *Flegeljahre*, Schumann's favourite novel, though these were dropped before publication. The quotation of the German popular tune *Grossvaterstanz* (later to become the *Thème du XVIIeme siècle*, representing the Philistines in *Carnaval*) and the clock striking 6 a.m. after a night of revelry, conspire to make *Papillons* a miniature precursor of *Carnaval* Op. 9. This is still the most famous and popular piano work of the composer, and is, in its combination of literary, musical and thematic elements, an archetypal German romantic piano work. The fashioning of many of the twenty-two pieces' melodic material out of the notes of Asch (the birthplace of one of Schumann's temporary girlfriends) was part of a long tradition by German composers of translating letters of the alphabet into musical notes. In German notation 'ASCH' can be translated in two ways:

Ex. 9.3 Schumann's 'ASCH' theme.

and the ingenuity with which Schumann treats this three- or four-note cell is indeed remarkable. The fact that few of these cell transformations are audible and that the score must be perused in order to see them is symptomatic of the increasing intellectualisation of much romantic music: music outwardly spontaneous, improvisatory, 'from the heart', but in fact carefully fashioned, almost crabbed thematically, the very embodiment of art concealing art. *Carnaval* also marked the public unveiling of the *Davidsbund*, those of like mind to Schumann battling against the commercialisation and trivialisation of music by the Philistines. The *Davidsbundlertänze* Op. 6 represent a more subtle and hidden aspect of the same struggle: here the eighteen pieces are untitled though some have intriguing and novel performance directions ('Impatiently', 'Wild and merry', 'As if from far away').

The thirteen movements of *Kinderszenen* Op. 15 may be regarded as music for the home, but they are essentially brief musical poems raised to glorious heights. Schumann rarely said so much in so little space, in the process imbuing each of these tiny movements with great emotional warmth and expressivity. 'Traümerei', the best and best-known of the collection, exemplifies a movement outwardly four-square in its phrase lengths, but in actuality teeming with subtle rhythmic and melodic details, suggestions of counterpoint in what appears to be mere tune-plus-accompaniment, and a pervasive use of thematic regeneration (where the opening melody reappears many times though in ever-changing varied forms). The *Arabeske* Op. 18, lengthier and stylistically lighter, demonstrates Schumann's ability to capture the essence of improvisatory thoughts and techniques by means of uncannily precise musical notation.

Kreisleriana Op. 16, eight pieces inspired by E. T. A. Hoffmann's Kapellmeister Kreisler, is perhaps the most esoteric and certainly the most harmonically advanced – at least by comparison with any of Schumann's German contemporaries – work from the 1830s. The movements, all markedly different from one another, coalesce into half-an-hour's music that paints perhaps the most complete picture of Schumann in a single work. Conversely, the eight pieces that make up both the *Phantasiestücke* Op. 12 and *Noveletten* Op. 21 are not linked to one another by some indefinable sense of spirituality, such as the composer demonstrated in Opp. 2, 6, 9 and 16, but are separate entities: each is a group of 'songs' rather than a song 'cycle'. Op. 12 is frequently played as a set, Op. 21 rarely so.

These 'romantic' collections are balanced by other works owing some allegiance to classical models. Three sets of variations date from the 1830s. The opening phrase of the 'Abegg' Variations, amongst the finest of all Opus Ones, is conveniently provided by the letters of its title. The Impromptus on a theme by Clara Wieck Op. 5 are in reality a set of variations. Here, Schumann was as interested in the bass as in the melody of the theme. His model here was the finale of the 'Eroica' Symphony: both sets of variations begin in a remarkably similar way. The magnificent *Etudes symphoniques* Op. 13 are rightly described by Hutcheson as 'one of the peaks of the piano literature, lofty in conception and faultless in workmanship'.[6] The work combines variation form, étude-like figurations, and in three of its twelve variations, implied homage to Bach, Mendelssohn and Paganini. The work is particularly innovative in that frequently only the first few notes of the theme permeate many of the variations: these opening notes then generate new melodies as the variation proceeds. The Toccata Op. 7, in both C major and sonata form, may well be a musical tribute to Czerny, famous at the time for *his* Toccata in C. However, the quiet ending of Schumann's Toccata makes it unique in this most energetic of musical genres.

Standing alone is Schumann's supreme masterpiece, the *Phantasie* Op. 17; originally intended as a tribute to Beethoven, it ultimately became the expression of the composer's passion for Clara Wieck. 'The secret listener' from Schlegel's prefatory four-line motto, added after the whole work had been composed, constitutes a clear reference to Clara. At the same time, the quotations from Beethoven's *An die ferne Geliebte* and other works[7] underline and emphasise the fact that while Beethoven was the starting point, Clara, as usual, was not far from Schumann's mind. The first of the three linked movements constitutes an extremely free sonata structure in which the chord of C major is often ingeniously side-stepped at those very moments when it is most expected, resulting in a yearning, aching atmosphere only relieved at the very end of the movement. A triumphant march and the lengthy final Adagio in their structural simplicity complement this complex opening movement, both thematically and harmonically. With *Kreisleriana*, the *Phantasie* reveals Schumann as a consummate master of both the *innig* and the personal, yet it also possesses the power to move any audience.

Schumann's music in the 1830s was truly innovative, even if Clara Wieck motivated almost everything the composer produced at this period. The tendency to aphorism and the four-bar phrase was the natural consequence of a composer steeped in German poetry who was to bring the *lied* to a high water mark of perfection. The regularity of such phrases is usually masked by subtleties of rhythmic detail and elaborate thematic regeneration that move the music inexorably forward. Schumann's highly personal employment of dominant and diminished seventh chords is often explicable by their placement in new contexts: unusual resolutions of the chord or sudden tonal shifts rather than more gradual modulations, involving pivot chords. Characteristic spacings of middle-register chords, sometimes with interlocking hands, may appear to make the music conventional, or even dull, on the page; when transmuted into sound, one then realises to the full what a sensitive ear for piano sonorities this composer possessed.

Johannes Brahms

Brahms's piano music spans a period of some forty years. It falls conveniently into three groups: the first includes the large-scale sonatas, several sets of variations and a number of miscellaneous movements; the second the ten pieces that comprise Opp. 76 and 79; and lastly the twenty relatively short pieces Opp. 116–19, most of which were written, or at least completed, in 1892. Brahms's successful career as a composer can be ascribed to several factors: his enthusiastic championship by the Schumanns, his early emergence into maturity, his considerable powers as a pianist that enabled him to propagate his own piano and chamber music, and his unrelenting self-criticism. Brahms was over twenty years younger than the composers so far discussed, and his piano music dates from a period when the flamboyance of many virtuosos in the first half of the century was starting to be replaced by the probity and scholarly attitudes to performance by pianists such as Clara Schumann, Carl Tausig and Hans von Bülow. Moreover, in Germany the salon was facing competition from the concert hall, for which much of Brahms's piano music was intended. Up to about 1880 he himself was frequently its foremost exponent; thereafter a number of Viennese pianist-friends of Brahms, such as Ignaz Brüll and Julius Epstein, undertook the premieres of the later piano works. Some pieces, notably the Waltzes Op. 39 and the easier and shorter late pieces, can be regarded as (superior) domestic music, but such pieces are very much in the minority, compared with those intended for the concert hall.

After the early sonatas where, in a sense, he exorcised the ghost of Beethoven, Brahms turned subsequently to variation forms, in which the seeming straitjacket of formal rigidity produced some of Brahms's most remarkable and spontaneous music. In the longer sets of variations, such as the twenty-five on a theme by Handel Op. 24, Brahms adopted an expedient from Beethoven rendered necessary by the large number of variations. Many of these form themselves into composite groups of two or three by virtue of a common motif, figuration or piano technique, thus avoiding the potentially scrappy effect of twenty-five separate, short 'movements'. Beethoven had realised such possible dangers in his Thirty-two Variations in C minor (WoO 80), a work that Brahms included in his repertory as a pianist. The Handel variations conclude with a fugue, an idea reminiscent not just of Beethoven's 'Eroica' Variations but also of Bach's C minor organ Passacaglia. The spirit of Bach also informs areas of the Variations on a theme of Schumann Op. 9 in which three of the sixteen variations are canonic; counterpoint is also a prominent feature in a number of other movements in the set. In addition, Brahms quotes the fifth of Schumann's *Bunte Blätter* Op. 99, combining it with the fourth, the theme of the variations itself. The two sets of variations Op. 21, one an original, the other on a Hungarian theme, both display Brahms's fondness for technical difficulties: not of the pianistic variety, but difficulties brought about by contrapuntal voice-leading and the resulting need for textural clarity. The two books of Paganini Variations Op. 35 are unique in Brahms's output in being concerned with piano technique: they were therefore originally entitled 'Studies for piano' and were a direct outcome of the composer's friendship with Tausig.

The first of the Four Ballades Op. 10 represents a rare excursion into the Lisztian world of avowed programme music. The Scottish story of Edward, which Brahms came across in Herder's *Stimmen der Völker*, resulted in one of his most powerful and evocative piano works. More importantly, the poetic metre of the poem's first verse matches the musical metre of Brahms's opening bars. This 'metric transmutation' of

Ex. 9.4 Brahms, Ballade Op. 10 No. 2.

[F   A   F]

poetry into music is a constant feature in Brahms. It would hardly be surprising in a composer of over 200 songs but it also permeates many
instrumental melodies: explicitly as here and in the Intermezzo Op. 117
No. 1 (also taken from Herder's collection), and implicitly (if unprovable)
in many of Brahms's tunes. The main theme of the second Ballade offers
in its F(♯)–A–F(♯) motif one of many examples whereby Brahms translated his personal motto 'Frei aber froh' ('Free but happy') into musical
notes by means, in this case, of an acronym (Ex. 9.4).

The Eight Piano Pieces Op. 76 and the Two Rhapsodies Op. 79 date
from the late 1870s, around the time of the Second Symphony and Violin
Concerto. By this time Brahms had refined his piano writing in the sense
that the awkward and occasionally unpianistic figurations, found in particular in the early sonatas, have by now disappeared. The writing is both
grateful and effective. The four capriccios and four intermezzos – for
Brahms a movement in moderate tempo – of Op. 76 are singularly satisfying when played as a group. The two works in Op. 79 may represent a pun
on the composer's part; neither is rhapsodic in a literal sense since the first
is in rondo, the second in sonata form.

Opp. 76 and 79 are closer stylistically to the late piano pieces than to
the earlier works. The twenty autumnal movements of Opp. 116–19 are
mostly capriccios and intermezzos, and though always tautly constructed
in whatever form Brahms deemed appropriate the spirit of improvisation
seems seldom far away. We see Brahms's flexible employment of sonata
form in Op. 117 No. 2 where the second subject is a thematic transformation of the first (Ex. 9.5), while in the recapitulation the function of
second subject is combined with that of coda. There is further thematic
transformation in Op. 119 No. 2 where the quietly urgent main theme
becomes, in the middle section, a sentimental Viennese waltz. Words are
again transformed into music in Op. 117 No. 1. In the two D minor
capriccios of Op. 116 we notice the familiar cross rhythms, one of the
composer's favourite devices for avoiding four-squareness. In the
Intermezzo Op. 118 No. 6 the main theme employs only three notes that
then herald a five-minute drama of symphonic spaciousness and remind
us that even as late as 1892 Brahms was able to invest the familiar diminished seventh chord with new, unsuspected dramatic colouring, at times
almost usurping the traditional function of the tonic chord. We see, in

Ex. 9.5 Brahms, Intermezzo Op. 117 No. 2.

short, the storm and stress of the composer's youth transformed into a twilight of calm in which the piano miniature became the channel for Brahms's most personal and intimate thoughts.

Fryderyk Chopin

It was fortunate for Chopin that Paris, where he came to live in 1831, was to remain his home for the rest of his life. The artistic environment, the publishers who were willing to print his music, the wealthy and the aristocratic who paid what Chopin asked for their lessons, all these factors helped to set the seal on his maturity as a composer. The publication of the *Douze grandes études* Op. 10 in 1833 can be said to confirm this maturity; since Chopin had been working on them for some four years they represent a remarkable achievement for a composer barely out of his teens. By 1830 many composers had written studies, but invariably they were for classroom rather than concert use. In his own teaching Chopin made use of studies by Moscheles: some of his études indeed point forward to Chopin in their harnessing of technical figuration and musical content, but they lack the poetry and finish of Chopin's. (Always more flamboyant when giving titles to his music, it remained for Liszt to invent the *étude de concert*, which at the time must have seemed a contradiction in terms.) The two collections of studies Opp. 10 and 25 equip any pianist with the technical groundwork to cope with all Chopin's music and that of most other later composers. Many of them are constructed on the monothematic ternary principle: a single theme, idea or figuration is omnipresent, with a contrasting middle section realised by changes in tonality or other means. (A few of the preludes operate on the same principle.) Not infrequently the last bar of a study seems to resolve itself naturally in the first bar of the next; although Chopin may not have intended each set of études to be played complete, it is likely that he did envisage three or four studies in succession as an artistic entity. Most standard keyboard problems can be found in Chopin's studies: extended arpeggios

(Op. 10 No. 1), double thirds (Op. 25 No. 6), repeated notes (Op. 10 No. 7), octaves (Op. 25 No 10), cross rhythms and phrasings (Op. 10 No. 10), three-hand writing (Op. 25 No. 5). Others at first glance may seem to propagate mere finger dexterity (Opp. 10 No. 8 and Op. 25 No. 2), though if this is the case they do so much more musically than Moscheles or Czerny.

Schumann described the preludes, with some justification, as 'the beginnings of studies'. Many of them propound a motif or figure in their opening bars that is then developed consistently throughout the prelude. The epigrammatic nature of some of these exquisite miniatures seems strangely at odds with the power and depth of the twelve-bar E major or the thirteen-bar C minor preludes. Only a few have extended middle sections. (The two most substantial are those in F♯ and D♭.) It is unlikely that Chopin ever meant the preludes to be played complete in a recital; as with the études, he probably intended small groups of them to be played as and when the occasion demanded, in salon or concert hall. Charles Rosen confirms this: 'It is clear that a complete performance of Opus 28 was not thinkable during Chopin's lifetime, either in the salon or in the concert hall; nor is there any evidence that Chopin played the whole set privately for a friend or pupil.'[8] However, the immensely powerful and virile last prelude in D minor certainly acts as the climax to the whole set of twenty-four.

Among the works that Chopin intended for concert use the four ballades and four scherzos stand supreme. The ballades in particular show how Chopin attempted a wholly personal amalgamation of sonata structure and ternary design with triumphant success. The overall ternary shape of three of the ballades is less obvious to the ear than the supremely satisfying organic growth of the musical material. The third ballade's principal theme on its final appearance is cleverly stated one bar early over dominant, rather than tonic, harmony with almost incandescent splendour. The fourth ballade, in F minor, is in effect a combination of rondo and variation forms. Only the second, Op. 38, is different structurally from the others; the almost bucolic calm of F major alternates with a stormy episode in A minor. In addition the piece ends in a different key from that in which it began: an example of Chopin's interest in progressive tonality. (The second key, rather than the first, is regarded as 'the governing tonal centre'.)[9] Chopin adopts the same principle in the Scherzo Op. 31. Chopin's scherzos are also original in design. Two of the contrasting trios are particularly interesting in that in Op. 20 the trio is a variant of a Polish folk tune, and in Op. 39 it is a combination of chorale and filigree passage-work.

The Barcarolle Op. 60 stands apart as an example of Chopin's rich harmonic palette coupled with an Italianate warmth of melody, employing the classic formula of long chains of thirds. Chopin had few models for the barcarolle genre except in Italian opera itself, where several examples pre-date Chopin's piece. For instance Chopin must have seen Daniel-François-Esprit Auber's *Fra Diavolo* (1830) and Ferdinand Hérold's *Zampa* (1831), both of which include barcarolles. Some of Chopin's nocturnes are barcarolle-like in mood, such as Op. 37 No. 2, Op. 55 No. 2 and many areas of the three nocturnes Op. 9. John Field invented the piano nocturne but it was Chopin who invested the genre with a greater variety of mood. The highly elaborate passage-work that adorns so many of these pieces can be traced to the melodic lines, both written-out and improvised, of Italian opera, as well as similar passages in Hummel and Field. While it is now generally accepted that Chopin's style was formed long before he could have heard a Bellini opera, he was certainly influenced by Italian opera generally. On the page the nocturnes may appear tenuous in texture but the sustaining pedal invariably contributes to the fullness of the overall sound. These pieces were essentially works for the salon, as were almost all of the waltzes. When transported from ballroom to salon many dance forms take on a considerable increase in speed; this is particularly the case with many of Chopin's waltzes. Many are slighter than the nocturnes, but all bear witness to the composer's unerring sense of finesse and charm, essential requirements for this genre.

Chopin's unique position as a great composer, despite the fact that virtually everything that he wrote is for piano, has rarely been questioned. For the performer, amateur or professional, the textures are invariably satisfying. Frequently what appears to be merely an accompaniment turns out to be hidden counterpoint, where tiny fragments of melody emerge at unexpected points (Ex. 9.6). The two-part writing in the Impromptu in A♭ is skilfully designed to sound full and rich, particularly when enhanced by careful use of the pedal. The harmonic audacity of many of the mazurkas (see chapter 10) was undoubtedly enhanced by their folk origin and if the non-Polish genres exhibit a less obviously recondite harmonic idiom they are, in compensation, perhaps more subtle, refined and endlessly fascinating. There can be few other composers who gained almost immediate popularity during their lifetimes and have subsequently retained it.

Franz Liszt

Most public performances of piano music up to the 1840s usually involved other forces, such as vocal, chamber or orchestral music (see

Ex. 9.6 Chopin, Prelude in B, bars 14–15.

chapter 4). It was mainly due to Liszt and Thalberg that the full-length piano recital was established; the cult of the 'artist as hero' and an audience demand for publicly displayed virtuosity were both symptomatic of these early recitals. Even Clara Wieck had to conform to public taste, at least until around 1850. For public taste was not often high: master works were often interspersed with lighter pieces, such as operatic transcriptions. It is not going too far to say that up to about 1850 'the piano was more influential in the dissemination of other music (in the form of transcriptions) than for its own literature'.[10]

Liszt's transcriptions of Bach, Beethoven and Wagner remain 'faithful' to the originals, in the sense that he attempted to transcribe as much from the originals as possible without his own fanciful re-harmonisations or counter-melodies. These transcriptions were intended to familiarise the public with 'great music'. The operatic transcriptions are numerous and some were undertaken after Liszt abandoned the virtuoso platform in 1847. In his old age the spareness of the pianistic textures and an increasingly recondite harmonic language lend such transcriptions as the polonaise from *Eugene Onegin* a visionary, almost self-questioning aspect. Tchaikovsky's original melodies are still present, but they are extended or otherwise cleverly manipulated so that Liszt's musical personality is superimposed. Where the opera as a whole is concerned, Liszt sometimes attempted to tell a condensed version of the original, as in his Reminiscences of *Norma* (Bellini) and *Don Giovanni* (Mozart). More often he takes perhaps a handful of themes, occasionally a single theme only, developing them in various ways to produce a kind of musical 'chiaroscuro', resulting in a structural working that is possibly simplistic but always effective. In transcribing Schumann's 'Widmung' Liszt had no compunction in adding two further verses to the song as well as indulging in other small changes. Similarly, in 'Auf Flügeln des Gesanges' the final verse breaks away from Mendelssohn's original; the melody soars to a climax by means of a long phrase extension: a truly Lisztian aggrandisement of Mendelssohn. Because they were so little known outside Austria, perhaps even Vienna, Liszt transcribed more than fifty of Schubert's Lieder, of which only a handful are relatively easy to play.

Liszt is virtually synonymous with programme music; almost every one of his pieces bears a poetic title. It was quite natural for him to link music with literature or painting, and thus this relationship is not a weakness, but a strength. The three collections of *Années de pèlerinage* contain twenty-six pieces, varying in technical difficulty more than merit. Many pieces in the first two *Années* are obvious concert pieces though some exhibit a salon-like intimacy of mood. On the other hand, in much of the third volume (1867–77) Liszt achieved a tenuity of texture by paring down the musical inessentials: in so doing he forsook much of the glitter and panache of an earlier age. The first (Swiss) volume concerns itself mostly with travel and nature, and includes a fine *Orage* (Liszt once remarked to Amy Fay that 'storms are my forte!') and the almost impressionistic *Au lac de Wallenstadt* and *Les cloches de Genève*, where the pedalling and blurred harmonies form the starting point for Liszt's own *Les jeux d'eau à la Villa d'Este* in the third *Année*. In turn this left its mark on Ravel's *Jeux d'eau* and many of the mature piano works of Debussy.

The second *Année*, mostly based on Italian literary and artistic subjects, contains the remarkable *Il penseroso*, inspired by Michelangelo's *Meditation*, a statue of Giuliano de' Medici; as has been frequently stated, its brooding chromaticism shows a remarkable foretaste of *Tristan und Isolde*. The most imposing piece in this collection is *Après une lecture du Dante*, in which the Italian *bel canto* style is combined with the striking bravura of *Orage*. The *Dante* Sonata, as it is sometimes called, can be regarded as the composer's most ambitious programmatic work for the piano. The rather loose sonata structure of exposition, development and recapitulation corresponds to the three *canticae* of Dante's original poem, which consists of over 14,000 lines.

Liszt was highly original in his attitudes to structure and was always concerned that in this respect his ideas should be as immediately intelligible to the listener as is consistent with the need for them. The Ballade in B minor, like the *Dante* Sonata, is also constructed as a free sonata-form movement where the exposition 'repeat' is in fact written out in full in B♭ minor: thus Liszt preserves the old-style exposition repeat but expresses it by radical means. In the same way, *Au bord d'une source* from the Swiss *Année* is a set of variations on a theme beginning in A♭ major but ending in B major. The seven variations are interrupted by three virtuoso interludes and the last variation has a distinct feeling of a 'sonata-form' recapitulation. Moreover, the variations are not consistent in length. Liszt thus takes a long-established structure and adapts it to his own ends, yet the result is

not amorphous. Additionally, the increasingly complex melodic ornamentation as the piece proceeds is in reality an integral part of the structure and assists in defining the form.

Three large-scale works from the early 1860s deserve some comment.
The Two Legends (*St François d'Assise: la prédication aux oiseaux* and *St
François de Paule marchant sur les flots*) are marked by a tradition that
Liszt first played them at Rossini's salon in Paris.[11] The *Mephisto Waltz No.
1* was transcribed from the original orchestral version into a concert masterpiece of story-telling:[12] the miracle is that the piano version is so masterly that it gives the impression of being the original rather than the
transcription.

Liszt's name is linked, along with Chopin's, with the transformation of
the humble classroom exercise (or study) into the concert étude that may
indeed form an indispensable aspect of conservatory study but is above
all a work for the concert platform. As a pupil of Czerny in Vienna in the
1820s Liszt wrote a number of studies and exercises of a mechanical
nature that were heavily indebted to his teacher. Twelve of these early
studies became, nevertheless, one of the high points of nineteenth-
century piano technique in the *Etudes d'exécution transcendante*, that
were eventually published in 1852 with a dedication to Czerny. (An intermediate version, published in 1839 as *Vingt-quatre grandes études* –
though only twelve actually appeared – is by far the most technically
demanding of the three versions: it was typical of Liszt to refine and sim-
plify unnecessary difficulties in order to produce a 'definitive' version.) All
but two of the études bear poetic titles, a clear line of demarcation
between the methods of Liszt and Chopin. The opening 'Preludio' is a
written-out improvisation of a type common at the time whereby 'to
prelude' meant to test the instrument and the player's technique by means
of one or more technical figuration exercises. By placing 'Mazeppa' and
'Feux follets' adjacent to each other and numbering them 4 and 5 (thus
they are centrally positioned in the set as a whole) Liszt was possibly
demonstrating the highest possible manifestations of two types of tran-
scendence: the one a massive bravura movement requiring physical
strength, the other an extreme example of double-note delicacy whose
filigree traceries produce a sound patterning reminiscent of, but highly
distinct from, Chopin's methods.

Chopin exerted a more noticeable influence on the *Trois études de
concert*, which make an effective concert trilogy when played as a group.
The F minor étude is particularly Chopinesque in its melodic figurations,
while the last, in D♭ and originally entitled 'Un sospiro', is a good example
of Liszt's sentimental though undeniably affecting Italianate melodic

line. The later *Zwei Konzertetüden* (1862–3) already show that paring down of textures that was to be such a feature of Liszt's last years.

The *Grandes études de Paganini*, which received their final form in 1851, had also gone through an earlier version a dozen years previously. Liszt's transfer of violinistic devices to equally effective keyboard equivalents demonstrates his uncanny skill and unerring instinct for what will work on the keyboard. The fourth étude is the most obvious manifestation of this, though the third and sixth are the most famous and popular: the former for its obvious bravura, the latter because Paganini's original attracted the attention of Brahms, Rachmaninoff, Lutosławski and Blacher, among others.

Nothing could be further removed from either salon or concert hall than much of the music of Liszt's last fifteen years. Increasingly recondite harmony, unresolved discords, first- and second-inversion chords to end a movement, unaccompanied melodies, frequently plainsong-like in outline, and a thinning of textures when in general musical density was becoming increasingly opulent: such procedures demonstrate Liszt's inventive and fecund musical imagination that was to prove such an inspiration for twentieth-century composers from Bartók to Busoni. *Unstern! Sinistre, disastro* and *Schlaflos! Frage und Antwort*, and many other pieces, are proof of the extraordinary journey that Liszt had undertaken over more than sixty years, when as a boy of eleven he contributed, along with approximately fifty other composers, a variation on Diabelli's celebrated waltz. Perhaps no other composer travelled so far.

Sonata and concerto

The development of these genres after the deaths of Beethoven and Schubert was symptomatic of the diversity in nineteenth-century musical styles. In particular, the sonata tended to develop along one of three main trajectories that might be described as the conventional, the radical and the revolutionary. To the first belong those numerous sonatas, by such composers as Moscheles, Hummel and Czerny, that were constructed on safe, formalistic lines. Contemporary audiences obviously liked this music, music that was usually played by its own composer. Individual passages can be interesting – the decorative passage-work in Hummel that frequently anticipates Chopin, for example – but as wholes such sonatas have an interest today for the scholar rather than the performer. Conversely, the young, radical Romantics, wary – perhaps fearful – of Beethoven's achievements adopted a rather different approach that was far from conventional. Mendelssohn wrote three sonatas in the 1820s, though two were possibly composition exercises not intended for publication. The third in E Op. 6 includes a barcarolle-like opening, reminiscent of the corresponding movement in Beethoven's Op. 101, and a highly elaborate slow movement, Adagio e senza tempo, with passages of recitative and long unbarred sections of music, highly rhapsodic in style. Schumann's three sonatas written in the 1830s exemplify a typical Romantic paradox of adhering to 'the rules' while at the same time exploring new paths. All three are in minor keys with their first movements' second subjects in the orthodox relative major key. (All three of Chopin's piano sonatas operate on the same principle.) Conversely, other areas venture into extremely remote tonalities. In the development sections the highly Schumannesque preference for lengthy stretches of music with an unrelenting obsession for persistent rhythmic patterns shows the composer's indebtedness to, but not dependence on, Beethoven. There are other major differences between Schumann and his conservative contemporaries. In Op. 11 the slow introduction to the initial Allegro refers (some twelve minutes later) to the succeeding slow movement, entitled 'Aria'. (This embryonic form of melodic interrelationship reached its peak a few years later in Schumann's D minor Symphony where all four movements form a work of remarkable subtlety, constructed on the cyclic principle that César Franck was to espouse forty years later.) Schumann's Third Sonata Op. 14, originally published as *Concert sans orchestre*, exists in two slightly different versions. Both imitate the textures of a piano concerto in a work that forms an interesting link between the rondo of Mozart's Sonata K311 and Alkan's Concerto for solo piano. (Chopin's apparently comparable *Allegro de concert* Op. 46 belongs to a different category: that of a first movement of an abandoned piano concerto, frankly arranged for piano solo.) The slightly later *Faschingsschwank aus Wien* Op. 26 (1839–40) is a five-movement sonata in lighter mood.

In the first movements of his sonatas Chopin dispensed with the recapitulation of the first subject, a daring experiment in the telescoping of traditional sonata-form structure. Op. 35 in B♭ minor includes the famous Funeral March and a short presto epilogue-finale written entirely in octaves. The larger B minor Sonata, with its concise scherzo and inventive and cumulatively textured finale, represents, along with Liszt's Sonata, also in B minor, the peak of the Romantic sonata repertory. Liszt's work, a supreme example of the rare revolutionary trajectory in sonata design, dates from 1852–3 and combines three movements into one continuous whole; an energetic fugato may be regarded as an 'introduction' to the 'finale'. In this work, both intricate and imposing, Liszt achieved his masterpiece for piano. It combines exceptional workmanship (most of the passage-work turns out to be thematic) with material of

the utmost nobility, much of which is developed by thematic transformation. (Here, as in other aspects of his music, Schubert proved extremely
influential. His 'Wanderer' Fantasy, a four-movement work in which thematic transformation emerges almost fully fledged, was a true precursor
both of Liszt's Sonata and – rather less obviously – of Schumann's D
minor Symphony; see chapter 8.) However, in no other work save the
Faust Symphony, with which the sonata has much in common, did Liszt
ever write anything less calculated to strike popular fancy. Indeed Liszt
himself rarely performed the sonata, except in private, because it was
always coldly received.

Brahms's three sonatas, written before he was twenty-one, make one
regret that he abandoned the genre at an early age. The first and last movements of the C major Op. 1 are built on ingenious transformations of the
same theme; the slow movement is a set of variations on a German folk
song. In Op. 2 in F♯ minor the slow movement is also a set of variations
joined to the ensuing scherzo, an additional variation on the same theme.
The imposing Sonata in F minor Op. 5 is in five movements and is
Brahms's most overtly romantic work: the slow movement is headed by
three lines of poetry from Sternau. (Two lovers stand in the moonlight,
their hearts entwined in passionate ardour.) After the energetic scherzo
the *Rückblick* (retrospect) seems to indicate, by its funeral march
rhythms, that some (unspecified) tragedy has occurred.

Brahms's two concertos of 1854–8 and 1878–81 have been described
as symphonies for piano and orchestra rather than genuine concertos.
They are indeed very unlike the typical Romantic concerto which, after
Beethoven, had become a contest between soloist and orchestra: the complete antithesis of the Classical concerto. It is true that obvious dramatic
elements dominate areas of Brahms's first concerto, though the solo part
is hardly virtuoso in the usual sense. However, the second concerto Op. 83
is basically a mellow blend of soloist and orchestra (exemplified by the
opening horn solo and the prominent solo cello in the slow movement),
where the four movements constitute one of the longest concertos in the
repertory. Liszt's two concertos are markedly different from each other.
The E♭ concerto, like the sonata, combines several movements into a
single unit using thematic transformation and ingenious, at times
chamber, orchestration as a unifying feature. The A major concerto, in
one movement and largely based on the opening theme, is also an
example of chamber scoring balanced by brasher virtuosic music for both
soloist and orchestra.

The first movement of Schumann's Piano Concerto, originally a separate *Phantasie*, propounds a single theme that goes through an astonishing
number of transformations, each one enacting important structural areas

as the movement unfolds: first and second themes, transitions, cadenza and coda. The succeeding intermezzo and waltz-like finale are also thematically linked to each other. The whole concerto is one of Schumann's best works, not least because of its effective, often restrained orchestration. The two early Chopin concertos took as their models works by Field and Hummel, not Beethoven, hence the slender orchestral accompaniments and unusually prominent and virtuosic solo writing. Their finales are indebted to Polish dance rhythms, and it is indeed their musical content that has kept the concertos alive, since the orchestral parts are scarcely rewarding to play. In a reduced format the Field and Chopin concertos were often performed in small venues, even salons. The programme for Chopin's Paris début in 1832, reproduced in the *New Grove*, vol. 4, p. 295, shows that the F minor Concerto and Op. 2 Variations were accompanied by the string quintet players who had opened the programme.

French music

Much French piano music from the second quarter of the nineteenth century was conceived for the salon, but, unlike that of Chopin, was often directed at the amateur market, though there are numerous virtuoso pieces too. Many of the composers, such as Herz, Hünten and Kalkbrenner, lived in Paris but were of German origin. Their music spoke fluently in the current idiom of the day, but little survives in the current repertory. After 1850, a more serious approach can be detected in the work of Camille Saint-Saëns, though the most interesting piano music dates from the last twenty years of the century.

César Franck, whose musical development was relatively slow, was only eleven years younger than Liszt, though his greatest music did not appear until the 1880s. Before this, Franck had composed a considerable amount of piano music, aimed at the salon and domestic markets. Much of this is both trivial and uninteresting and it was not until the surprisingly late impact of Liszt and Wagner on Franck's music which, allied to his 'serious' Walloon origins, resulted in two late masterpieces for piano. These revealed Franck as a force to be reckoned with in French music, even though his outlook and techniques were Germanic in concept. The *Prélude, choral et fugue* (1884) offers a modern equivalent of a baroque prelude and fugue extended into a triptych by a dignified chorale. As in other works of his maturity, Franck here revivified those cyclic elements from Schubert and Liszt by a learned display of contrapuntal thematic combinations. Towards the close, the principal rhythmic patterns of the prelude are combined with both chorale and fugue. In addition, there are numerous cross-references between one theme and another as the work proceeds. In the slightly later and similarly ternary-structured *Prélude, aria et final* (1886–7) the close of the aria is combined with the prelude's principal melody towards the end of the whole work. Inevitably, the magnificence and nobility of these two pieces were beyond the comprehension of the majority of the concert public when they were first performed at the Société Nationale.

Gabriel Fauré (1845–1924), musically and temperamentally Franck's opposite, stands in many ways as a representative of those peculiarly French characteristics of reticence, subtlety and restraint. His piano works and *mélodies*, though intended for the salon, are epitomised by an exquisite harmonic palette allied to continually varied keyboard textures, both of which underpin a superb gift for melody. Overall, Fauré's music demonstrates a craftsmanship worthy of Brahms, allowing for necessarily different compositional methods.

In his piano writing Fauré's supreme achievement was to develop and extend the scope of the nocturne and barcarolle to unsuspected heights after Chopin's highly personal treatment of these genres. Fauré composed no fewer than thirteen of each, the first seven nocturnes and the first six barcarolles spanning the period *c.*1875–98. At first slightly influenced by Chopin's pianistic textures, Fauré soon developed a highly original style. Elaborate accompaniments are divided ingeniously between the hands, along with sinuous melodies centrally placed in the texture. Counterpoint plays an important role, resulting in a free employment of accented passing and chromatically altered notes. In addition, Fauré made an important contribution to the development of harmony, a development brought about in particular by his modulatory techniques. He was fond of moving rapidly from one unrelated (diatonic or chromatic) chord to another, frequently 'looking at' rather than stating a new key. Fauré's undoubted interest in modal harmonies, supposedly derived from the Niedermeyer School where he was taught, has sometimes been over-emphasised. The most popular works of Fauré tend to use modal themes, though he often introduced chromatic notes foreign to the prevailing mode. In fact, Fauré was a late-romantic composer, whose aim was never to subvert tonality and 'thus it is not so much the language which is new, it is rather the syntax, the order of words'.[13] The sixth and seventh nocturnes (1894 and 1898) are truly symphonic utterances, written on a grand scale but never descending to the grand manner. In fact they start to demonstrate an austerity and tenuity of texture that were to be the hallmarks of Fauré's final period. Here, sobriety coupled with considerable technical difficulty results in music that is popular neither with performer nor audience. Nevertheless, Fauré's piano music is sufficiently varied to challenge the best of Chopin and Debussy. One or two pieces, such as the *Ballade* Op. 19 and *Thème et variations* Op. 73, enjoy fairly frequent hearings. But it was in the salon where Fauré knew that his refined and aristocratic style could best be appreciated and the atmosphere of this milieu is today a relic of a bygone age. However, this music, as represented by Fauré, remains unsurpassed and unapproached.

Emmanuel Chabrier (1841–94), again an artistic personality very different from both Franck and Fauré, wrote little for piano though what he did write is significant. He was among the first to bring genuine wit and ebullience into French music, resulting in what has been described as a 'café-concert atmosphere'. Yet his music, underneath its sparkle and tender warmth, was highly influential on later composers, especially Ravel and 'Les Six'. Influenced by Wagner's seventh and ninth chords and the folk melodies and rhythms of his native Auvergne region, the result was a highly original music that nevertheless was immediately popular. The *Dix pièces pittoresques* (1881) were a landmark in French piano music in their skilful combination of innovative harmony and original though often short-breathed melody, combined with superbly effective (if occasionally orchestral) piano writing. 'Idylle', 'Improvisation', 'Menuet pompeux' and 'Scherzo-valse' are the best-known movements. It is a rare though rewarding experience for both pianist and audience to play and hear all ten pieces in sequence. The *Bourrée fantasque* (1891), Chabrier's last completed major work, stands by itself as an example of flamboyant virtuosity, with extreme contrasts of nervous energy and tender, sentimental melody.

Claude Debussy, though born in 1862, was a twentieth-century composer in techniques and outlook, whose most significant piano writing dates from after 1900. Nevertheless, two works from the 1890s deserve mention. In its three movements with baroque titles, the *Suite bergamasque* pays homage to earlier French harpsichord composers; the oddly contrasting slow movement is the well known 'Clair de lune'. *Danse*, more original, lively and inventive, is the best of the early piano works. The nervous energy of its pentatonic opening contrasts with an astonishingly spacious middle section, achieved by long vistas of swirling arpeggios allied to slow changes of harmonic rhythm.

The nineteenth-century duet repertory

'Piano duets' are defined in the *New Grove* as 'of two kinds: those for two players at one instrument, and those in which each of the two pianists has an instrument to himself.'[14] In fact, a piano duet invariably implies two people at one piano, as does 'four-hand music' also; if two instruments are involved, the term 'for two pianos' is usual. With few exceptions, piano duets in Germany were intended for domestic use (in France and Russia, the salon), whereas the two-piano repertory everywhere was for concert performance. With two pianos, both players are virtuosos in their own right, a relatively cumbersome proceeding when only one instrument is involved. After Schubert, the original repertory for both types was relatively small. The succeeding five paragraphs discuss the repertory for two players at one instrument.

Mendelssohn's *Allegro brillante* in A Op. 92 is a rare and rather taxing example of the virtuoso duet and inevitably different from Schumann's contributions to the repertory. These include the *Ballszenen* Op. 109 (1851) and *Kinderball* Op. 130 (1853). Both contain movements in national style (French, Scottish, Hungarian, etc.) though they are eclipsed by the *Bilder aus Osten* Op. 66 (1848), not especially oriental and described as six impromptus for four hands. Schumann writes imaginatively and gratefully for the two players here, and the collection affords a panoramic view of his sober late style. Just before the composer attempted suicide in 1854 he sketched a theme that in his hallucinatory state he believed he had received from the spirits of Schubert and Mendelssohn. Brahms took this for his Variations on a theme of Schumann Op. 23 (1861), which ends with a funeral march. Much better and better-known are the four books of Hungarian Dances, composed between 1852 and 1869. Brahms claimed only to have arranged these popular tunes, though it is believed some of the (best?) melodies are of his own invention.

As one would expect, the French repertory is quite different: keyboard colouring and sonorities assume greater prominence, and collections and pieces both tend towards poetic titles. For much of the time, as always, French composers were engrossed in opera and ballet. It was not until the last thirty years or so of the century that the repertory started to come into its own. One of the earliest and best works is the twelve short pieces *Jeux d'enfants* (1871) by Bizet (1838–75), in which each title is supplemented by a generic term. The whole collection is distinguished by its epigrammatic humour and wit. Bizet orchestrated five numbers ('Trompette et tambour, marche'; 'La toupie, impromptu'; 'La poupée, berceuse'; 'Petit mari, petite femme, duo'; 'Le bal, galop') to form a Petite Suite, today invariably entitled *Jeux d'enfants* also. As with everything that Bizet wrote, both versions are distinguished by clear textures, melodic charm and harmonic piquancy.

Somewhat in the same vein, though as a result rather different from his other works, is the 'Dolly Suite' (1894–6) by Fauré. The opening 'Berceuse' owes something to Bizet and the final 'Le pas espagnol' to Chabrier; apart from the canon in the middle section of 'Tendresse', the whole suite shows the composer in unusually light-hearted mood. Debussy's youthful contributions to the repertory were relatively slight; they include the popular *Petite Suite* (1886–9) and the *Marche écossaise sur un thème populaire* (1891) in which the faint suggestions of the whole-tone scale, a genuine Scottish melody and Borodin-like pedal points in the central section all co-exist very happily. The two sets of Slavonic Dances Op. 46 (1878) and Op. 72 (1886) did for Dvořák what the Hungarian Dances had done for Brahms. (For the coffers of their mutual publisher, Fritz Simrock, all four collections did even more.) In similar mood are Grieg's attractive Four Norwegian Dances Op. 35 (1881), exhilarating mood pictures that utilise Norwegian folk idioms.

A striking anticipation of Hindemith's *Gebrauchsmusik* principle was provided in 1879 by the paraphrases on 'Chopsticks' by Anatol Liadov, Nikolay Sterbatcheff and three members of 'The Five' (see chapter 10). At a party a little girl had remarked that her favourite piece was something that *she* could play:

Ex. 9.7 'Chopsticks' theme.

The five composers proceeded to write a set of paraphrases on this theme; actually a series of ostinato movements, since the theme is repeated unaltered many times over. (It is always at the top of the texture, thus the whole composition might be fancifully designated a 'sky treble' since it is exactly the opposite concept of a ground bass.) There are twenty-four variations and finale, followed by sixteen genre pieces (march, fugue, polka, waltz, etc.). For the second edition Liszt contributed a paraphrase, cheating in the process since he repeated small sections of the theme to suit his purpose. The hilarity of the piece does not detract from the composers' overall inventiveness; it is strange that the work is now virtually forgotten.

The two-piano repertory is considerably smaller, though musically more valuable. Chopin is ill-represented by his Rondo in C Op. 73, a post-humous work and rare in this genre since the first piano part is more difficult than the second: it was Chopin's intention to play it with a less able friend. Schumann's Andante and Variations in B♭ Op. 46 (1843) was originally written with additional parts for two cellos and horn, a version not published until 1893. One of the great works in the repertory, Brahms's Sonata in F minor Op. 34b, exists in the equally fine version for piano quintet (the original conception was for string quintet). Amongst its many qualities the first movement bears clear testimony to Brahms's unobtrusive contrapuntal skill; the slow movement is influenced by similarly mellow and serene Schubert songs. The Scherzo is one of Brahms's most exciting, while the faintly Hungarian finale is a masterpiece of unexpected, though subtle, changes of mood: the last two bars surprise, yet are somehow inevitable. Brahms and Tausig gave the (unsuccessful) premiere in 1864. Equally fine and also existing in an alternative version (orchestra) are the Variations on a theme of Haydn Op. 56b (1873) whose theme, despite the Haydnesque irregular phrase lengths, is probably not by Haydn. (It is usually known today as the 'St Anthony' Chorale.) The eight variations are extremely diverse in mood, despite remaining close to the theme throughout. They are followed by a passacaglia finale in which the *basso ostinato* consists of an ingenious combination of the melody and bass of the original chorale.

Its closest French equivalent is Saint-Saëns's Variations on a theme of Beethoven Op. 35 (1874), one of the composer's best works. (Preceded by a slow introduction, the theme is the trio section of the third movement of Beethoven's Sonata Op. 31 No. 3.) The piece is difficult though rewarding to play, and the final fugue, often a sterile academic exercise with Saint-Saëns, is exhilarating. Chabrier's *Trois valses romantiques* (1883), as usual with this composer, are both ebullient and humorous. An interesting curiosity was provided in 1877 by Grieg's 'accompaniments for a second piano' (very much in his own style) to three Mozart sonatas (K533/494, K545 and K283) and the Fantasia and Sonata K475 and K457. Other important works include suites by Anton Arensky (1861–1906) and Rachmaninoff.

Finally, an important aspect of domestic music-making in the nineteenth century was the numerous arrangements for piano duet of string quartets, orchestral works and so on. For many this was the only way it was possible to hear and get to know such pieces until the arrival of the gramophone record and piano roll. Arrangements were good, bad and indifferent. Some of the best were of the Beethoven and Schumann symphonies for two, four and eight hands by Ernst Pauer. Mendelssohn's orchestral music somehow transcribes well for piano duet, and it is worth remembering that the original version of the overture *A midsummer night's dream* was in this form.

Conclusion

The music discussed in this chapter represents only a small fraction of the large repertory of salon, domestic, concert and teaching music written for the piano between *c.*1830 and 1900. That repertory is larger by far than that for any other instrument. Even when the trivia are discarded, the remainder is impressive in quality, quantity and variety. In 1830 the solo pianist could be heard only as an assisting artist. By 1850, Liszt and Thalberg – and a little later Clara Schumann – had made the piano recital what it is today: one of the most popular forms of musical entertainment. It is obvious that without the repertory this would not have been possible. It is less obvious that for some 150 years such popularity has shown little sign of declining, though various composers have inevitably been 'in' or 'out' of public esteem. Despite the proliferation of radio, television, CDs and other forms of electronic reproduction there seems little doubt that the piano recital will survive for some time yet. While the salon is now relegated into the museum of history, domestic music – whether played on a real piano or (increasingly) its electronic equivalent – continues to thrive, taking its repertory from the music of all periods, a repertory in which the piano, or its keyboard predecessors, stands supreme.

10 Nationalism

J. BARRIE JONES

Introduction

Nationalism used to be portrayed, mistakenly, as an offshoot of nine-teenth-century Romanticism, portrayed, moreover, almost exclusively as an eastern European phenomenon. We can see now that Weber's *Der Freischütz* and Wagner's *Der Ring des Nibelungen* are German nationalist in concept in much the same way that Mikhail Glinka's (1804–57) *A life for the Tsar* and Modest Musorgsky's (1839–81) *Boris Godunov* are Russian nationalist works. However, it is true that musical nationalism seems most apparent in those countries where there had been virtually no previous traditions of art music, such as one can point to in France, Italy or the German-speaking areas of western Europe. This is, of course, not to say that music was uncultivated in eastern Europe. Far from it: the Slavonic peoples have for the most part been intensely musical. Bohemian instrumentalists were justly celebrated in the second half of the eighteenth century and, as in most countries, eastern Europe enjoyed a rich cultural heritage of folk song and dance. Nor should we ignore the importance of church music, which had a strong impact on nineteenth-century Russian music. Since eastern European folk music and church music are much less familiar to western ears they seem to have acquired an exoticism and mystique that formerly contributed to the myth of musical nationalism as a purely eastern phenomenon. And one might add that in the nineteenth century social and political forces were strong factors in the emergence of nationalist sentiments: political unrest was endemic throughout Europe, particularly between about 1830 and 1870.

Nationalist feelings are expressed most forcibly in the setting of words. Thus opera and song were primary targets of many nationalist compos-ers. The symphonic poem also proved fruitful in delineating folk tales and national heroes. Coupled with the general nineteenth-century pre-occupation with orchestral opulence and colour, the piano proved less of an attraction to many nationalist composers. However, a great deal of piano music was produced, much of it aimed at the salon or domestic market rather than the concert hall.

Poland

Polish music is inevitably centred on Chopin, whose mazurkas and polonaises exemplify some of the earliest overtly nationalist sentiments in music. The mazurka epitomises the dance of the common people, one of the reasons, perhaps, why it appealed mostly to Polish or Russian composers. The polonaise, like the mazurka in triple time, was originally of folk origin, but was transformed into a processional by the nobility. This gentrification made it internationally popular: it was a regular movement in the baroque suite, and even in the classical era a number of examples were composed by Wilhelm Friedemann Bach, Beethoven, Weber and Schubert.

Unquestionably it was Chopin who put the mazurka on to the European musical map. Despite the sophistication that he acquired after his move to Paris, Chopin retained a deep and abiding love for Poland. It would be wrong to describe him as a countryman, but he was familiar with Polish folk songs and as a youth had enjoyed hearing the rustic bands that played *al fresco* in the countryside. The more than fifty mazurkas were a direct outcome of Chopin's patriotism and first-hand experience, and they span the whole of his creative career. They are too numerous to discuss in detail, but a survey of the entire collection reveals a remarkable diversity of moods and techniques within the limited confines of the mazurka genre. As with the waltz, some of these dances acquired a degree of sophistication that befitted their performance in the salon; on the other hand many are obviously danceable (though never, of course, in salons!). The original dance was variable as to tempo, frequently with stresses on either the second or third beat of the bar. Now and again, such syncopated stresses could vary within a single piece. At times the slower mazurkas require a (not always indicated) increase in speed for their middle sections. Formally, the mazurkas are ternary in design, frequently with a coda that may introduce a short-lived new tune (Op. 59 No. 3). Chopin tended to publish his mazurkas in sets of three or four, and in every case the set gains by being performed complete.

The earlier sets (Opp. 6–33 and many of the posthumously published Opp. 67 and 68 sets) tend to a harmonic palette simple yet bold. The iconoclastic defiance of those chains of consecutive dominant sevenths in the coda of Op. 30 No. 4 (Ex. 10.1) and the extraordinary final VIb chord of Op. 17 No. 4 (Ex. 10.2) are typical examples. Chopin was particularly interested in modal experiments in the earlier sets: Op. 24 No. 2, ostensibly in C major, is actually in the Aeolian mode with a brief Lydian episode from bars 21 to 36. Now and again we see exotic scales, such as the 'gypsy' scale (with raised fourth) in Op. 68 No. 2 (Ex. 10.3) and in the remarkable

Ex. 10.1 Chopin, Mazurka Op. 30 No. 4, bars 125–33.

Ex. 10.2 Chopin, Mazurka Op. 17 No. 4, end.

Ex. 10.3 Chopin, Mazurka Op. 68 No. 2.

middle section of Op. 7 No. 1, where the gypsy melody is supported by an unrelated pedal drone on G♭. At the opposite extreme stands the tonic/dominant music of much of Op. 33 No. 2. Many of the mazurkas are organised almost in cells, short phrases of two or four bars that repeat either exactly or with only minimal variation, a procedure known as cell development technique: a frequent mannerism in Slavonic music.

The later mazurkas, while still rustic, become somewhat more stylised, though they are certainly more sophisticated harmonically. Phrases will sometimes cut across set harmonic patterns to produce an individual form of syncopation. Very occasionally, tempo and mood become almost a *valse triste*, as in Op. 63 No. 2 and Op. 68 No. 4. Since the danced

Ex. 10.4 Chopin, Mazurka Op. 17 No. 4, bar 18.

mazurka was performed in couples, imitation is sometimes used to depict what has been described as 'la fuite de la danseuse devant le danseur' ('the dancer's flight from her partner') as in Op. 50 No. 3. In Op. 63 No. 3 the imitation is at one beat's distance and sufficiently exact to form a canon. This, and that in Mozart's Sonata K576, are instances of the somewhat rare one-beat canon. As Thomas Fielden remarks in his edition: 'The *danseur* must have been close to the *danseuse*!'[1]

Pedal effects are frequent to imitate the village band, as in Op. 6 No. 3, but on occasion are also used structurally to help define the form, as in Op. 17 No. 4, and Op. 68 No. 3, where complete middle sections are built upon pedal points. Chopin sometimes imitates the characteristic sounds of clarinet or violin; the pianistic *fioriture* of Op. 17 No. 4 clearly had their origin in violin portamento (Ex. 10.4). Chopin very occasionally borrows folk tunes, but more usually he imitates them, assimilating folk idioms into characteristic melodies entirely his own. Chopin is more obviously folk-like (that is, Polish) in the mazurkas than elsewhere in his music, rather in the way that Beethoven is in the 'Pastoral' Symphony, compared with the other eight. However, in neither case are these 'nationalistic' works in any way at odds with the composers' individual identities in their music as a whole.

The larger structures of Chopin's polonaises have made them more familiar concert works than the mazurkas. The composer's first efforts were more tentative: several early examples, including the three in Op. 71, later published posthumously in 1855, were not intended for immediate publication. Apart from the boyish G minor Polonaise, which was published in 1817 more or less as a stunt, the first polonaises that Chopin deemed worthy to see the light of day were the two in Op. 26. Certainly both display a finish lacking in their predecessors. That they are still relatively early works is perhaps demonstrated by a rudimentary coda in No. 2 and by no coda at all in No. 1. Even so, Chopin – great melodist that he was – rarely surpassed himself in the superb arches of melody that grace the trio in No. 1. Conversely, the second in E♭ minor is a rare example in Chopin – though it is common in Beethoven, most remarkably in the first

movement of the 'Eroica' Symphony – of a structural edifice more dependent on a masterly agglomeration of short motifs than on *cantabile*
melody; even the trio consists of short phrases more remarkable for their
rhythmic patterns than for memorable cantilena. The two polonaises Op.
40, as has often been said, may well have been written to represent the
greatness and the downfall of Poland. To avoid bombast in the A major
and ensure pathos in the C minor, the tempo should be similar for both
works; Hutcheson reported such constant tempos in Paderewski's
playing.[2] The A major polonaise, again devoid of a coda, seems as a result
to come to a rather lame halt at the end; on the other hand, in the C minor,
the manner by which the brief coda grows naturally from what precedes it
is strangely impressive. In the three succeeding works, the coda was to
assume increasing importance.

   The Polonaise in F♯ minor Op. 44 is one of the longest in the series, and
is unique in that its middle section takes the form of a mazurka, and like
Opp. 53 and 61 the introduction is thematic, not merely annunciatory.
Op. 53 in A♭, one of the most resplendent and heroic of all polonaises, is
celebrated for its ♩♫♫ left-hand ostinato in the middle section. Its execu-
tion requires an extremely supple wrist, and this episode contrasts tell-
ingly with the succeeding quiet passage where the polonaise rhythm all
but disappears, making the final return of the principal theme all the
more effulgent. The magnificent Polonaise-fantaisie Op. 61 stands in a
class by itself. Neither appreciated nor really understood until many years
after Chopin's death, its harmonic richness and the wealth of thematic
ideas so convincingly brought together in the final peroration, suggest
new directions that the composer might well have taken had he lived
longer. After Chopin, much of the piano music produced in Poland was of
the salon type, exemplified by the Scharwenka brothers, Xaver
(1850–1924) and Philipp (1847–1917), and Moszkowski, who spent
much of his life in Paris. Stanisław Moniuszko (1819–72) can be compared with the Russian Glinka in that he concentrated his energies on
attempting to establish Polish opera as a viable expression of nationalist
feeling. The one worthy pianistic successor to Chopin was Karol
Szymanowski (1882–1937).

Bohemia

In the early nineteenth century the early Romantic piano piece was pioneered by Tomášek and Voříšek, but the nationalist movement was initi-
ated, then dominated, by Bedřich Smetana (1824–84), and later Antonín
Dvořák (1841–1904). Neither of these later masters appears at his best in

the piano repertory. This is surprising in Smetana's case, since he was a virtuoso pianist who in his earlier years composed voluminously for the instrument, attempting to do for the polka what Chopin had done for the mazurka. Most of his early pieces are of the superior salon type and of considerable technical difficulty. Smetana's piano style, though effectively written for the instrument, demonstrates in the occasional massiveness of textures the composer's predilection for orchestral writing. This is still apparent in his piano masterpiece, the Czech Dances of 1877. The collection begins with four polkas, more refined and pianistic than many of their earlier namesakes, that are then followed by ten large-scale dances, five of which re-work genuine folk melodies. (In the first polka, the sliding chromatic sequences make for an interesting comparison with bars 5–8 and elsewhere in Chopin's Mazurka Op. 6 No. 1.) As with many nationalists, however, those melodies of his own invention that Smetana introduces could well be taken for real folk songs. This set of dances, rarely played yet singularly effective as a whole, seems to epitomise the Czech spirit in all its moods. Even when the music is at its liveliest, there is sometimes an undercurrent of poignancy, nostalgia, even melancholy.

Dvořák was an eclectic genius who profited from a close study of Smetana's music, and also learned much from Schubert, Brahms and Wagner. His best piano writing occurs in the chamber music. Solo pieces were relatively a side issue, but in so prolific a composer, such pieces are numerous. Many are somewhat trivial and were aimed at the domestic market, though the Eight Waltzes Op. 54 have an undeniable charm. The best of the earlier works is the Theme and Variations Op. 36 (1876), clearly modelled on the first movement of Beethoven's Sonata Op. 26. Other pieces include the thirteen Poetic Tone Pictures Op. 85 (1889) – the title may well have been borrowed from Grieg's Op. 3 – containing the charming 'Goblins' Dance' and an energetic 'Furiant'; the Humoresques Op. 101 (1894), the seventh of which made Dvořák's publisher, Simrock, many millions; and the Suite Op. 98 (1894), probably the composer's masterpiece for piano. Largely moulded in five relatively substantial movements, its piano idiom is typical of many works: alternately pianistic and straining for quasi-orchestral effects. Dvořák in fact orchestrated the suite himself, to its great advantage, and it is in this form that it is more likely to be heard. As in most eastern European music, Czech music abounds in dance-like rhythms and short phrases that are often repeated, exactly or with minimal variation. There is, though, an element of greater musical continuity (often brought about by sequence) at times, reminding us that German influences were stronger on the Bohemians than on the Slovaks and eastern Moravians such as Janáček.

Russia

As in other lands, most composers of nationalist inclinations pursued a greater interest in opera and song than in 'nationalist' piano works. A considerable quantity of piano music was produced, however, mostly for the salon market. Within its limitations, some of this music was well written, though much is also now forgotten. Glinka, by general consent the 'father' of Russian music, was not particularly attracted to the piano and what he wrote for it is relatively trivial. In addition to the standard salon repertory of dances and occasional pieces, he also composed paraphrases on popular Italian operas, a genre to which he always responded with enthusiasm.

Russian music took a great step forward with the succeeding generation of composers. 'The Five' (or 'The Mighty Handful') were not, as a group, instinctive writers for the piano. César Cui (1835–1918) produced numerous salon pieces overtly facile in character, while Nikolay Rimsky-Korsakov (1844–1908) probably saw his relatively few piano works as composition exercises, since they mostly comprise fugal and other contrapuntal pieces avowedly academic in style. Alexander Borodin (1833–87) wrote relatively little in any genre, but his *Petite Suite* (1885) is certainly characteristic. An unhackneyed piece, ideal as an encore, might be salvaged in his deft and humorous Scherzo in A♭ (1885). There is a famous recording of this by Rachmaninoff.

The piano music of Mily Balakirev (1837–1910), the leader and mentor of this group of composers, is perhaps long overdue for revival. Unlike his colleagues he appears at his best in instrumental music: although he produced some choral works and over forty songs, his one attempt at opera survives only in fragments. He is best known for his forbiddingly difficult oriental fantasy *Islamey* (1869, second version 1902), based on Caucasian folk tunes. There is, however, a large corpus of piano pieces, many of which date from the last decade of Balakirev's life, when, in his retirement and after numerous earlier spells of depression, he felt impelled to return to composition. The bulk of his piano music may well have been conceived for concert use, though its manner is frequently of the salon. Like Smetana's, the music is technically difficult, but it bears the undeniable stamp of the composer's personality rather more than does his Bohemian contemporary's. Factors that have told against it are the relative sameness of much of the music and, during that last decade, the fact that in style it was some forty years or so behind the times. There are undoubted mannerisms: a fondness, not to say obsession, for music in five flats (both sonatas are in B♭ minor), widespread left-hand arpeggios, thin textures and melodies permeated throughout with similar intervallic shapes. But the music is pianistic, clearly textured and beautifully crafted. Balakirev was attracted to the mazurka, producing seven all told: No. 5 exists separately as the second movement of the Sonata No. 2, while No. 6 interestingly ends with a *krakowiak* in a different key (A♭) from that in which the movement began. (The *krakowiak* was a folk dance in duple time from the Cracow region of Poland.) In this piece, in order to retain the same key signature for the start and finish Balakirev's first theme is in his favourite D♭ tonality, though since he oscillates between D♭ and A♭ in the first section, a four-flat signature does duty for both keys. There are also seven waltzes, three nocturnes and numerous other pieces including a charming Berceuse in the same D♭ tonality as Chopin's. Balakirev's piano writing is pianistic though at times awkward, is difficult technically but not obviously so in the manner of Liszt or Rachmaninoff: hence its neglect by present-day concert pianists. But it merits an urgent revival.

Musorgsky was the only one of The Five to produce a masterpiece for the piano, *Pictures from an exhibition* (1874), perhaps the only monumental Russian solo piano piece in the entire century. As in his colleagues' best works, Musorgsky here demonstrated his uncanny skill at painting those thumbnail sketches so essential in brief descriptive pieces such as these. The short stories and sketches of Gogol and Pushkin were as influential here as any work by Glinka or didactic instruction from Balakirev. As with Borodin and Rimsky-Korsakov, such small-scale workings made Musorgsky more responsive to the setting of words than to purely instrumental music, yet *Pictures* triumphs over the awkward piano writing by the sheer brilliance of the whole concept, its immediacy, and the originality of its harmonic and melodic content. The work was inspired by drawings in a memorial exhibition of the composer's friend, the architect Victor Hartmann. It was a master-stroke to conceive of an introductory 'Promenade', which basically consists of one melodic shape, to represent a visitor to the exhibition, whose thoughts and emotions change while walking from picture to picture. Thus the movement recurs several times in varied melodic and harmonic guises. The theme itself embodies the Russian folk idiom *par excellence*. The various movements epitomise many of the nationalist techniques of Russian music: the unbroken tonic pedal in 'Il vecchio castello', sudden changes of mood and texture in 'Gnomus', clanging bells in 'La porte des Bohatyrs de Kiew' and persistent phrase repetitions in 'La cabane sur des pattes de poule'. There is also what might be described as the reverse of the coin from those simple repetitive folk tunes that utilise gapped melodic intervals, often fourths: the development of a more chromatic harmony, with melodies derived from them. This type of harmony, frequently non-functionally chromatic and often used for colouristic purposes, stemmed from the whole-tone scale, found occasionally in Glinka and developed more systematically by Rimsky-Korsakov and Musorgsky in particular. Where description or word-setting is involved, whole-tone harmonies frequently portray magic or malevolence. In *Pictures*, non-functional chromatic harmony abounds but is particularly direct and forceful in 'Catacombae sepulchrum Romanum'. The trio section of 'Ballet des poussins dans leurs coques' is mostly based around colourfully exotic whole-tone harmony. The achievement of The Five is all the more remarkable in that only Balakirev was a professional musician; the others were initially trained in other fields, Borodin and Cui remaining active in those fields throughout their lives.

Tchaikovsky, more versatile than any of The Five, pursued a wider range, being attracted equally to both vocal and instrumental music. Since Tchaikovsky thought primarily in orchestral colours, he is not seen at his best in his piano writing except in avowedly easy pieces (such as the Children's Album Op. 39, one of the best of its kind) or when writing in a virtuoso manner (as in the three concertos, Fantasia for piano and orchestra and piano trio). Many of the shorter pieces, grouped into small collections, were intended for salon audiences who were attracted particularly to stylised dance forms. Tchaikovsky was able to produce such pieces without undue difficulty; thus there is a wealth of waltzes, mazurkas, polkas, Russian dances and so on. Often melodically attractive, the accompanimental figures and textures are relatively stereotyped and tend to the banal. The Twelve Pieces ('of moderate difficulty') Op. 40 (1878) are a fair specimen of such examples. More serious are the six pieces (prelude, fugue, impromptu, funeral march, mazurka and scherzo) based on a single theme Op. 21 (1873), an interesting extension of the Lisztian thematic metamorphosis principle. Better known than any of these are the set of twelve pieces, *Les saisons* Op. 37b, commissioned by a monthly periodical for each month of the year 1876. The June ('Barcarolle') and November ('Troika') movements became especially popular. The Eighteen Pieces Op. 72 move in a new direction. They were composed soon after Tchaikovsky had made his first draft of the *Pathétique* Symphony in March–April 1893 and break away from the essentially superficial textures of his earlier piano music. They include two waltzes, a mazurka and an over-bombastic polonaise. The pieces are unequal and less obviously melodic than usual but Tchaikovsky took particular care to extend the routine nature of his accompanimental figures, with the result that the set as a whole exhibits a careful workmanship that raises it above the normal salon level of his compositions. Two of the best pieces are No. 5 ('Méditation'), whose compound triple metre is reminiscent of the slow movement of the

E minor Symphony, and No. 8 ('Dialogue'), a passionate duet between two lovers.

Tchaikovsky is often regarded as a westernised Russian, but he knew and appreciated Russian folk song as well as any member of The Five. He tended to favour folk idioms in the more intimate genres; thus he is often more obviously 'Russian' by these methods in his chamber music, some at least of his piano music, in his songs and in *Eugene Onegin*, which for all the glitter of the famous ballroom scenes is a surprisingly intimate and restrained opera for the late nineteenth century.

Hungary

Hungarian piano music centres essentially on Liszt, whose interest in folk music of all countries is obvious merely from an inspection of any work-list. During his years as a virtuoso pianist he composed variations or para-phrases on most of the European national anthems as compliments to his foreign audiences. It comes as no surprise that the three collections of *Années de pèlerinage* were inspired by Italy and Switzerland and that the original version of the first collection made use of Swiss folk melodies. Similarly the supplement to the second collection (*Venezia e Napoli*) is largely a brilliant re-working of Italian popular tunes and at least one aria by Rossini. In the same way, we find pictures of Poland's 'downfall' and 'glory' in the two polonaises in C minor and E major of 1851, essentially gloomy and bright tonalities. Written on a larger scale than Chopin's, the C minor has a particularly beautiful second subject, and overall pro-pounds a strong undercurrent of melancholy, despite some bravura pas-sages. Its companion could hardly be more different. Even the A minor trio section is heroic in tone, while the main theme's reprise is a glittering coruscade of fragmentation allied to thematic metamorphosis, and is a classic example of filigree passage-work in the highest register of the instrument. The slightly earlier *Mazurka brillante* demonstrates in its very title the exact antithesis of Chopin's conception of the dance.

Liszt's interest in specifically Hungarian idioms belongs, on the whole, to his later years. The third *Année* (1867–77) includes 'Sunt lacrimae rerum', sub-titled 'en mode hongrois', and utilises what has come to be known as the 'Hungarian' scale – basically the harmonic minor scale with a sharpened fourth, though in practice the seventh note also oscillates between a sharpened and naturalised form. The *Historische ungarische Bildnisse* ('Historical Hungarian portraits') depict seven national artists and politicians; though composed in the 1870s and 80s the set was not published till 1956. Long after the national dance, the csárdás, had first

Ex. 10.5 Liszt, *Csárdás macabre*, bars 58–65.

appeared in the 1830s, Liszt wrote three of his own. The dance, taken up in operetta and ballet, is generally bipartite (slow–fast), both sections being in duple metre. Liszt's examples bear only the remotest resemblance to 'folk style'. The title *Csárdás obstiné* (1886) might well be a pun since the work is basically constructed on ever-present ostinato patterns, in the best tradition of folk music. The *Csárdás macabre* (1881–2) propounds an extraordinary succession of chromatically moving bare parallel fifths (Ex. 10.5): a twentieth-century (*sic*) version of organum years ahead of its time. Its trio is based on a Hungarian folk song, a number of which Liszt arranged in sensitive settings around this period.

The one conspicuous Hungarian piece from earlier in Liszt's career was the seventh of the *Harmonies poétiques et religieuses*, the eloquent *Funérailles*, which bears the inscription 'Oktober 1849' and was intended as a tribute to those who had died in the Hungarian revolution of that year. It stands as the finest obsequial piece ever composed for solo piano and though resplendent in quasi-orchestral sonorities they are always achieved by purely pianistic means.

There remain the nineteen Hungarian Rhapsodies which, despite their somewhat misleading name, are still the most famous Hungarian works ever written. Ever the cosmopolite, Liszt misunderstood the true nature of Hungarian folk music, describing it in his book *Des bohémiens et de leur musique en Hongrie* (1859) as synonymous with gypsy music, a misconception that earned him many enemies. The whole question is complicated since Hungarian folk and gypsy music continually interacted; but put somewhat simplistically, Hungarian folk music is like that of any other country, that is, creative, whereas gypsy music is essentially a style of playing. That style was propagated by gypsy fiddlers, and achieved by their taking pre-existing pieces (folk songs from Hungary and elsewhere, popular music of the day, well-known 'art' music, etc.) and dressing them up in a highly rhapsodic, improvisatory and virtuoso manner so that these pieces became almost new works in their hands. The *verbunkos*, an eighteenth-century dance primarily employed as a musical method of recruiting soldiers, played an important role in all this, since it was often performed by gypsy groups who treated well-known pieces in their characteristic style. The basic slow–fast formula (or *lassu friss*, to use the Hungarian terms) eventually developed into the csárdás, though Liszt's contributions here lack the introductory *lassu*.

Liszt's rhapsodies are in reality gypsy, not Hungarian, music. They take the form and style of the *verbunkos*, though the structure is often extended from two to several sections. The last four rhapsodies date from the composer's old age and are virtually unknown. Most of the remaining fifteen, the majority of which were published in the 1850s, have remained familiar to concert audiences and there can be few pianists who do not include at least a handful in their repertory. It will probably never be known how many of these tunes, alternately catchy and melancholy, were of Liszt's own invention and which were already generally familiar to Hungarians. This scarcely matters: Liszt transformed these essentially commonplace melodies by combining a wealth of harmonic treatments, frequently juxtaposing major and minor triads, and exciting rhythmic pungencies involving syncopation and Scotch snaps, all woven into dazzling pianistic effects. There are ingenious contrived imitations of the cimbalom and violin in the process. The cimbalom is the 'national' instrument of Hungary, but was also an important component of the gypsy band. Not all the rhapsodies, however, are virtuoso. No. 3, in ternary form, presents a melody that oscillates between B♭ major and minor, with a contrasting G minor episode suggesting the violin and cimbalom. No. 5, entitled *Héroïde-élégiaque*, is a dignified funeral march, written in sonata form minus development section. No. 6, however, is more typical of the genre: the *lassu* and *friss* constitute sections three and four of the piece, which begins with a march-like Tempo giusto and a short Presto, directed to be played twice. Liszt's own favourite was No. 13, though the public favoured (in the nineteenth century as now) No. 2 or No. 15, a grandiose version of the Rákóczi March, a popular tune from *c.*1810 and also used by Berlioz in *La damnation de Faust*. The unnumbered *Rapsodie espagnole* (1863) is a magnificently structured fantasia on *La folia* and the popular *Jota aragonesa*. Busoni arranged this work for piano and orchestra, and Liszt himself made a similar arrangement of No. 14. This version is known as the Hungarian Fantasia. Liszt also orchestrated several of the rhapsodies himself. Many critics have dismissed the rhapsodies as superficial, but when first heard they must have seemed ultra-new, exotic and flamboyant, and their fascinating if slightly misplaced national character is all part of the immense variety and richness of nineteenth-century music.

Scandinavia

The four Nordic countries came late to the composition of nationalist music. The Finnish contribution in effect begins with Jean Sibelius (1865–1957); the salon music of the Danish Niels Gade (1817–90) has long been forgotten, while Swedish composers, as with Sibelius, came to the fore only in the twentieth century. The Norwegian composers, Johan Svendsen (1840–1911) and Christian Sinding, were completely over-shadowed by their compatriot Edvard Grieg.

If Grieg was, as many assert, foremost a miniaturist, this is mostly due to his Norwegian environment. It would be absurd to look for the Wagnerian 'unending melody' in the sort of music that he set out to write. Actually, Grieg was pragmatic rather than dogmatic in his attitude to large structures, as is the case with many composers. Though he studied at the Leipzig conservatory, he later claimed to have learnt little in Germany, but his acquaintance there with Mendelssohn's and Schumann's piano music lent his earliest compositions an assured competence and possibly gave him confidence to attempt large-scale pieces then and later. Grieg's early meeting with the Norwegian violinist Ole Bull (1810–80) fired him with a lasting enthusiasm for Norwegian folk music, in which the most characteristic feature is a falling leading note. This is exemplified by the famous ♩ opening of the Piano Concerto, and found thereafter in numerous works by Grieg. It permeates many Norwegian folk melodies and it is this that lends to Grieg's music that tinge of exotic melancholy, an attribute that made Grieg particularly popular in France and England.

Grieg is perhaps at his most personal in his songs, but the piano music provides an equally comprehensive view of his musical personality. Most of it was published in Leipzig. The *Vier Stücke* Op. 1 demonstrated what the composer could do with neo-Schumannesque textures of a pre-dominantly simple nature. However, as early as the *Six poetic tone-pictures* Op. 3[3] there is a distinct advance in musical style, though here we see both Grieg's strengths and weaknesses. There is an over-reliance on section repetition in No. 4 and on phrase repetition overall. But these faults are outweighed by a harmonic and melodic freshness, the effectiveness of the piano writing and the overall conception of the music. (Curiously, in his chamber music with piano, Grieg sometimes seems to be striving for an orchestral massiveness in the piano accompaniments.) No. 6 in E minor shows traces of the elfin fleetness of Mendelssohn's scherzos. Here, the E minor tonality is significant: this piece stands in a direct tonal line from Mendelssohn's Scherzo in E minor Op. 16 No. 2, continuing in Grieg's Lyric Pieces Op. 12 No. 4 and Op. 54 No. 5.

Specifically Norwegian pieces can be explicit, for example the extremely pianistic arrangements of genuine folk melodies such as the twenty-five in Op. 17 (1869) and the nineteen in Op. 66 (1896). In a class of their own stand the magnificent *Slåtter* Op. 72, composed in 1902–3, which are arrangements of peasant tunes as played on the Hardanger fiddle by Knut Dale. These are Grieg's most dissonant pieces, strongly twentieth-century in outlook, where the 'emancipation of the dissonance' may have had some influence on Bartók. In addition to the free employment of seventh and ninth chords, which had been a hallmark of Grieg's style for many years, the frequent added-note chords look ahead to Stravinsky. The Ballade Op. 24 (1875–6), a set of variations on a Norwegian folk tune, is one of Grieg's most ambitious works for piano. The *Holberg Suite* Op. 40 is an unusually successful essay in recreating a baroque suite in Norwegian style.

Norwegian colouring is implicit in most of Grieg's remaining piano works, the most distinctive of which are the ten books of Lyric Pieces composed at regular intervals between 1864 and 1901. These pieces made Grieg internationally famous. Their greatest weakness lies not so much in the short-breathed melodies as in the composer's unwillingness to re-compose the last section of an ABA formal scheme. The A:‖: B A:‖ structure may well tempt some performers to omit the second repeat, always much longer than the first, but in many cases Grieg actually writes out the B A repeat in full as though to forestall any curtailment on the part of the performer. Occasionally there may be a coda ('She dances' Op. 57 No. 5) but usually Grieg is content either with nothing or with just a few bars to round off the movement. A through-composed piece such as 'Phantom' Op. 62 No. 5 is very much the exception. That said, Grieg never ceases to astonish by the variety of his conceptions: in the memorability of the melodies and, in particular, the resourcefulness of the harmony, often presented with so light a touch and in so transparent a texture that its audacities go unnoticed. Very occasionally, as in 'Bell ringing' Op. 54 No. 6, there is a foreshadowing of impressionism, though here this is an avowed imitative exercise for colouristic purposes.

After a long period when the cultivation of music in the home made these pieces universally familiar, Grieg's piano music has become relatively obscure, there being a wealth of twentieth-century music to take its place. Grieg's harmonic colourings were taken up by Delius, Warlock and Grainger and, less attractively, by twentieth-century composers of light music, revues and film scores, so that what was at first original eventually became merely hackneyed, superficial or sentimental in the hands of third-rate imitators. This, needless to say, in no way detracts from Grieg's overall achievement.

Sonata and concerto

On the whole, these genres did not attract the nationalists: Chopin's and Liszt's contributions are universal as opposed to specifically nationalist. Balakirev, as might be expected of a composer instinctively drawn to piano music, wrote two sonatas in B♭ minor. The second, though written mostly between 1900 and 1905, presents in its second movement a reworking of its equivalent in the first sonata of nearly fifty years earlier. The fugal elements of the first movement and the fiery energy of the finale enclose a mazurka and nocturne in a wholly attractive work. As usual, the player's technique needs to be formidable, and since all four movements end quietly it is easy to see why concert pianists fight shy of it.

After an early sonata, written in 1865 but not published till 1900, Tchaikovsky composed a second sonata in G, of imposing dimensions and considerable difficulty, in 1878 contemporaneously with the Violin Concerto. The sonata is much maligned but it is unsatisfactory more because of the ultra-massive textures of its chordal passages, which are too orchestral, than for any inadequacies in the material as such. As so often, the more lyrical episodes are wholly delightful and characteristic; the slow movement and scherzo, despite the awkward and unpianistic nature of the latter, are the most convincing areas of the work.

Grieg's solitary Sonata in E minor Op. 7 (1865, revised 1887), though hardly showing the composer at his best, has a faded charm and can convince an audience if the player is in sympathy with the piece. Neither Smetana nor Dvořák contributed to the sonata repertory, save for an early essay by Smetana that remained unpublished during his lifetime.

Dvořák wrote his single piano concerto in 1876, a spacious, not to say prolix composition, as was so often the case with works from his early period. It has attractive themes and succeeds in the concert hall, though its relatively unvirtuoso (by nineteenth-century standards) textures have not commended it to most pianists. Balakirev produced two concertos, one early, the other late in his career, though both are relatively insubstantial. However, Rimsky-Korsakov produced in his solitary concerto in C♯ minor (1882–3) a strikingly original one-movement work based on a Russian folk song: its opening high bassoon solo almost suggests Stravinsky's *Le sacre du printemps*. Like most Russian music the concerto is episodic, a charming succession of mosaics – and none the worse for it.

It was Tchaikovsky, however, in his B♭ minor Concerto (1874–5) who produced by far the finest concerto of all the nationalists. It stands as a classic example of the traditional contest between soloist and orchestra. The extremely original opening movement is rather longer than the two remaining movements combined. The lengthy introduction, with a 'big tune' in the 'wrong' relative major key of the work's tonality as a whole (a tune that never returns thereafter), is followed by a sonata allegro whose principal theme is borrowed from a folk tune. The slow movement juxtaposes two wildly differing sections with complete conviction, while the energetic finale is symptomatic of a number of late nineteenth-century concertos in that the most memorable melody of the whole work occurs in the second theme: quietly the first time round, *grandioso* in the coda. This is true of Bruch's three violin concertos, Rachmaninoff's first two concertos and Grieg's Concerto (1868, revised 1906–7). Tchaikovsky's concertos in G and E♭, understandably overshadowed by the B♭ minor, are by no means negligible works that deserve more frequent hearings.

Grieg's Piano Concerto, probably modelled on Schumann's, is nonetheless a remarkable piece in its own right. Its first movement is full of memorable, if short-lived, themes with one of the most subtly integrated cadenzas of any concerto. This is followed by a compact and rapt slow movement, much of whose piano writing is improvisatory in style, and a lively folk-style finale using the rhythms of the *halling*, a duple metre dance derived from the Scottish reel.

Coda

The nineteenth century saw two very different American composers who may both be described as nationalists. Louis Moreau Gottschalk, a virtuoso pianist and composer, made his debut in Paris at the age of fifteen playing Chopin's E minor Concerto in the composer's presence. His compositions were influenced by black American rhythms, and his numerous salon and concert pieces foreshadow both ragtime and jazz. Conversely, Edward MacDowell (1860–1908), conventionally trained in Germany and heavily swayed at first by European influences, became both university professor (at Columbia) and America's most celebrated composer. There is a considerable corpus of piano music including two concertos, four sonatas and a quantity of genre pieces bearing poetic titles. Traces of Grieg, the virtuoso manner of Liszt and an almost puritan style that is wholly New England American, combine to produce a composer with a personal voice: racy and fantastical in his scherzo movements; with a solemnity and poise, not unlike that of Elgar, in the more *nobilmente* moods. MacDowell's music is now out of fashion but scarcely deserves its neglect. He stands as a salutary reminder that, despite the immense fame that he enjoyed during his lifetime, the vagaries of fashion have now deemed his music unworthy and inconsequential, a fate that has overtaken a number of other composers.

11 New horizons in the twentieth century

MERVYN COOKE

'Take it for granted from the beginning that everything is possible on the piano, even when it seems impossible to you, or really is so.'[1] So wrote Busoni two years before the beginning of the twentieth century, prophesying the extraordinary explosion of compositional innovation which the new epoch would bring, and in which the development of the piano's technical and sonorous capabilities would play a crucial role. Yet in spite of the apparent desire on the part of several composers at the turn of the century to break firmly with tradition and cultivate an almost avant-garde approach to pianoforte composition, with hindsight it now seems abundantly clear that the exciting new developments in piano music in the early years of the century were firmly rooted in nineteenth-century precedent.

By 1916 the piano's impact on compositional developments had become sufficiently evident for E. J. Dent to publish an article entitled 'The pianoforte and its influence on modern music',[2] in which he expressed the opinion that Liszt had been the 'foundation of modern pianoforte-playing and pianoforte composition' in spite of his various 'shortcomings as a composer of real music'. The influence of Liszt's technical virtuosity and harmonic experimentation is to be seen clearly enough in Ravel's *Jeux d'eau* (1901), which owed much to the water-figurations of Liszt's *Les jeux d'eau à la Villa d'Este* (1877). The impressionistic application of virtuoso figurations to create atmospheric effects was adopted by Debussy in his piano music from the *Estampes* (1903) onwards, and Ravel's *Gaspard de la nuit* (1908) marked the apparent limits to which such technically demanding figurations could be stretched. Although Debussy had independently found a use for Lisztian models as early as 1888, when his First Arabesque borrowed both its key and pentatonic triplets from Liszt's *Sposalizio* (1858), his debt to Chopin proved to be of more lasting significance; Chopin's extended residency in Paris from 1831 until his death had resulted in the strong influence of his piano style on many later French composers, Fauré in particular. Liszt was posthumously to influence one further strand of twentieth-century piano music, however, through the absorption of his style by a new generation of Hungarian composer–pianists. Dohnányi's piano music represents the conservative side of this influence, owing as much to Brahms as to Liszt,

Ex. 11.1 Beethoven, Sonata Op. 31 No. 2, first movement.

but Bartók extracted certain modernistic and folk-inspired features from Liszt's style and went on to create a new nationalism, ultimately taking Hungarian music well away from the Austro-German domination under which it had languished during the nineteenth century.

The emancipation of the sustaining pedal

Nineteenth-century influences on the piano music of the early twentieth century were not confined to matters of virtuosity alone. One specific area of technique which was soon liberated from all restraints, an emancipation signifying both the new harmonic freedom and a widespread interest in cultivating innovative sonorities, was the use of the sustaining pedal. The first major composer to have been aware of the creative potential of blurred pedalling was Beethoven. Oft-cited examples are the recitative from the first movement of the Sonata in D minor Op. 31 No. 2 (Ex. 11.1), or the first movement of the Sonata in C♯ minor Op. 27 No. 2. These striking passages are prophetic not only of later impressionistic pedalling effects, but are also symptomatic of Beethoven's fondness for harmonic experimentation, since the prolonged depression of the sustaining pedal results in a confused blur of unresolved harmonies. Pedal techniques were further refined by Chopin, from whose example many of Debussy's innovations seem to stem. Margeurite Long (Professor of Piano at the Paris Conservatoire from 1920 until 1940) famously recalled that Debussy shared Chopin's conviction that subtle use of the sustaining pedal could simulate a kind of musical 'breathing'.[3]

Although Debussy's colouristic use of pedalling has often been singled out for praise, it is a singular fact that his piano scores are almost entirely devoid of clear pedalling instructions to the performer. 'Pedalling cannot be written down . . . entrust it to your ear', was Debussy's advice,[4] and his strict avoidance of the conventional markings 'Ped.' and '*' verged on the obsessional. Instead, Debussy attempted to convey the subtlety of his harmonic blurring or promotion of lingering sonorities by the use of ties which imply that the sound of a note or chord is to be prolonged well into the succeeding rests; the precise sequence of pedal changes is left to the performer's discretion. In cases where a bass note is to be sustained in this fashion, Debussy sometimes breaks notational rules by using both bass clef and treble clef simultaneously on the left-hand stave. An early example of this unorthodox procedure is to be seen in the 'Prélude' from the suite *Pour le piano*, written in *c*.1895 (bar 15; cf. also Example 11.2, bar 2). In later piano works he generally preferred to notate the music on three staves instead of two (see, for instance, *D'un cahier d'esquisses* from 1903) – a notational convenience which proved increasingly useful and was widely adopted by later composers as the texture of their piano music attained still higher levels of complexity (cf. Example 11.3).

The wide variety of impressionistic effects created by both Debussy and Ravel in their subtle use of the pedals may partly have been inspired by the playing of the Catalan pianist Ricardo Viñes, who settled in Paris in 1887 and went on to give the premieres of almost all their significant piano works during the first decade of the twentieth century. Poulenc, who studied with Viñes, declared that his pedalling was sufficiently striking to draw attention to its status as 'an essential feature of modern piano music', and Viñes himself recalled discussions with Ravel on the correct pedal techniques to employ in the latter's *Jeux d'eau*.[5] Ravel suggested that the sustaining pedal should be used in the upper register to emphasise 'the hazy impression of vibrations in the air', thereby drawing attention to a fundamental discovery associated with the pedal's acoustical function that underlies much twentieth-century piano music. As Dent observed in 1916,

> It is in fact the right-hand pedal which gives the pianoforte an advantage possessed by no other instrument to any appreciable extent. A pianoforte without the pedal would be almost as limited in its effects as a violin without a bow. For the principal value of the pedal is not merely to sustain sounds when the finger is for some reason obliged to release the key, but to reinforce sounds by allowing other strings to vibrate in sympathy with them.[6]

One reason why Debussy was so strongly attracted to the sonorities of Javanese gamelan music when he heard it at the Paris Exposition in 1889 was undoubtedly the extraordinary 'vibrations in the air' generated by tuned percussion instruments, an effect he emulated in 'Pagodes' from the 1903 *Estampes* (see Ex. 11.2). The implied pedalling in the second bar demonstrates the mechanism's dual function, serving both to prolong sonorities and to emphasise the harmonic daring arising from the composer's systematic use of the anhemitonic pentatonic scale and consequent avoidance of familiar triadic patterns. The elevation of unprepared and unresolved major-second clashes to the status of a new consonance is

Ex. 11.2 Debussy, 'Pagodes' from *Estampes*, bars 39–40.

typical of the close connection between sonority and harmony in Debussy's keyboard music. (Dent described the ubiquitous use of dyads comprising major or minor seconds as 'playing on the cracks'.)[7]

The structure of gamelan music further inspired Debussy to devote greater attention to effects of 'layered' polyphony in his piano music, suggesting the resonance of deep Indonesian gongs by the sustained pedalling of low piano tones above which various ostinato patterns are superimposed. Younger French composers – principally Ravel, Poulenc and Messiaen – came to share Debussy's fascination with gamelan techniques. It was Messiaen who, perhaps more than any other composer, went further than Debussy in developing an approach to the composition of piano music that arose largely from an awareness of the instrument's sonorous potential. Messiaen's early *Préludes* for piano (1929), while recalling Debussy's two sets of *Préludes* (1910, 1913) in numerous respects, first experimented with what the composer termed 'added resonance'. Not content to achieve acoustical effects by the use of the sustaining pedal alone, Messiaen went so far as to include deliberately 'wrong' notes (played more softly than the prevailing musical material) which function as an illusory extension of the natural sympathetic vibrations set up by the release of the pedal. Ex. 11.3, in which liberal pedalling is again implied with Debussian ambiguity rather than explicitly stated, gives an instance of this 'added resonance' in the final bars of the first prelude, 'La colombe'.

Colouristic harmony

Debussy's major innovation in the sphere of harmony lay in his cultivation of so-called 'non-functional' chords, present for the sake of their individual sonorities rather than as part of a traditional harmonic progression involving tension and release from dissonance to consonance.

Ex. 11.3 Messiaen, 'La colombe' from *Préludes*, end.

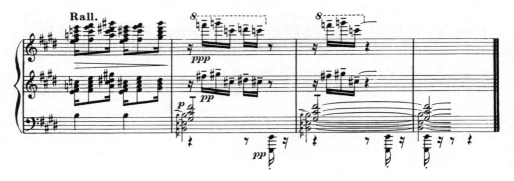

The chains of parallel unresolved dominant ninths with which Debussy habitually improvised are a notorious and simple example, and in more sophisticated applications of the same harmonic concept it seems evident that novel pianistic techniques (including generous use of the sustaining pedal) were inextricably linked with harmonic experimentation. Emile Vuillermoz recalled: 'Debussy's playing was one long harmony lesson ... no one else had his gift of transforming a dissonant chord into a little bell made of bronze or silver, scattering its harmonics to the four winds'.[8] A comparable, but much more extreme, instance of a composer's experimentation with innovative harmonies as sonorous elements in their own right is to be found in the early piano works of Schoenberg. Although Schoenberg arrived at his piano idiom without the catalyst of Debussian influence, the non-functional atonal chord patterns explored in the Three Pieces Op. 11 (1909) represent the fruits of a similar artistic impulse. In the last of the Six Little Pieces Op. 19 (1911), Schoenberg composed a miniature tone-poem commemorating Mahler's funeral which, in its simple but resonant reiteration of a dissonant chord, also suggests a 'bell ... scattering its harmonics to the four winds'.

On a more prosaic level, certain of Debussy's and Schoenberg's influential harmonic experiments were especially well suited to the piano. The equal-tempered scale employed on modern keyboard instruments was essential to Schoenberg's desire to make all chromatic tones of equal importance (in contrast, a string player or vocalist tends to sharpen or flatten notes by various degrees according to their status in the prevailing tonal context). The whole-tone scale frequently used by both Debussy and (in early works) Schoenberg was a natural by-product of equal temperament. Pentatonicism, too, has its simplest manifestation in the black keys of the piano, a property exploited by Debussy (cf. Ex. 11.2) while once more following Chopin's pioneering example in his G♭ major Etude Op. 10 No. 5. In 1946, Zoltán Kodály (1882–1967) composed a set of Children's Dances which put the euphonious properties of black-note pentatonicism to educational use (an interest also developed in Carl Orff's method of class improvisation): although printed without key signatures, the music is to be performed exclusively on the black notes.

The piano as percussion instrument

According to Margeurite Long, Debussy continually strove to make the piano sound as if it had no hammers ('sans marteaux'), a challenge partly met by constant use of the sustaining pedal which releases all dampers simultaneously and allows notes to decay naturally into silence. This preoccupation was again probably connected with Debussy's admiration for gamelan music, in the finest examples of which the players miraculously manage to create mellifluous effects, even in virtuoso passage-work, in spite of the need to strike every single note with a hand-held mallet. The piano is, of course, a percussion instrument; Debussy's concern for furthering the illusion of a capability for sustained tone (which in reality it does not possess) goes directly against its intrinsic nature. In contrast, Bartók's most important technical innovation in his compositions for piano was his emphasis on the instrument's essentially percussive tone-quality. In 1927 Bartók declared, 'The neutral character of the piano tone has long been recognised. Yet it seems to me that its inherent nature becomes really expressive only by means of the present tendency to use the piano as a percussion instrument.'[9] As Bartók's mention of 'the present tendency' implies, he had not been alone in cultivating a percussive style of piano writing. The early *bravura* idiom of Sergey Prokofiev (1891–1953), displayed markedly in his first two piano concertos (1912–13), presents a notable comparison. After the first performance of Prokofiev's second concerto, one commentator observed that the audience had been 'frozen with fright, hair standing on end'.[10]

After producing a number of early works immersed in the influence of Liszt (a model especially prominent in the Rhapsody Op. 1, dating from 1904), Bartók's highly original keyboard style emerged in the period 1908–11. As with Debussy and Schoenberg, Bartók's innovations in keyboard technique were inseparable from matters of musical substance. The Fourteen Bagatelles Op. 6 (1908) were widely condemned as being too 'modern', an epithet which in this context effectively meant that they were anti-Romantic. In his use of the pentatonic scale and other modes, Bartók here revealed his recent discovery of Debussy's music (which he also emulated in the Ten Easy Pieces composed at the same time), and his pre-occupation with chords built from seconds, fourths and sevenths indicates a comparable interest in non-functional harmonic sonorities. Busoni rightly hailed the Bagatelles as heralding a new era in piano composition; among their many features of interest was the downward arpeggiation of chords, a technique common in eighteenth-century harpsichord music, for which Bartók later devised a new notation. The percussive piano writing which was to become Bartók's trademark was rationalised in the notorious *Allegro barbaro* (1911), where prolonged ostinato passages again reveal a close kinship with Debussy in spite of the turning away from all superficial impressionistic effects which the work ostensibly represents.

Many poor performances of Bartók's piano music emphasise its percussive quality to the detriment of all else. Anyone who has heard recordings of Bartók's own playing, or indeed who has taken time to study the wide range of subtle articulation markings printed in the composer's scores, will surely agree with Roy Howat's verdict that he was 'a pianist of lyrical Romantic tradition – never a hard hitter – with an exceptional ear for fine nuances of timbre, rhythm and melody'.[11] Bartók's pupil Júlia Székely (who studied at the Budapest Academy in the 1920s) recalled that he showed meticulous attention to detail in matters of pedalling and articulation, especially when teaching the piano music of Debussy by which his own approach to the instrument was so strongly influenced.

Bartók's adaptation of musical material borrowed from folk music is well documented, and first surfaces in his piano writing in the collection *For Children* (1908–9). It seems plausible that his development of a percussive piano style owed something to an interest in the sonority of the cimbalom, a folk zither (played with two hammers) used in much east-European folk music. Stravinsky, who had also arrived at a percussive style of piano writing independently from Bartók and Prokofiev, included the cimbalom in several works written in this period. The highly percussive ballet score *Les noces* (1914–23) went through several orchestrations, involving at various times the use of two cimbaloms and a mechanical piano (or pianola, an invention dating from 1895) before achieving its definitive scoring for four pianos and percussion. In the *Ragtime* for eleven instruments (1919), Stravinsky used a cimbalom to represent the clattering sonority of a honky-tonk upright piano. The latter, somewhat surprisingly, was in later years to become a featured instrument in its own right, especially in music-theatre pieces: it appeared in the opera *Wozzeck* (1925) by Alban Berg (1885–1935), and went on to figure prominently in a series of works by Peter Maxwell Davies (b.1934) written during the 1960s.

Even in his ostinato-based percussive style, Bartók had not strayed too far from historical precedent. He entertained a passionate interest in pre-Classical music, and the 'strummed' repetitions of dissonant chords often to be found in his piano music directly recall similar devices in the more adventurous of Domenico Scarlatti's harpsichord sonatas. Bartók's early musical development had been largely founded on a solid diet of Austro-German keyboard repertory, including Beethoven, Mendelssohn, Brahms and Liszt; but even here he would have encountered examples of per-cussive accompanimental figurations, especially in instances as striking as the opening of Beethoven's 'Waldstein' Sonata Op. 53 (1804), a work which he learnt at the age of ten. The culmination of Bartók's early *martellato* style is reached in the hammered ostinato patterns of the First Piano Concerto (1926), but soon afterwards his idiom became tempered by the admixture of neo-classical influences. Stravinsky (for whose work in this area, see below) had successfully reinterpreted baroque rhythmic vitality and textural clarity in his Concerto for piano and wind instruments (1924). This work was performed in Budapest in 1926, and subsequently had a profound impact on Bartók's style; its influence is felt most prominently in his Second Piano Concerto (1931).

Clusters, glissandi and harmonics

Bartók's other innovations in the growing arsenal of permissible keyboard techniques included the cultivation of black-note and white-note groupings as contrasting harmonic resources (see, for example, the sixth Improvisation of 1920). These sometimes take the form of black- and white-note 'clusters', a device he is reputed to have borrowed consciously from the American composer Henry Cowell (1897–1965) whom he encountered in London during 1923.[12] Clusters of black and white notes are often directly opposed to create extreme harmonic tension, as in the second movement of the Second Piano Concerto (Ex. 11.4). In bars 91–2 the opposing clusters encompass all twelve degrees of the chromatic scale. The chordal trill encountered here was one of the many devices Bartók borrowed from Debussy, who had concluded his spirited *L'isle joyeuse* (1904) with an uncharacteristically percussive application of the technique (Ex. 11.5) which includes a dissonant sharpened fourth (D♯) foreshadowing Bartók's folk-inspired use of the Lydian mode. In the slow movement of the Sonata for Two Pianos and Percussion (1937), a work in which the percussion instruments reinforce the pianos' percussive tendencies, Bartók employs simultaneous glissandi on black and white notes. (He was not the first composer to have explored this technique: black- and

Ex. 11.4 Bartók, Second Piano Concerto, slow movement, bars 88–93 (piano part only).

Ex. 11.5 Debussy, *L'isle joyeuse*, end.

Ex. 11.6 Schoenberg, Three Pieces Op. 11 No. 1, bars 14–16.

white-note glissandi had both been used by Berg as early as 1910 in the piano accompaniment to the last of his Four Songs Op. 2.) Many of Bartók's cluster and glissando effects are concentrated in his famous passages of 'night music', in which the impressionistic suggestion of nocturnal sounds reflects the composer's lasting debt to Debussy and Ravel. His continuation of the quest for novel sonorities inspired by the piano's acoustical properties is further to be seen in his adoption of a method for producing 'harmonics' by sympathetic vibration first used by Schoenberg as early as the first of the Three Pieces Op. 11 (1909, see Ex. 11.6). Keys indicated by void diamond note-heads are silently depressed in order to release their dampers, while the conventional playing of lower notes causes the liberated strings to vibrate in sympathy with the overtones thus produced. A simple example of Bartók's application of this device may be seen in No. 102 of the *Mikrokosmos* (1926–39), his celebrated collection of 153 educational pieces which comprise a veritable compendium of pianistic and compositional techniques.

Ragtime and jazz influences

Another manifestation of the gradual turning away from both nine-teenth-century German models and early twentieth-century impression-ism in keyboard music was the influence of ragtime and, later, jazz styles of piano playing (see also chapter 12). Ragtime (of which the first pub-lished example for solo piano was *Mississippi Rag by* William H. Krell (1873–1933), printed in Chicago in 1897) became popular in Europe around 1900–5 in instrumental arrangements performed on the interna-tional concert tours undertaken by Sousa's band, and it was probably from this source that Debussy encountered the idiom during the first decade of the century. His witty imitation of both the 'stride' (that is, 'oom-pah') left hand accompanimental chords and the syncopated melodic style of ragtime in the 'Golliwog's Cakewalk' from *Children's Corner* (1908) was an early example of the influence of popular music on keyboard styles, and Charles Ives (1875–1954) followed suit with a more ambitious and eccentric reworking of the ragtime idiom in his First Sonata (composed in 1909 but not performed publicly until 1949). Stravinsky, perhaps following the example of Erik Satie (1866–1925) – whom he went on to praise in his autobiography for 'opposing to the vagueness of a decrepit impressionism a precise and firm language stripped of all pictorial embellishments'[13] – experimented with an abstract and characteristically distorted mixture of ragtime elements in his *Piano-Rag-Music*, commissioned by Artur Rubinstein in 1919. The rag idiom also surfaces in *Suite, 1922* by Paul Hindemith (1895–1963) and *Trois Rag-Caprices,* (1923) by Darius Milhaud (1892–1974), by which time it had already been eclipsed in popularity by the emergence of jazz. The relationship between concert works and popular music did not merely involve a one-way process of influence, however. Debussy's har-monic language itself came to influence jazz musicians, as shown by the piano solo *In a Mist* (1927) composed by Bix Beiderbecke (1903–31), which clearly owes its title, non-functional harmonies and use of the whole-tone scale to French impressionism.

Structure versus sonority

From the 1920s onwards, trends in piano composition fell broadly into two major areas. On the one hand, many composers moved away from overtly colouristic effects to cultivate a more abstract keyboard idiom as a vehicle for complex musical structures. Others continued to experiment with the piano's sonorous potential by introducing further innovative methods of sound production – some of which come dangerously close to mere gimmickry. The distinction between these two categories is not, of course, absolute: in the work of the finest composers of piano music since Debussy and Bartók there is often a high degree of integration between timbre and structure.

The development of an approach to piano composition characterised by a tendency towards abstraction and a deliberate shunning of superficial colouristic devices stemmed from the work of two composers, for both of whom this had represented a partial rejection of their earlier idioms. Stravinsky's neo-classicism, which finds its purest manifestation in his Piano Sonata (1924) and Serenade in A (1925), incorporated a strong – though characteristically idiosyncratic – element of tonal harmony. Textures were clarified, either using a contrapuntal idiom redolent of baroque models or simple accompanimental patterns recalling early classical keyboard works. Buoyant, repetitive motifs typical of baroque toccatas propelled the music forwards with a rediscovered sense of rhythmic momentum. At around the same time as Stravinsky's early neo-classical works, Schoenberg published his first dodecaphonic serial music in the guise of the Suite for Piano Op. 25 (1923). This draws equally heavily on contrapuntal methods and structures borrowed from previous epochs and marks a significant textural contrast to the earlier piano works by Schoenberg discussed above. Although fundamentally divergent in terms of tonal language and textural complexity, both Stravinsky's and Schoenberg's keyboard music in this period nevertheless appear to be pursuing similar artistic aims.

The influence of neo-classicism on later keyboard music varied according to the different responses to the two tonal extremes represented by Stravinsky and Schoenberg. Hindemith's 'utility music' promoted a clarity of contrapuntal texture still based on simple rhythmic patterns but couched in his own elusively modal harmonic language. In addition to completing a set of three contrasting piano sonatas in 1936, his crowning contrapuntal achievement was the monumental *Ludus Tonalis: studies in counterpoint, tonal organisation and piano playing* (1943). This comprises a cycle of twelve fugues linked by transitional interludes, the entire work framed by a prelude and postlude (the latter a retrograde inversion of the former). Shostakovich's Twenty-four Preludes and Fugues Op. 87 (1951), written to commemorate the 200th anniversary of the death of J. S. Bach, are an extended essay in diatonicism. The first fugue is an ingenious attempt to compose a piece entirely on the white notes.

Followers of Schoenberg's atonality, however, felt less constrained to adopt clearly recognisable baroque or classical models in their keyboard music. The innovations of Anton Webern (1883–1945) in matters of texture and structure proved to be highly influential on post-war composers, although these would scarcely have been conceivable without the prior example of Schoenberg's dissolution of conventional melody-plus-accompaniment textures in his Opp. 11 and 19 piano pieces (a radical step against which Schoenberg himself later reacted by re-admitting traditional textures in the 1920s, as we have seen). Taking Schoenberg's renewed commitment to contrapuntal techniques as a starting point, Webern developed a wholly new approach to textural transparency which owed as much to silence as to sonority. Fragmented intervallic gestures are organised in highly systematic patterns which rarely allow the formation of chords containing more than two or three notes, and each movement or piece (invariably of minuscule dimensions) is unified by a forbidding cogency of serial technique. Webern sometimes assigns a different dynamic marking to almost every note, suggesting a refined sense of sonorous contrast which is only fully revealed in the composer's ensemble music, with its technique of *Klangfarbenmelodie* ('tone-colour-melody', a term coined by Schoenberg) in which equally fragmented textures are orchestrated with a pointillistic allocation of a different timbre to each note. Webern's mature piano writing is confined to a single work, the Variations Op. 27 of 1936. Ex. 11.7 shows the opening of the second movement, where each hand is strictly confined to its own thematic strand (one the exact inversion of the other). The posthumous influence of Webern's radical textures was to prove formidably wide-spread, and quite out of proportion to the modest quantity of his own piano music. Not all developments of his innovations have been equally successful, however. In his solo piano piece *Herma* (1961), described by Susan Bradshaw as 'the most difficult piano piece ever written',[14] Iannis Xenakis (b.1922) devoted lavish attention to the differentiation of individual semiquavers by extreme contrasts of dynamic and register. Some adjacent semiquavers to be played by the same hand are as much as two octaves apart and marked *ppp* and *fff*, but the composer's efforts are wasted when his frenetic metronome marking (180 crotchets per minute) self-evidently renders the rapidly leaping contrasts impossible to play.

Messiaen went one stage further than Webern by applying strict organisational principles not only to pitches but also to each note's

Ex. 11.7 Webern, Variations Op. 27 No. 2.

duration, register, dynamic and mode of attack (staccato, accented, etc.). This precursor of what soon became labelled 'total serialism' was unleashed in the *Modes de valeurs et d'intensités*, one of a set of four *Etudes de rythme* (1949), which presents a texture recalling Webern in its sparseness but tending to use long notes and ties to achieve greater continuity of sonority. Messiaen did not follow up the far-reaching implications of this style, however, choosing in the 1950s to devote increasing attention to capturing the melodic idiom of birdsong in highly decorative keyboard figurations. This new departure resulted in music exhibiting a technical virtuosity of which Liszt would surely have been proud, and the re-admission into Messiaen's piano music of a wide variety of more colourful techniques (sometimes literally 'colourful' in their symbolic depiction of various shades of plumage). The culmination of his mature piano style is to be seen in the thirteen movements of the *Catalogue d'oiseaux* (1958). Messiaen commented (of his 150-minute solo piano cycle *Vingt regards sur l'enfant Jésus*, composed in 1944) that it is possible to make sounds on a piano that are 'more orchestral than those of an orchestra',[15] and in returning to a more impressionistic piano idiom in later works he rejoined the strong tradition of highly atmospheric French piano music.

Orchestral imitation, a feature of piano writing since at least the work of Beethoven, had ceased to be a meaningful concept when Ravel published a series of works in distinct versions for either piano or orchestra (examples include the *Valses nobles et sentimentales* and *Le tombeau de Couperin*) of which it is impossible to judge on purely musical evidence which version was composed first.

If Messiaen retreated from the radical suggestions of his own experimental music in the early 1950s, it was his pupil Pierre Boulez (b.1925) who was destined to pick up the emerging techniques of total serialism where his teacher had left them. Boulez composed his first volume of *Structures* (1952) for two pianos in a similar vein to that of Messiaen's *Modes de valeurs et d'intensités.* Boulez's First Sonata for solo piano (1946) had already shown strong traces of Messiaen's influence alongside a development of Webern's lean contrapuntal textures. Whereas Boulez's counterpoint generally falls into two parts in the First Sonata, his Second Sonata (1948) explores denser contrapuntal textures and achieves passages of expressionistic violence (the novel verbal directions include markings such as 'pulveriser le son' – 'pulverise the sound') and considerable virtuosity. Boulez began a third sonata in 1957 which experimented with a mixture of pre-established serial forms and random structural selection: one movement, entitled 'Constellation', requires the pianist to select from material printed in different colours. Boulez's three sonatas have earned themselves a firm place in the repertory, largely through the medium of best-selling recordings by artists of the stature of Maurizio Pollini and Charles Rosen.

In 1951 Stockhausen heard a recording of Messiaen's *Modes de valeurs et d'intensités* and was inspired to abandon his early style to concentrate on developing the more radical implications of Messiaen's experiments. *Klavierstücke* ('Piano Pieces') *I–IV* (1952–3) suggest the continuing influence of Webern, whose music Stockhausen was analysing at this time, while *Klavierstücke V–X* (1954–5) explore contrasting methods of attack and pedal technique. These works also adopt the method of producing harmonics by sympathetic vibration pioneered by Schoenberg and Bartók. Stockhausen's experimentation with pure piano sonorities provided a foil to his simultaneous work in the sphere of electronic music. He developed techniques of playing clusters with the palm of the hand or the elbow, and utilised a cluster glissando (performed with special gloves) on white and black notes. Cluster effects and chordal glissandi reach their zenith (or perhaps nadir) in the explosive patterns of *Klavierstück X*. *Klavierstück XI* (1956) is an aleatory work to be formed from nineteen segments; the performer is permitted to make fundamental decisions governing structure, tempo, dynamics and mode of attack. After

Klavierstück XI, there ensued a lengthy abstention from piano music before the composer began to rework ideas from his operatic projects in a new sequence of *Klavierstücke* commencing in 1979.

Experimentation with various methods of augmenting the piano's timbral possibilities has been widespread, but was initially concentrated in the USA. It began with Ives's remarkably precocious (and, at the time, largely unnoticed) attempts to overcome the limitations created by the pianist's finite number of fingers by using the entire arm or a strip of wood to play cluster chords, as in the 'Concord' Sonata of 1911. Cowell, whose influence on some of Bartók's more radical techniques has already been noted, was the first systematic pioneer of unconventional timbral effects. Tone-clusters (for which Cowell devised a special notation) are first encountered in his piano music at around the same time as Ives was writing his 'Concord' Sonata, and a ferocious *ffff* opposition of white- and black-note clusters appears in *Antimony* (1917). In the 1920s Cowell went on to experiment with still more eccentric effects. A series of works requires the pianist to play the strings inside the piano, thus bypassing altogether the mechanical action of the keys and hammers; Cowell coined the term 'string piano' to describe the instrument when played in this way. Simple pizzicato is used in *The Aeolian harp* (1923) and *Pièce pour piano avec cordes* (1924). In *The banshee* (1925), where the composer stipulates that the sustaining pedal be depressed throughout, a sweeping motion across the strings produces an effect like a harp glissando; by raising only certain dampers (depressing the relevant keys with the other hand) various combinations of notes are produced. Muting of the strings and stopping them at nodal points to produce genuine harmonics (corresponding to those possible on stringed instruments rather than those caused by sympathetic vibration) were introduced in *Sinister resonance* (1930).

The prepared piano

To meet the increasing desire for more eccentric sonorities, the phenomenon of the 'prepared piano' emerged in the late 1930s. This blanket term describes the use of various gadgets to modify the normal piano timbre, and the concept reaches back at least as far as experiments by Satie and Ravel which involved placing strips of paper between the strings in order to produce a sound approximating to that of a harpsichord (or, in the case of Ravel's *Tzigane* (1924), to imitate the clattering sonority of a cimbalom). Some of Cowell's innovations significantly modified the instrument's timbre by requiring the strings to be stopped manually or to be

Figure 11.1 Interior of a prepared piano, according to directions given by John Cage in the introduction to his *Amores* (1943).

struck by using hand-held mallets or plectra, but it is John Cage (1912–92) who deserves the credit for turning the piano into a source of a myriad of sound effects. Cage began by adopting certain of Cowell's more adventurous techniques, modifying the internal glissando played on the 'string piano' by using a gong beater and metal rod to strike the strings in the *First construction in metal* (1939) – a suitably modernistic title reflecting the influence of the visual arts. He then introduced the 'prepared piano' in *Bacchanale* (1940), a work influenced by the Balinese gamelan, which he had encountered through Cowell's interest in ethnomusicology. This work requires twelve strings to be prepared, using 'fibrous weather stripping' and screws with nuts by way of muting. Cage produced a stream of works for this bizarre instrument over the course of the next fourteen years, creating new timbres by the use of wedges placed between the strings to restrict their vibrations, or by the use of metal nuts and bolts (which may either be fixed or left to vibrate), or rubber erasers. In the accompaniment to the song *The wonderful widow of eighteen springs* for voice and 'closed piano' (1942) the performer is instructed to strike the piano's frame in different locations. In all these enterprises, Cage's confessed aim was to construct an instrument of unique timbral characteristics which would not be associated with the conventional piano. His timbral experimentation was not necessarily allied to avant-garde musical material, however, and a work for 'prepared piano' such as *Amores* (1943; Fig. 11.1) is heavily dependent on simple modality and ostinato figurations reflecting Cage's post-Debussian interest in the gamelan.

At around the same time as Cage was introducing his 'prepared piano', his fellow American Lou Harrison (b.1917) – who studied with both Cowell and Schoenberg – created a metallic piano sonority by the simple ploy of sticking drawing pins into the felt covering of the hammers. (In a less artistically pretentious context, the ragtime and stride pianist Winifred Atwell – famous for her spirited version of George Botsford's *Black and White Rag* – did something similar to intensify the honky-tonk sound of upright instruments.) In more recent years, there has continued to be an astonishing diversity of novel piano sonorities produced by unorthodox means. Innovators include Lukas Foss, Mauricio Kagel, Roberto Gerhard, Robert Sherlaw Johnson, David Bedford and Peter Maxwell Davies: their techniques range from the extreme of removing the interior of the piano altogether so that it can only be played like a cimbalom, to the simple but effective device of requiring the pianist in chamber music to keep the sustaining pedal depressed when not playing so as to promote sympathetic vibrations from notes sounded by other instruments (for example, in works by Xenakis). In his *Sequenza IV* (1967), Luciano Berio (b.1925) made explicit use of the modern grand piano's sostenuto pedal (which releases only selected dampers rather than the whole range – a useful mechanism which is often neglected even by professional pianists) to sustain a background chord progression. In the early 1960s some composers grew dissatisfied with the restrictions of equal temperament, and constructed new keyboard instruments capable of microtonal tuning or of a return to just intonation.

One composer who has managed to adapt some of Cowell's innovations and has shown them to be capable of considerable atmospheric suggestion without gimmickry is George Crumb (b.1929), whose *Vox balaenae* ('The voice of the whale', 1971) for piano, flute and cello is an especially fine example of the sensitive application of unconventional pianistic techniques not requiring special accessories apart from electronic amplification. The quest for timbral novelty has since the 1950s been increasingly diverted into the field of electronic music, with some early examples of works for tape taking piano sonorities as their basis. Composers have gradually returned to more conventional methods of playing the piano. This must have come as a welcome reaction for those in the piano trade concerned with the upkeep and renovation of instruments. As one author has laconically noted, 'almost any physical action will produce novel, interesting sounds from the piano, though some damage may result'.[16]

12 Ragtime, blues, jazz and popular music

BRIAN PRIESTLEY

Throughout the multifarious developments in the field of composition during the twentieth century, the piano has clearly retained its high profile, and its central role in European-style music making. The divide between broadly 'popular' and so-called 'serious' music, however, has widened irrevocably and, even though the boundaries may fluctuate from time to time, this has come about through changes in Western society.

It is undeniable that the distinct personality of twentieth-century popular music reflects the stylistic contribution of African–American idioms. While such idioms originally developed unhindered, the last one hundred years have seen a gradual but remarkable takeover of the popular field. The arrival of a powerful sheet-music publishing industry was followed (in chronological order of their greatest impact) by radio, sound films, commercial recording and television. Although in each medium the powers that be initially resisted black composers and performers, they eventually capitulated and thereafter played a crucial role in spreading previous minority preferences among the mainstream.

Further consideration of this fascinating process lies outside the scope of the present volume, but two other factors must be borne in mind. Firstly, those responsible for each musical innovation were not merely the elite who form the breeding ground for innovation in any artistic sphere, but a performing minority within a racial minority. Thus, despite the accelerated rate of change brought about by technological developments, the dissemination of musical innovation was a three-stage process. There had to be some acceptance among black American listeners, and then by white musicians; if these stages occurred, the rest of the world got to hear the results. This staggered popularity is distinct from the generation gap it causes – the way in which white teenage fans of swing music in the 1930s still liked it as adults in the 1950s, the period when their own teenage children were absorbed in rock-and-roll (both sets of teenagers being a decade in arrears compared with the relevant innovations of black musicians).

Secondly, some of the music discussed here represents stylistic features that, though not widely popular in themselves, nevertheless became part of the vocabulary on which later developments were based. To use the European terminology (for the last time in this chapter), popular music contains its own significant areas of 'serious' music, lacking widespread acclaim but eminently worthy of attention by piano aficionados.

The growth of ragtime

An instance of the first phenomenon is ragtime. Although now seen to have reached its artistic peak during the first decade of the twentieth century, it developed out of a variety of nineteenth-century popular music ranging from brass bands to minstrel-show banjo tunes. The vitality of 'classic' ragtime between 1899 and 1909 produced most of the instrumental compositions that are still remembered. But this regional style engendered widespread activity by New York songwriters in the following decade (when 'Alexander's Ragtime Band' was published) and, continuing the process of international popularisation, the often bland music of the 1920s 'jazz age' still echoed the style of ragtime. The same transition took place in Europe, with British composers such as David Comer ('Hors d'oeuvre', 1914) and Billy Mayerl ('Marigold', 1929) mirroring the gradual softening of the original style.

Whatever its historical antecedents – and they are the subject of some debate – classic ragtime was essentially a music for solo piano. Some of those who first popularised the style were also songwriters still working in the minstrel-show tradition, such as Ben Harney, a light-skinned African American who 'passed for white'. The most fondly remembered writer of piano rags, however, was the uncompromising Scott Joplin (1868–1917), whose ultimate ambitions lay in the diametrically opposed direction of operatic composition (his *Threemonisha* was finally staged fifty-five years after his death). For many decades, the most widely known of his prolific output of piano pieces was 'Maple Leaf rag' (1899), overtaken in popularity since the 1970s by 'The entertainer' (1902) which was used in the film *The sting*.

The style brought to fruition by Joplin and his pianist–composer colleagues, initially in the mid-Western town of St Louis, has several features crucial for understanding all of the music discussed here. Much jazz and popular music has an ambivalent relationship to European harmony, but the influence of the latter was still extremely strong one hundred years ago. Further, the inheritance of European compositional structures was never more visible than in ragtime, which adopted from martial and folk-dance music the practice of employing several melodic strains (usually sixteen bars long) and one or at most two key-changes to make a piece hold together. The architecture of 'Maple Leaf rag' may be described as AABBACCDD, with a change of key up a fourth (subtly engineered by

Ex. 12.1 Joplin, 'Maple Leaf rag', bars 1–16.

starting on the V chord of the new tonality) for the third strain, and a return for the last strain (disguised by starting on the IV chord of the 'new' key).

The harmonic, and especially rhythmic, subtlety is seen most clearly in the first strain, with the surprising use of the ♭VI chord in parts of bars 5 and 6 followed by the suspenseful broken-chord of bars 7–8 (Ex. 12.1). The latter coincides with a 'break', whereby the steady rhythm of the left hand is halted for two bars, only to return with correspondingly greater momentum. In the opening melodic phrase (similarly, in the opening phrase of 'The entertainer'), it is important to hear the repetition of melodic cells moving 'across the beat', which leads to the accentuation of every third note.[1] Known at the period in question as 'secondary ragtime', and roughly equivalent to the Greek term 'hemiola', such rhythmic counterpoint is absolutely central to the kind of syncopations heard in popular music to this day.

Whatever the pre-1890s growing pains of ragtime, it burst upon the conventional music world through the medium of sheet-music publication, and 'Maple Leaf rag' for instance went on to sell a million copies. In the period before the arrival of the mass media described above, music making was done in the home far more than in the concert hall and, for ragtime to achieve such great popularity, it had to be available in printed form and also to be re-edited in simplified editions (some of which are still around – see under 'Repertory' p. 224). The first passive 'home entertainment' medium was the player-piano or pianola, whereby a roll punched with holes passed through a mechanism akin to that of a barrel-organ, and the instrument's proliferation in the early decades of the century meant that many rolls were engraved by merely reproducing the sheet music. A process was soon developed whereby performers could play on a piano in order to cut rolls directly, which gave us recordings of several European classical composers as well as important American writers.

Joplin died too soon, after making only a handful of rolls, although the majority of his sixty compositions were made available in this format. But in the period from 1915–25, before the radio networks began to hold sway, many recordings were made directly by composer–performers of the post-Joplin generation such as Eubie Blake (1883–1983), James P. Johnson (1894–1955), his pupil Thomas 'Fats' Waller (1904–43) and Ferdinand 'Jelly Roll' Morton (1890–1941). All of them also went on to make numerous disc recordings, but their piano-rolls profoundly influenced younger musicians.

Post-ragtime developments

Preserving their work without prior notation was of course crucial, for it was only in the classic ragtime style that the player was intended to adhere exactly to the written composition. The generation just mentioned considered an element of improvisation essential in establishing the styles of individual performers, and this became increasingly true as time went by. The existence of recordings of the composer–improvisers themselves was invaluable not only for preserving nuances of performance which would have escaped the printed page, but for disseminating these among other professional performers whose learning was less and less involved with studying notation.[2]

What links the work of Blake, Johnson and Waller is the post-ragtime style known as 'Harlem stride piano', taking its name from the locality of its development and from the manner of playing. In other words, where the left hand in classic ragtime had displayed a fairly genteel motion between the single bass notes and the intervening middle-register chords, the Harlem performers went in for a much larger 'striding' motion and were more apt to thicken the bass notes with octaves or tenths. They were also partial to breaking off the stride pattern to play moving bass lines, or to conflate the two by having the left hand play across the beat (in the manner previously described for the right hand in 'Maple Leaf rag'). More immediately noticeable to the casual observer was the increase in virtuosity of the right-hand figuration, and the variations introduced during repeats.

These are readily heard in comparing different versions of Johnson's 'Carolina shout', recorded several times by the composer as well as by Fats Waller. Alone among these artists, Waller achieved considerable popularity in the years before his premature death. Although this was largely on the strength of his entertaining singing style, many of his listeners appreciated the fact that he was a commanding pianist whose work was a summary of several decades of development. (The style, of course, did not die away but survived in debased form through such players as Winifred Atwell in the 1950s and Russ Conway in the 1960s.) Of his own piano showpieces, 'Alligator crawl', 'Viper's drag' and 'Clothes line ballet' live on (the last two incorporating tempo changes, which is relatively unusual in this field) but Waller's song compositions entered the general repertoire more readily, because they are more open to improvised variation. His non-vocal recordings of 'Honeysuckle Rose (a la Bach, Beethoven, Brahms and Waller)', is inaccurately sub-titled but shows excellent musicianship.

The above-mentioned 'Jelly Roll' Morton was one of many performers who enjoyed success in the 1920s but whose career was decimated by the Depression of the 1930s. His composing style has its ragtime inheritance in common with the Harlem pianists but, in a series of recordings with his 'Red Hot Peppers' groups, he proved more expert at adapting it to the organisation of larger groups (in a way which stands outside the main concerns of the present book). More importantly for our purposes, his playing represents the importation into ragtime of two other influences which were essential for the development of both jazz piano and popular music in general.

Because of his stylistic interest, it is often forgotten that Morton was a virtuoso player fond of using percussive octaves in the right hand, influencing Waller and many others. But he was perhaps more virtuosic in the rhythmic arena and, rather than merely breaking his left-hand pattern as described above, he often engendered much greater fluidity and interplay between the left and the right, approaching the complexity of some Caribbean and Latin-American styles. Morton originated from New

Orleans, which unlike Harlem had direct contact with the Caribbean, and two generations later – when his 'Spanish tinge' had solidified – a new school of New Orleans piano gave us the work of Roy 'Professor Longhair' Byrd (1918–80), Antoine 'Fats' Domino (b.1928) and their disciple Mac 'Dr. John' Rebennack (b.1941). Secondly, the importance of Morton's Southern heritage may be seen in his unaffected incorporation of the blues influence.

Blues and boogie-woogie

Like ragtime, the blues is a genre which has permeated twentieth-century popular music and, indeed, its continued influence on contemporary forms such as soul and hip-hop is much more readily audible than that of ragtime. The blues also coalesced around the end of the nineteenth century from a variety of prior sources. Unlike ragtime, it was and remains a predominantly vocal form, and it has always been closer to folk music and considerably less susceptible to notation. By the time that standard material such as W. C. Handy's (1873–1958) 'Beale Street blues' and 'St. Louis blues' was being published in the 1910s, it was as far removed from the folk roots as 'Alexander's Ragtime Band' was from its sources. If there was a blues equivalent of turn-of-the-century classic rags, it would be a raw vocal music, either unaccompanied or with a skeletal backing from banjo or guitar.

The playing of blues has always been more associated with stringed instruments, as well as harmonicas and latterly saxophones, but was often transferred to the piano. The music was thought of as rural, but that was one of its main attractions – even as the black population was gradually urbanised. When social gatherings were held in Chicago tenements or small Harlem clubs, the music would often be rural in tone and the pianist would be called upon to evoke the playing of folk artists. Whether the performance was solely instrumental or constituted the accompaniment to a vocal (often by the same person who was playing), its approach was deliberately unsophisticated musically. As such, repetition was one of its main resources, especially if intended also as dance music.

This is no doubt the reason for the longevity of the blues form. Ragtime displayed the comparative complexity of different melodic strains (with possible key-changes) alternating within a single piece, in the manner of the folk dances of various European immigrant groupings in the USA. But the blues restricted itself to a single twelve-bar strain with, in its basic form, only three chords (I, IV and V) used in a circular harmonic stasis, and it remained in the same key throughout lengthy performances recreating the trance states of African traditional music.[3] Often the left hand's repeated patterns would be a hypnotic ostinato much more rudimentary than anything in ragtime, and even the variations in the right hand would be minimal, and more rhythmic than melodic. In the work of a pianist–singer such as Jimmy Yancey (1898–1951), however, the extreme simplicity was both charming and moving, like that of folk artists anywhere.

Inevitably perhaps, the possibilities of the instrument seduced many of the more energetic performers to expand their role within this strictly limited framework. Like the Harlem stride outgrowth of ragtime, the development of boogie-woogie cannot be easily separated from the parent style of blues piano, and many later players alternated between the two. The introduction of more varied, and often more virtuoso, left-hand patterns did not detract or distract from the relentless twelve-bar blues chord-sequence. Nor did the increase of invention in right-hand parts alter the fact that emotional release was the aim, rather than empty display. Despite the fact that pieces such as 'Honky tonk train blues' by Meade 'Lux' Lewis (1905–64) or 'Chicago breakdown' by 'Big' Maceo Merriweather (1905–53) make excellent concert items today, the piano was still being treated (to repeat an oft-used phrase) as 'eighty-eight tuned drums'.

Jazz and composition

During the 1920s the distinctive areas of ragtime and blues began to merge, in what would be only the first of many cross-influences between the different branches of African–American music.[4] The 'jazz age' begat much popular music which was to be forgotten, alongside many classic recordings which are cherished to this day. There was also much repertory composed during the decade which has survived and been endlessly reinterpreted, but the impending maturity of the music is evidenced more by the records than the printed scores. Doubtless it was because of this, and because of the evanescent nature of the countless performances not preserved on record, that there was considerable interest on the part of European composers.

There were, of course, other less welcome reasons for the attention turned on American popular music, which were bound up with the disintegration of the tonal system and the resulting stylistic confusion. Just as Picasso's interest in African masks mirrored Debussy's enthusiasm for Balinese gamelan, so curiosity about jazz may often have been mixed with a desire to end the impasse in European music. If so, it must be said that the beneficial results were few and far between.[5] Whether one looks at orchestral work such as Milhaud's *La creation du monde* or keyboard compositions such as Stravinsky's *Piano ragtime,* the importation of jazz effects failed to solve the writer's structural problems (as might indeed have been foreseen). It also managed to reduce what was becoming a lively and self-sufficient art to the status of local colour in a travelogue. If one looks for examples which actually breathe the air of jazz and blues, while yet remaining successful works within the European compositional tradition, the list might well begin and end with Ravel's Piano Concerto in G.

Again, it might have been foreseen that the best use of ragtime and blues material in larger-scale composition would be made by musicians more intimately associated with the relevant traditions, such as George Gershwin (1898–1937). Now that *Porgy and Bess* has been acknowledged as a classic twentieth-century opera and his *Rhapsody in Blue* has been accepted into the European concert repertory, his success has finally become self-evident. As with miniatures such as the Three Preludes, the reason is clearly that his varied uses of 'third-note accentuation' and of blue notes came naturally, not as a stick-on effect. During his early days as a songwriter and demonstrator of others' songs, Gershwin had developed an excellent ragtime playing style and, though not an originator in this field, his surviving recordings and piano rolls show an idiomatic performer at work.

Gershwin also introduces another significant strand of this story, for subsequent performers have found numerous interpretations of his songs of which the composer himself was not aware. His 'I got rhythm' is just one example, but thousands upon thousands of jazzmen have taken the bare bones of the song, often discarding the given melody at the very outset and improvising endlessly upon the underlying chord sequence. Gershwin himself wrote a concert piece for piano and orchestra called 'Variations on 'I got rhythm'', which pales before his long-distance contribution to the creativity of several generations of jazz players.

His black counterpart, Edward 'Duke' Ellington (1899–1974), went considerably further in working out the development of orchestral jazz from the inside. He too aspired to be first a ragtime player and then a writer of songs, and the original, piano-concerto form of his 1943 'New world a-comin' also deserves consideration alongside *Rhapsody in blue.* His involvement with the piano is often deemed less crucial than his instrumental writing for the many other musicians who populated his various bands. Nevertheless his chromatic writing for ensemble, and his often astringently experimental piano interjections to band compositions, exercised a great long-term influence on keyboard players.

Stylistic diversification

In the early blues and boogie-woogie period, the piano was usually the sole instrument to fulfil the function of what is now known as the 'rhythm section' and, even if played alongside an acoustic guitar, it would predominate. The fussiness of ragtime was found to be excessive when used alongside other instruments, but the pattern of blues and boogie-woogie for accompaniment purposes survived with little modification in the jazz-influenced rhythm-and-blues bands of later generations. The great model in defining the piano's place within the jazz ensemble was William 'Count' Basie (1904–84), whose rare solo spots often employed the same minimal but propulsive gestures that he used when accompanying the rest of his group. Most succeeding players found there to be more of a serious dichotomy between what they were required to do in the rhythm section, that is, when in a backing role, and what they wished to do when allowed the space to play a solo.

From this period on, the solo improvisation was usually not unaccompanied but the work of a single player backed by other group members, and most pianists' right-hand work began to mirror the sounds of other jazz instruments. By the time that Basie was making his mark in the 1930s, his discretion stood out in stark contrast to most other established jazz players. His informal teacher, Fats Waller, was at the height of his powers, while the more daring Earl Hines (1903–83) was also leading his own band. Hines was able to imply rhythm with the left hand but use it as a percussive adjunct to highly syncopated flights of fancy essayed by his right. This has proved to be the conventional division of labour ever since, and many pianists of later generations have become so addicted to left-hand punctuations as to be unwilling to play any regularly repeated rhythm. It is, however, a by-product of Hines's original desire to make the melodic improvisation of the right as incisive, and rhythmically self-sufficient, as a trumpet or other wind instrument capable of producing only one note at a time. Since wind players, from Louis Armstrong onwards, have usually been the pacesetters in jazz, there has been an inevitable non-keyboard influence on the pianist's approach.

One unique performer took these developments for granted, and was also admired by such as Horowitz and Godowsky for his sheer dexterity. Art Tatum (1909–56) had a brilliant musical mind which enabled him, often in the course of a single short piece, to incorporate flashes of smoothed-down stride, the anti-stride discontinuity of Hines, and his own chromatic harmonies (full of ninth and thirteenth chords) which were to influence later players, even wind players. Just occasionally, he would play a genre piece such as his 'Tatum-pole boogie' (recorded in

1949) or his virtuoso arrangement of 'Tiger rag' (1932–3). Tatum's speciality, however, was to take a familiar melody, reharmonise it and decorate it with arpeggios and complex runs, sometimes in a *rubato* manner which was new in a jazz context and which made his in-tempo passages all the more effective. In this way the piece became a completely new experience, and two excellent if untypical examples are his versions of Massenet's 'Elegie' (which manages to incorporate a bizarre quotation from 'The Stars and Stripes forever') and of Dvořák's 'Humoreske'.

Hines and Tatum belonged to the first generation who chose to base their improvisations on the popular songs of the day. They wrote little original material, simply because their reworkings of others' material became sufficiently original to be easily distinguished from their fellow performers. They were also of sufficient middle-class upbringing to be given excellent conventional tutoring in the European repertory before branching out into the vernacular, and this is true of the vast majority of players who followed them. There continued to be important exceptions, however, such as Erroll Garner (1921–77). Singled out in early childhood as having an exceptional ear and being able to reproduce both piano rolls and pieces from his elder siblings' classical lessons after a single hearing, he deliberately distanced himself from conventional learning. He was also an exception stylistically in that, almost alone of his generation, he maintained a steady left-hand rhythm. This was only abandoned at climactic moments or when he simulated the ensemble playing of big-band jazz by phrasing with both hands together, a technique known as 'block chording' which is still widely used today.

Post-war developments

The ascendancy of Hines, Tatum and then Garner came during the immediate post-Depression years and the second world war, when the wider field of popular music was more indebted to jazz than ever before or since. But pianists never attained the contemporary fame of the white bandleaders who played wind instruments, such as Benny Goodman or Tommy Dorsey. Even the pacesetters of the piano were most admired by fellow musicians, and their wider significance has only become obvious with the passage of time. As is often the way in the popular arts, many other performers of less impressive pedigree achieved greater renown, but only for shorter periods. Now totally forgotten, people like Maurice Rocco and others appeared in the three-minute-long sound films produced for use with early jukeboxes (a forerunner of today's promotional videos). In wartime, even Hollywood looked favourably on black female pianists such as Hazel Scott and the still-active Dorothy Donegan, who produced a palatable blend of jazz elements with embellishments echoing their classical upbringing.

The end of the war, and the ensuing collapse of more favourable attitudes towards black citizens, coincided with the emergence of a new style of jazz which turned its back on the very idea of courting popularity. For a period in the late 1940s 'bebop' – a deliberately frivolous name comparable to that of the Dada movement in art – attempted to expand on trends inherent in the work of Tatum and others, in an atmosphere free from the dictates of commerce. Needless to say, commerce soon intruded (as in the art world) but, in the meantime, two players emerged who between them dictated the main directions of development followed by creative pianists ever since.

Earl 'Bud' Powell (1924–66) might be likened to a jet-propelled Earl Hines, whose glittering tone and helter-skelter lines rivalled the saxophone of bebop's icon Charlie Parker, just as Hines emulated Louis Armstrong. Though still undervalued for his far-reaching influence, Powell laid such an emphasis on the right hand's melodic improvisation that few subsequent developments (of whatever precise stylistic inclination) have questioned the proposition that the main goal of jazz or a jazz-influenced pianist should be linear invention, in the manner of a wind instrumentalist. The main exceptions belong to the school of Powell's contemporary, Thelonious Monk (whose first name, not a nickname, has now graced three generations of the same family).

Monk (1917–82) apparently began his career as a more conventional jazz player but, by the time he gradually became to make a name for himself, he had pared away all the smoothness and introduced fascinating discords, voicing these in a strangely sparse way often alleged to be caused by a lack of fluency. However, a study of his characteristic vocabulary, and especially of the comparatively large amount of original material he created, reveals a highly coherent method which is all cut from the same cloth. Monk and his few followers were openly inspired by the harmonic pungency of Duke Ellington. Equally enamoured of Monk and Ellington is Cecil Taylor (*b.*1929), whose hyperactive atonal clusters might be likened to the school of action painting, although this is a simile which he would undoubtedly reject as too flippant. Indeed the 1960s, which saw him become a force to reckon with, was the period when the continuous development from ragtime through to avant-garde jazz began to be described as 'black classical music', in order to distinguish it from more popular forms.

Each of three aforementioned artists lived to witness (as indeed did

Earl Hines and Erroll Garner) the gradual move of serious jazz performance away from the backing of dancers and the entertainment of
nightclub audiences towards concert-hall presentation. This move, which
has involved certain losses as well as considerable gains, had already
begun immediately after the height of the bebop period. An early innova-
tor in putting on concerts for college audiences, Dave Brubeck (b.1920) is
a rather heavy-handed improviser whose success in the 1950s was even an
early inspiration for Cecil Taylor and, like Taylor, he came to jazz comparatively late, after a background in the European classics. The player of the
same generation whose playing is more idiomatic, yet possesses a fiery
fluency that communicates easily to non-specialist listeners, is Oscar
Peterson (b.1925). He is also an excellent group player, but the height of
his achievement lies perhaps in his unaccompanied performances which
often resemble a more intense version of Art Tatum.

Jazz and popular music

It may come as a surprise to learn that the role model for the young
Peterson (and for most players of his age) was the singer–pianist Nat
'King' Cole (1917–65). Since it was Cole's singing which was promoted at
the expense of his keyboard work, he all but abandoned the latter in
order to stand at the microphone and perform face-to-face with the mass
audience. The recordings he made in the 1940s, however, when he
accompanied himself at the piano, reveal tantalising hints of the jazz
pianist he used to be. And they provide one reminder that, as in the field
of European composition, much that was intended as purely functional
or commercial music – with no other aim than entertaining its con-
sumers – may stand the test of time and reveal hidden gems decades later.

Little matching that description survives from the 1950s, with the
notable exception of another singer–pianist who was initially one of the
many performers enamoured of Cole. However, Ray Charles (b.1930) had
a much closer affinity with the vocal and instrumental blues, and effected
a dramatic transformation of both blues and pop by marrying them with
the influence of gospel music. The vocal results, which led to the development of 1960s 'soul', lie outside the field of the present book but the piano
work was highly influential. By taking the left-hand octaves and the
ringing right-hand triads previously only heard in black churches (and
typified by Mildred Falls, the long-time accompanist of gospel singer
Mahalia Jackson), Charles brought a new sound to popular piano music.
One has to look for small nuggets within his predominantly commercial

recordings but, having been blind since childhood, unlike Cole he has continued to perform from the piano bench.

If Cole and Charles underline the frequent background role of the keyboard in the popular field, two sometime jazzmen emerged in the 1960s to sudden success with avowedly 'light music' approaches. Peter Nero played in a glib and glossy manner which was distantly reminiscent of players such as Tatum and Peterson, and which gave him access to frequent prime-time television appearances. German pianist Horst Jankowski (*b.*1936), who led a fine radio orchestra and had accompanied many leading jazz players, will be forever associated with a trifle entitled 'A walk in the Black Forest'. Yet, though these efforts easily went in one ear and out of the other, their professional backgrounds assured technically excellent performances which inspired many younger performers to raise the standards for popular music.

Another example of the piano being relegated to the background, yet nevertheless making a distinctive contribution, is within the field of Hispanic–American music. Already a cliché by the 1950s, the percussive running octaves of pianists in Latin bands made them stand out from the general rhythm-section sound without giving them solo space as such. This gradually changed as the 'salsa' style coalesced in the 1960s, largely thanks to the work of Charlie Palmieri and later his brother Eddie (both of Puerto Rican descent), both of whom led bands dominated by their flamboyant keyboard work. Their serious approach was perhaps a Latin equivalent of jazz, but more widely popular throughout the world were two Brazilian players. The frothy vocal and instrumental combination of Sergio Mendes's Brazil '66 group (subsequently Brasil '77) was heightened by his piano work, while the celebrated songwriter and musical director Antonio Carlos Jobim made highly effective use of his minimal single-note piano in many of the original 'bossa nova' recordings.

European and exotic influences

A similar sensibility to that of Jobim has been at the heart of much jazz piano of the last thirty years and more, and the reason for this lies in the enormous influence exerted by Bill Evans (1929–80). As Earl Hines's development is linked to that of Louis Armstrong, Evans will be eternally associated with one aspect of the work of trumpeter Miles Davis – as typified by the classic recording *Kind of blue*, which Evans stamped with his ensemble style. The particular combination of delicacy and strength produced by his chord voicings, taken together with soaring but oblique right-hand lines, was a leap forward to the same extent as Cecil Taylor's, but much more readily accepted. At his most reflective, he often plays what one might expect from Erik Satie, if Satie were a contemporary jazz performer, especially when occasionally abandoning the chord sequences of his favourite popular songs to improvise on a modal base. This was a widespread shift during the 1960s (and in soul music from the following decade onwards), and examples of Evans's work in this vein are 'NYC's no lark' (1963) and 'Peace piece' (1958).

Evans, like Powell before him, was less known for his original material, whereas McCoy Tyner (*b*.1938), the chief collaborator of saxophonist John Coltrane, followed Monk in largely preferring his own composi-tions. Because of the association with Coltrane, Tyner's work was far more tempestuous than that of Evans and, whereas Evans's extended har-monies sometimes echoed Debussy, Tyner's adaptation to the modal approach resulted in heavily accented chords built up in fourths, not thirds. Not only did these two between them affect the future course of jazz, but the frequently less demanding fusion known as 'jazz-rock', which took root from the 1970s, was populated with pianists whose chief requi-site was a stock of Evans and Tyner phrases. Of course, the nature of the context meant that they were usually importing this vocabulary to one of the many electronic keyboards, which lie beyond the scope of our discussion.

Several of the most individual players who had success in the fusion field, however, were originally jazzmen whose first love was the conven-tional piano, now frequently and solecistically known as the 'acoustic piano' (or, by those who strongly prefer it, by the ironic name of 'steam piano'). Two of the musicians concerned are Herbie Hancock (*b*.1940) and Armando 'Chick' Corea (*b*.1941), who as well as frequently leading rock-influenced electric bands have repeatedly returned to their original outlet, sometimes even touring as a duo. Both, of course, were trained in the European repertory, and both have written works for piano that reflect classical influences. In their 'acoustic' jazz work, both represent amalgams of Evans and Tyner, with Hancock emphasising more of an awareness of blues phraseology while Corea more often exploits his Puerto Rican roots.

Perhaps the performer who has come to represent the epitome of jazz piano for many people – enjoying a widespread acceptance comparable only to that of Brubeck thirty years ago – is Keith Jarrett (*b*.1945). His scope and his output have been enormous and, in addition to his early work as a stimulating ensemble player leading his own quartets, he made his reputation with a decade of solo concerts in which he drew on a huge range of influences. Post-Evans jazz, blues, gospel, ethnic music and seemingly the whole of European composition from baroque to atonal – all are grist to the millstone around his neck, that of creating a whole evening's performance with no preconceived material. The 1975 *Köln concert* remains a classic, but many of his attempts to repeat its success plough remarkably similar furrows, thereby negating some of the benefits of free improvisation. It is worth noting, too, that he has inspired a new genre of less demanding solo piano work by players such as George Winston, who helped to found the kind of uplifting meditative music known as 'new age'.

The piano central to all styles

In working his way out of an artistic impasse in the 1980s, Jarrett adopted several ploys. He not only reverted to trio versions of the popular-song repertory favoured by Bill Evans but became one of the few jazz performers (apart from Benny Goodman and Wynton Marsalis) to record repertory from the European canon, such as the Goldberg Variations. Whatever the genuine insights into this material discerned by his reviewers, it is perhaps of more interest that he has drawn admiration from some classical players for his jazz work. What is an even more remarkable and very recent development is the serious interest on the part of classical players in becoming involved in jazz performance.

Back in the 1950s, there were inroads made by Friedrich Gulda (*b*.1930) (who has recorded with Chick Corea) and André Previn (*b*.1929), both of whom have maintained an association with the jazz field while continuing their careers in 'straight' music. But there were few high-profile colleagues who cared to join them in this very difficult and rather risky activity. During the last ten years, however, many factors including the double-barrelled approach of Jarrett and the acknowledged respectability of Joplin and Gershwin have led to a more wide-ranging involvement by classical performers. One of the results is the performance of transcriptions of Garner and Monk by the British pianist Joanna MacGregor. The French player Katia Labèque (who partners her sister Marielle in a piano duo) has played works by Evans and Hancock and has commissioned works from other jazz writers.

It would be a mistake, though, to think that popular music is somehow justified by the endorsement of figures from the classical world, when it is the technique and traditions of the music which are their own justification. Popular piano today can mean all sorts of things, from simplistic playing-down to the audience by someone such as Richard Clayderman to the real down-market thumping of an Elton John. But it can also mean lightweight jazz from the likes of a Dave Grusin, or the genuinely widespread appeal of someone with high artistic ideals such as Keith Jarrett. Much of this broad spectrum of activity will live on into the next century and, although for reasons already explained sheet-music is of limited use to the explorer of this territory, recordings continue to provide more and more listeners with a challenge to the ear and to the hands.

Repertory

Because popular music at its most creative is essentially a performer's art and not a composer's art, its representation in printed form is slender. Most of what has been made available must be regarded as unreliable, because it usually takes the form of simplified arrangements aimed at other would-be performers. The only publications recommended here are those intended as accurate transcriptions of the way the music was actually played by its creators. Although even here small errors are often found, the volumes below do offer an insight into the performance of popular music at a high artistic level.

Brubeck, Dave, *Time Out* and *Time Further Out* (Derry Music, 1962)

Corea, Chick, *Piano Improvisations* (Advance Music, 1990)

Evans, Bill, *Bill Evans plays* (Tro Ludlow Music, undated)

Evans, Bill, *Bill Evans 3* (Tro Ludlow Music, undated)

Garner, Erroll, *Erroll Garner songbook* (Cherry Lane Music, 1977)

Hancock, Herbie, *Classic jazz compositions and piano solos* (Advance M, 1992)

Jarrett, Keith, *The Köln concert* (Schott, 1991)

Joplin, Scott, *Collected piano works* (4th edn, New York Public Library, 1981)

Kriss, Eric (ed.), *Six blues-roots pianists* (Oak Publications, 1973) (includes pieces by Jimmy Yancey and five others)

Monk, Thelonious, *Jazz masters* (Amsco, 1978)

Morton, Jelly Roll, *Collected piano music* (Smithsonian Institution, 1982)

Priestley, Brian (ed.), *Jazz piano*, vols. 1–6 (IMP, 1982–90) (each volume contains pieces by ten or more pianists, covering 53 different performers in all)

Richards, Tim, *Improvising blues piano* (Schott, 1997) (includes 'Honky tonk train blues' by Meade 'Lux' Lewis)

Tatum, Art, *Jazz masters* (Amsco, 1986)

Tyner, McCoy, *Artists transcription series* (Hal Leonard, 1992)

Glossary

action: the mechanism by which a hammer is made to strike the strings when a key is depressed. In the late eighteenth and nineteenth centuries most grand actions were of two fundamentally different types. In the 'Viennese' action (Figs. 2.2a and 2.2b) the hammer mechanism is mounted on the key itself, whereas in the English and similar actions (Figs. 2.3a and 2.3b) the hammer is mounted on a separate frame. The modern grand action (Fig. 6.3) is derived from the English grand action. **Upright** piano actions comprise the same component parts as grands, but arranged differently to suit the vertical orientation of the strings.

agraffe: a metal stud pierced with as many holes as there are unison strings to a note, invented by Sebastien Erard in 1808, whose function is to prevent the hammer pushing the strings upwards when they are struck (Fig. 6.2).

base board: the wooden underside of an early piano.

bassoon: a tone-modifying device operated by **handstop**, **knee lever** or **pedal** by means of which a strip of parchment, silk or other material is pressed against the bass strings of the piano, causing them to make a buzzing sound (see Fig. 2.7).

belly rail: the substantial wooden frame member which runs the width of the piano and supports the end of the **soundboard** nearest to the performer.

bentside: the long, curved side of the grand piano to the right of the performer. In some early pianos the wood curves into the body of the piano and is joined to the (straight) **tail** of the instrument (see Figs. 1.2 and 1.5). In other pianos, there is a continuous 'S' shape, referred to as a 'double bentside' (see Fig. 2.1), which incorporates the tail of the piano.

bichord: stringing of the piano in which there are two strings per note.

bracing: a system of wooden or metal supports which strengthen the piano.

bridge: the strip or strips of wood which are fixed to the **soundboard**, and over which the strings pass, whose function is to transmit the vibration of the strings to the soundboard.

cabinet pianos: see **upright pianos**.

capo d'astro **bar**: a metal bar which presses down on the strings and performs the same function as the **agraffes**.

case: the outer shell of the piano.

check: the part of the **action** which 'catches' the **hammer** immediately after it has struck the strings. Some early piano actions have no check, some have individual checks for each note (Figs. 2.3a, 2.3b and 6.3) while in other actions there is a single check rail for all of the hammers (Figs. 2.2a and 2.2b).

combination piano/harpsichords: instruments which contain harpsichord and piano mechanisms by means of which the strings can either be plucked (harpsichord) or struck (piano), as the performer chooses. Combination piano/harpsichords were made by several makers up to *c*.1780.

combination piano/organs: instruments which contained piano and organ mechanisms. They were made until *c*.1800.

cottage pianos: see **upright pianos**.

cross-stringing (overstringing): on modern upright and grand pianos the bass strings do not lie parallel to the treble strings, but pass over them, allowing for greater string length in uprights, and a more central position of the **bridge** on grands. Cross-stringing was developed in the nineteenth century (see Fig. 6.1).

damper: most commonly a piece of felt, but generally leather or cloth on early pianos, whose function is to damp the vibration of the strings of an individual note.

damper rail: the strip of wood which guides the dampers in place on some pianos (see Fig. 2.6).

double escapement action: an **action** patented by Erard in 1821, and sometimes referred to as his 'repetition' action, which allows the performer to repeat a note before the key has been completely released. The modern grand action is a modification of Erard's action.

English grand pianos: grand pianos with distinctive **actions** and **case** constructions that were made in England in the eighteenth and nineteenth centuries and whose original design had much in common with Cristofori's pianos. The fundamental design elements were used in many parts of continental Europe, especially in France, and formed the basis of modern grand piano design.

escapement: the part of the **action** which allows the **hammer** to 'escape' as the string is struck, allowing it to fall back to a low resting position. Some early pianos (especially squares) have no escapement (see Figs. 1.1, 2.2a, 2.2b, 2.3a, 2.3b, 6.3).

giraffe pianos: see **upright pianos**.

hammer: the part of the **action** which strikes the string (see Figs. 1.1, 2.2a, 2.2b, 2.3a, 2.3b and 6.3). On most eighteenth- and early nineteenth-century pianos, the hammer heads were covered with leather (see Figs. 2.2a and 2.3a), although some early hammers were made of bare wood. In the course of the nineteenth century, the practice of covering hammer heads with felt was introduced.

handstop: the means of operating tone-modifying devices on some early pianos (see **pedal**). Handstops are either situated inside the case of the piano (on squares – see Fig. 1.4b), or they project through the **nameboard**.

hitchpin plate: the metal plate into which are set the **hitchpins** (on pianos after *c.*1830).

hitchpins: the small metal pins around which the strings are looped at the end of the strings opposite the **tuning pins**.

intermediate lever: part of the **action** of some pianos which lies between the key and the **hammer**, whose function is to increase the rate of acceleration of the hammer towards the string (see Fig. 1.1, component 'E' and Fig. 6.3).

kapsel: wooden or metal component in which the **hammer** rests (Figs. 2.2a and 2.2b)

knee levers: levers which are operated by the knee to perform the same function as **pedals**. Knee levers were used on many types of continental piano instead of pedals until the early nineteenth century.

lute: a tone-modifying device operated by a **handstop**, **knee lever** or **pedal** which causes a strip of leather or other material to be pressed against the strings, inhibiting their vibration.

moderator: a tone-modifying device operated by a **handstop**, **knee lever** or **pedal** in which tongues of leather or cloth are interposed between the **hammers** and strings, muffling the sound, but leaving the strings free to vibrate (see Fig. 2.6).

nameboard: the piece of wood immediately behind the keys on which is usually found the piano maker's name.

overstringing: see **cross-stringing**.

pedal: foot-operated lever operating the tone-modifying devices of the piano. See **bassoon**, **lute**, **moderator**, **sostenuto**, **sustaining**, **Turkish music** and *una corda*.

reproducing piano: a piano with a mechanism for recording a performance (see Fig. 5.1).

ribs: pieces of wood glued to the underside of the **soundboard**.

sostenuto: the sostenuto pedal is found on some grand pianos from the second half of the nineteenth century onwards. Its purpose is

selective sustaining and its mechanism causes to be sustained only the notes that are depressed by the performer at the time the pedal is pressed: all other notes are damped in the usual way while the pedal remains depressed.

soundboard: a large panel of softwood supported on the underside by **ribs** glued across the board.

square piano (Tafelklavier): the rectangular form of the piano that was most commonly used for domestic purposes in the eighteenth and nineteenth centuries (Figs. 1.4a and 3.4).

sticker: a component of the **action** used in **upright pianos** in which the **hammers** are placed some distance above the level of the keyboard. Lengthy strips of wood transmit the motion of the key to the hammer mechanism (Fig. 3.7).

sustaining: the sustaining **handstop(s)**, **knee lever(s)** or **pedal(s)** which raise all of the **dampers** from the strings.

Tafelklavier: see **square piano**.

tail: the end of a grand piano opposite the performer.

trichord: stringing of the piano in which there are three strings to each note.

tuning pins (wrest pins): the metal pins around which the strings are wound at the end of the strings nearest the performer on a grand piano. The tuning pins are set into the **wrestplank** and are rotated in order to slacken or tighten the strings in tuning.

Turkish music: a device, or collection of devices, operated by a **knee lever** or **pedal** that was fashionable in the early nineteenth century. It comprises a combination of various drum, cymbal and triangle effects.

una corda: a tone-modifying device operated by a **handstop**, **knee lever** or **pedal** which causes the keyboard to move laterally, allowing the hammer to strike one or two, rather than all of the strings. On many early grands a small wooden block to the side of the keyboard controls the extent of the keyboard shift – to one or two strings – whereas on more recent grands the shift is limited to two strings.

upright piano: in almost all forms of upright piano the strings lie perpendicular to the floor. The form in general use today was often referred to as the 'cottage piano' in the nineteenth century (see Fig. 3.8) and had shorter strings than the grand piano. In the 'giraffe' and 'cabinet' (Fig. 3.6) forms of the upright piano the strings are similar in length to those of a grand and rise from floor level upwards. In upright grands, the strings rise upwards from the level of the keyboard (Fig. 3.5). Some early experiments were made with upright square pianos by William Southwell, but not many instruments of this design were made.

'Viennese' piano: grand pianos with distinctive actions and case construction. 'Viennese' pianos were made in Austria and southern Germany in the late eighteenth and nineteenth centuries.

wrest pins: see **tuning pins**.

wrestplank: the block of wood into which the **tuning pins** are set.

Notes

1 The piano to *c.*1770

1 The development of piano actions prior to Cristofori is discussed in Stewart Pollens, *The early pianoforte* (Cambridge, 1995), chs. 1 and 2.

2 Giuliana Montanari, 'Bartolomeo Cristofori', *EM*, 19 (1991), pp. 383–96; Pollens, *Pianoforte*, p. 45.

3 Montanari, 'Cristofori', p. 385; Pollens, *Pianoforte*, p. 45.

4 Pollens, *Pianoforte*, p. 45.

5 Maffei's description is published in full along with a detailed description of Cristofori's surviving instrument in Pollens, *Pianoforte*, p. 232.

6 Ferrini's keyboard instruments are discussed at length in Luigi Ferdinando Tagliavini, 'Giovanni Ferrini and his harpsichord "a penne e a martelletti"', *EM*, 19 (1991), pp. 399–408 and Stewart Pollens, 'Three keyboard instruments signed by Cristofori's assistant, Giovanni Ferrini', *Galpin Society Journal*, 44 (1991), pp. 77–93. His harpsichord/piano is described in Pollens, *Pianoforte*, ch. 5.

7 Pollens, *Pianoforte*, ch. 5.

8 Pollens, *Pianoforte*, p. 119.

9 Charles Burney, *The present state of music in France and Italy* (London, 1771), ed. Percy Scholes (London, 1959), p. 152.

10 Pollens, *Pianoforte*, p. 58.

11 Joel Sheveloff, 'Domenico Scarlatti: tercentenary frustrations', *MQ*, 72 (1986), pp. 90–118.

12 Pollens, *Pianoforte*, p. 57.

13 Pollens, *Pianoforte*, p. 119.

14 Lorenz Mizler, *Neu eröffnete musikalische Bibliothek*, vol. 3, part 3 (Leipzig, 1747), pp. 474–7; Friedrich Wilhelm Marpurg, *Kritische Briefe über die Tonkunst*, vol. 3, part 1 (Berlin, 1764), pp. 81–104.

15 See Sarah Hanks, 'Pantaleon's Pantalon: an eighteenth-century musical fashion', *MQ*, 55 (1969), pp. 215–27.

16 For further information on the keyed pantalon, see Michael Cole, *The pianoforte in the classical era* (Oxford, 1997).

17 Johann Heinrich Zedler, *Grosses vollständiges Universal-Lexicon* (Halle and Leipzig, 1732–50), vol. 5, pp. 135–40.

18 Jacob Adlung, *Musica mechanica organoedi*, 2 (Berlin 1768), p. 116, tr. in Hans T. David and Arthur Mendel, *The Bach reader* (rev. edn, New York, 1966), p. 259.

19 Johann Nikolaus Forkel, *Ueber Johann Sebastian Bach's Leben* (Leipzig, 1802), pp. 25–6.

20 Silbermann's surviving grands are described in detail in Pollens, *Pianoforte*, pp. 175–84.

21 *Spenersche Zeitung* (11 May 1747), tr. in Christoph Wolff, 'New research on Bach's *Musical Offering*', *MQ*, 57 (1971), p. 401.

22 Wolff, 'New Research', p. 403.

23 All of these upright grands are described in Pollens, *Pianoforte*, pp. 107–114, 186–202.

24 Heinrich Christoph Koch's *Musikalisches Lexicon* (Frankfurt, 1802) s.v. 'Fortbien' gives 1758 as the date of Friederici's invention of the square: the date of a square by Socher (1742) is unreliable.

25 The action of one of J. H. Silbermann's pianos is shown in Rosamond Harding, *The Piano-forte: its history traced to the Great Exhibition* (Old Woking, 1978), p. 38.

26 Carl Philipp Emanuel Bach, *Versuch über die wahre Art das Clavier zu spielen*, part 1 (Berlin, 1753), tr. and ed. by William J. Mitchell (London, 1949), p. 36.

27 Jacob Adlung, *Anleitung zu der musikalischen Gelahrheit* (Erfurt, 1758), p. 563.

28 Charles Burney, *The present state of music in Germany, the Netherlands, and United Provinces* (London, 1775), ed. Percy Scholes (London, 1959), p. 39.

29 Burney, *Germany*, p. 96.

30 Burney, *Germany*, p. 160.

31 Burney, *Germany*, p. 200.

32 Johann Adam Hiller in *Anhang zu dem dritten Jahrgang der Nachrichten und Anmerkungen die Musik betreffend*, part 4 (Leipzig, 24 July 1769), p. 32.

33 Abraham Rees, *The Cyclopaedia; or Universal Dictionary* (London, 1819), s.v. 'Harpsichord'.

34 Ibid.

35 Slava Klima, Garry Bowers, Kerry Grant (eds.), *Memoirs of Dr. Charles Burney, 1726–1769* (Lincoln, 1988), pp. 72–3.

36 Rees, 'Harpsichord'.

37 *Memoirs of Dr. Charles Burney*, p. 73.

38 Paget Toynbee and Leonard Whibley (eds.), *The correspondence of Thomas Gray* (Oxford, 1971).

39 Thomas Mortimer, *Universal director* (London, 1763), p. 50.

40 David Wainwright, *Broadwood by*

appointment: a history (London, 1982), p. 41.

41 Charles Burney, *Music, Men and Manners in France and Italy*, ed. H. Poole (2nd edn, London, 1974), pp. 19–20.

42 Warwick Henry Cole, 'Americus Backers: original forte piano maker', *The Harpsichord and Pianoforte Magazine*, 4 (1987), pp. 79–85.

43 Alvaro Ribiero (ed.), *The Letters of Dr Charles Burney* (Oxford, 1991), vol. 1, p. 163.

44 Edward Francis Rimbault, *The pianoforte, its origins, progress and construction* (London, 1860), p. 133.

45 Information from London newspapers given to me by Richard Maunder.

46 Information from London newspapers given to me by Richard Maunder.

47 Gillian Sheldrick, *The accounts of Thomas Green 1742–1790* (Hitchin, 1992).

48 Eugène de Bricqueville, *Les ventes d'instruments de musique au XVIII siècle* (Paris, 1980), p. 11.

49 Hiller, *Jahrgang der Nachrichten*, 24 July 1769.

50 William Dowd, 'The surviving instruments of the Blanchet workshop', in Howard Schott (ed.), *The historical harpsichord*, 1 (1984), p. 89.

51 Frank Hubbard, *Three centuries of harpsichord making* (Cambridge, MA, 1965), p. 293.

52 Hubbard, *Harpsichord making*, p. 294.

53 Hubbard, *Harpsichord making*, p. 311.

54 Burney, *France and Italy*, p. 27.

55 Denis Diderot, *Correspondence*, ed. G. Roth (16 vols., Paris, 1955–70), vol. 11, pp. 197, 213.

56 In Ernest Closson, *La facture des instruments de musique en Belgique* (Brussels, 1935); tr. Delano Ames, ed. Robin Golding as *History of the piano* (2nd edn, London, 1974), p. 86.

57 Marie-Christine and Jean-François Weber, *J. K. Mercken* (Paris, 1986), p. 22.

58 Hubbard, *Harpsichord making*, p. 295.

59 Wainwright, *Broadwood*, p. 62.

60 See J. Gallay, *Un inventaire sous la terreur. Etat des instruments de musique relevés chez les émigrés et condamnés par H. Bruni* (Paris, 1890).

61 See Voltaire's letter of *c.*15 December 1774 in Theodore Besterman (ed.), *Correspondence and related documents of Voltaire* (Banbury, 1975), vol. 41.

2 Pianos and pianists *c.*1770–*c.*1825

1 Friedrich Kalkbrenner, *Méthode pour apprendre le pianoforte* (Paris, 1830); Eng. tr. Sabilla Novello (London, 1862), p. 10.

2 The merits of pianos by Walter, Stein/Streicher and Schanz are discussed by Schönfeld in his *Jahrbuch der Tonkunst von Wien und Prag* (1796), sections of which are translated in Eva Badura-Skoda, 'Prolegomena to a history of the Viennese fortepiano', *Israel Studies in Musicology*, 2 (1980), p. 94.

3 It is discussed in detail in Kurt Wittmayer, 'Der Flügel Mozarts', *Mozart-Jahrbuch* (1991), pp. 301–12.

4 Carl Czerny, *Supplement (oder verte Theil) zur grossen Pianoforte Schule* (Vienna, 1842), tr. and ed. P. Badura-Skoda (Vienna, 1970), p. 10; and Emily Anderson (ed. and tr.), *The Letters of Beethoven* (London, 1961), p. 82.

5 David Wainwright, *Broadwood by appointment: a history* (London, 1982), p. 60.

6 *AMZ*, 5 (1802), cols. 196–8.

7 Richard Maunder, 'Mozart's keyboard instruments', *EM*, 20 (1992), p. 214.

8 Maunder, 'Mozart's keyboard instruments', p. 214.

9 Richard Maunder and David Rowland, 'Mozart's pedal piano', *EM*, 23 (1995), pp. 287–96.

10 Emily Anderson (ed. and tr.), *The letters of Mozart and his family* (3rd edn, London, 1985), p. 340.

11 Anderson, *Letters of Mozart*, pp. 339–40.

12 *Caecilia*, 10 (1829), p. 238.

13 Anderson, *Letters of Mozart*, p. 793.

14 *AMZ*, 5 (1802), cols. 196–7.

15 For a discussion of these works and other details of pedalling, see David Rowland, *A history of pianoforte pedalling* (Cambridge, 1993).

16 Czerny, *Supplement*, p. 97.

17 Alfred James Hipkin's notebooks, quoted in Wainwright, *Broadwood*, p. 75.

18 Wainwright, *Broadwood*, p. 75.

19 Wainwright, *Broadwood*, p. 76.

20 See, for example, Howard Allen Craw, 'A biography and thematic catalog of the works of J. L. Dussek (1760–1812)', (diss., University of Southern California, 1964), pp. 109–13.

21 Leon Plantinga, *Clementi: his life and music* (London, 1977), ch. 6.

22 1789, col. 270 and 1790, col. 72.

23 *AMZ*, 2 (1799), October Intelligenz-Blatt, no. 2.

24 Rowland, *Pedalling*, ch. 9.

25 These are described in William Newman, *Beethoven on Beethoven: playing his piano music his way* (New York, 1988), pp. 50–4.

26 Anderson, *Letters of Beethoven*, p. 292.

27 Newman, *Beethoven*, pp. 54 ff.

28 According to Beethoven's teacher, Neefe, in a letter to Cramer's *Magazin der Musik* (Hamburg, 1787), p. 1386, translated Elliot Forbes (ed.), in *Thayer's Life of Beethoven* (2nd edn, Princeton, 1967), p. 86.

29 Forbes, *Thayer's Life of Beethoven*, p. 105.

30 See, for example, Anderson, *Letters of Beethoven*, pp. 82–3, 101, 269, 523.

31 Czerny, *Supplement*, p. 38.
32 Carl Czerny, *Erinnerungen aus meinen Leben* (MS 1842), tr. by Ernest Sanders in *MQ*, 42 (1956), p. 309.
33 Rowland, *Pedalling*, pp. 136–9.
34 Johann Nepomuk Hummel, *Ausführliche theoretische-practische Anweisung zum Piano-forte Spiel* (Vienna 1828), tr. as *A complete theoretical and practical course of instructions on the art of playing the pianoforte* (London, 1828), part 3, p. 40.
35 Franz Gerhard Wegeler and Ferdinand Ries, *Biographische Notizen über Ludwig van Beethoven* (Koblenz, 1838), tr. by Frederick Noonan as *Remembering Beethoven* (London, 1988), p. 94.
36 Carl Maria von Weber, 'Tempo-Bezeichnungen nach Mälzl's Metronom zur Oper Euryanthe', *AMZ*, 50 (1848), col. 127, tr. Newman, *Beethoven*, p. 112.
37 Kalkbrenner, *Méthode*, p. 10.
38 Kalkbrenner, *Méthode*, p. 12.

3 The piano since c.1825
1 See, for example, Rosamond Harding, *The piano-forte: its history traced to the Great Exhibition of 1851* (2nd edn, Old Woking, 1978), Appendix C, and Edward Francis Rimbault, *The pianoforte, its origins, progress and construction* (London, 1860), pp. 149–57.
2 I am indebted to David Hunt for this information.
3 David Wainwright, *Broadwood by appointment: a history* (London, 1982), p. 127.
4 Harding, *Piano-forte*, p. 200, and information received from David Hunt.
5 Deborah Wythe, 'The pianos of Conrad Graf', *EM*, 12 (1984), p. 454.
6 *New Grove*, s.v. 'Pianoforte'.
7 Rimbault, *Pianoforte*, p. 168.
8 Daniel Spillane, *History of the American pianoforte* (New York, 1890, repr. 1969), ch. 7.
9 Rimbault, *Pianoforte*, p. 168.
10 Harding, *Piano-forte*, pp. 237–9. See also Peter and Ann Mactaggart (eds.), *Musical instruments in the 1851 Exhibition* (Welwyn, 1986), p. 35.
11 Wainwright, *Broadwood*, p. 328.
12 Harding, *Piano-forte*, pp. 179–80.
13 Mactaggart, *Musical instruments*, p. 18.
14 Wythe, 'Graf', p. 456.
15 Alfred Dolge, *Pianos and their makers* (Covina, 1919, reprinted New York, 1980), pp. 97ff.
16 Cyril Ehrlich, *The piano: a history* (London 1976), pp. 81–2, 140–1.
17 Mactaggart, *Musical instruments*, p. 34.
18 Mactaggart, *Musical instruments*, p. 96.
19 *Le piano d'Érard a l'Exposition de 1844* (Paris and London, 1844), p. 4; reprinted in *Dossier Erard* (Geneva, 1980).
20 Harding, *Piano-forte*, p. 318; *AMZ*, 31 (1829), col. 596.
21 *AMZ*, 38 (1836), col. 129–33.
22 *New Grove*, s.v. 'Pianoforte'.
23 *Perfectionnemens apportés dans le méchanisme du piano par les Érard* (Paris and London, 1834), pp. 4–5: reprinted in *Dossier Erard*.
24 Mactaggart, *Musical instruments*, p. 15.
25 George Grove (ed.), *A dictionary of music and musicians* (London, 1879–89), s.v. 'Pedals'. For further details see David Rowland, *A history of pianoforte pedalling* (Cambridge, 1993).
26 John Broadwood & Co., *Pianofortes* (London, 1892), p. 32.
27 Personal communication from the firm.
28 See, for example, Edwin Roxburgh's *Labyrinth for Bösendorfer piano* (1970).
29 Ehrlich, *Piano*, p. 113.
30 Ehrlich, *Piano*, p. 124.
31 Ehrlich, *Piano*, pp. 192–3.
32 *New Grove*, s.v. 'Yamaha'.
33 Quoted in Rimbault, *Pianoforte*, pp. 159–60.
34 Ehrlich, *Piano*, p. 91.
35 Ehrlich, *Piano*, p. 185.
36 Wainwright, *Broadwood*, p. 327.
37 Wainwright, *Broadwood*, p. 151.
38 Wainwright, *Broadwood*, p. 327.
39 Ehrlich, *Piano*, p. 52.
40 A more extended description of cabinet and giraffe pianos can be found in Edwin Good, *Giraffes, Black Dragons, and other pianos* (Stanford, 1982), pp. 103–12.
41 Harding, *Piano-forte*, pp. 63–4.
42 These pianos are described in detail in Harding, *Piano-forte*, pp. 221–4.
43 Harding, *Piano-forte*, pp. 221–59.

4 The virtuoso tradition
1 Artur Rubinstein, *My young years* (London, 1973), p. 444.
2 Emily Anderson (ed. and tr.), *The letters of Mozart and his family* (3rd edn, London, 1985), p. 793.
3 Carl Czerny, *The art of playing the ancient and modern pianoforte works* (London, c.1848). Thalberg probably got the idea for his arpeggio effects from the harp virtuoso Elias Parish-Alvars. The *Moses* Fantasy is more or less directly copied from a Parish-Alvars piece of the same name.
4 Daniel Ollivier (ed.), *Correspondance de Liszt et de Madame d'Agoult* (Paris, 1933), vol. 1, p. 190.
5 Eduard Hanslick, *Music criticisms*, tr. Henry Pleasants (New York, 1988), p. 107.
6 Carl Lachmund, *Living with Liszt*, ed. Alan Walker (Stuyvesant, NY, 1995), p. 35.

7 François-Joseph Fétis, 'Sur l'industrie musicale', *Revue musicale* 10 (1830), pp. 193–205.

8 Martin d'Angers, 'Des pianistes et de la musique de piano', *Revue et gazette musicale*, 45 (1845), p. 367.

9 La Mara (ed.), *Franz Liszts Briefe* (Leipzig, 1893), vol. I, p. 25.

10 Carl Czerny, *A systematic introduction to improvisation on the pianoforte*, tr. Alice Mitchell (New York, 1983), p. 6.

11 A recording of Hofmann's entire recital, which took place in the Casimir Hall, Philadelphia on 7 April 1938, can be found on IPA. 5007/8.

12 Trans. Charles Suttoni, *Journal of the American Liszt Society*, 12 (1982), pp. 12–13.

13 Richard Zimdars (ed.), *The piano master classes of Hans von Bülow* (Bloomington, IN, 1993), p. 44.

14 Zimdars, *Bülow master classes*, p. 67.

15 Charles Hallé, *Life and letters* (London, 1896), pp. 88–89.

16 Robert L. Jacobs and Geoffrey Skelton (trs.), *Wagner writes from Paris* (London, 1973), pp. 133–4.

17 Angèle Potocka, *Theodore Leschetizky*, tr. Lincoln (New York, 1903), p. 90.

18 Sigismund Thalberg, *L'art du chant appliqué au piano* (London, c. 1853).

19 Adrian Williams, *Portrait of Liszt* (Oxford, 1990), pp. 290–1.

20 The nature of teacher–pupil performance styles is examined further in chapter 5.

21 Lina Ramann, *Liszt-Pädagogium* (Leipzig, 1901), new edn with foreword by Alfred Brendel (Wiesbaden, c.1986); August Göllerich, *Franz Liszt Klavierrunterricht von 1884–1886*, ed. Wilhelm Jerger (Regensburg, 1975), tr. Richard L. Zimdars as *The Piano master classes of Franz Liszt, 1884–1886* (Bloomington, IN, 1997); Frederic Lamond, *The Memoirs of Frederick Lamond* (Glasgow, 1949); Emil Sauer, *Meine Welt* (Stuttgart, 1901). For Lachmund, see note 6.

5 Pianists on record in the early twentieth century

1 Roland Gelatt, *The fabulous phonograph* (2nd edn, London, 1977), p. 114; James Methuen-Campbell, *Chopin playing from the composer to the present day* (London, 1981), pp. 76–7.

2 Larry Sitsky, *Busoni and the piano* (New York, 1986), p. 328, from Ferruccio Busoni, *Letters to his wife*, tr. Rosamond Ley (London 1938, repr. New York, 1975), p. 287.

3 A. J. and Katherine Swan, 'Rachmaninoff: personal reminiscences', *MQ*, 30 (1944), p. 11.

4 Frederick William Gaisberg, *Music on record* (London, 1946), p. 174.

5 *MT*, 52 (1911), p. 189.

6 Larry Sitsky, *Busoni*, p. 326.

7 Quoted in Edward Lockspeiser, *Debussy: his life and mind* (London, 1965) vol. 2, p. 35.

8 See Robert Philip, *Early recordings and musical style* (Cambridge, 1992), pp. 28–9.

9 *The Observer*, 26 March 1922, quoted in Malcolm Gillies, 'Bartók in Britain: 1922', *ML*, 63 (1982), p. 222.

10 Hamish Milne, *Bartók: his life and times* (Tunbridge Wells, 1982), p. 67.

11 Robert Donaldson Darrell, *Gramophone shop encyclopedia of recorded music* (New York, 1936).

12 Gaisberg, *Music on record*, p. 260.

13 Interview with Bernard Keeffe, 30 August 1965, BBC Sound Archives LP29683.

14 See Philip, *Early recordings*, pp. 51–3.

15 See note 13.

16 Henry Pleasants (ed.), *Music criticisms 1846–99* (rev. edn, Harmondsworth, 1963), p. 237.

17 Decombes was in Chopin's circle and heard him play many times, but he was not a pupil. See Methuen-Campbell, *Chopin playing*, p. 42.

18 In an interview with Dan Zerdin in *The ideal pianist*, BBC Radio 4, August 1972, quoted in Brian Crimp, *Solo: The biography of Solomon* (Hexham, Northumberland, 1994), p. 105.

19 *Piano questions answered* (London, 1909), reprinted with *Piano playing* (New York, 1976), p. 25.

20 Tobias Matthay, *Musical interpretation* (London, 1913), p. 63.

21 Hofmann, *Piano questions answered*, p. 100.

22 'Paderewski on tempo rubato', in Henry Theophilus Finck, *Success in music and how it is won* (New York, 1909), p. 459; Denise Restout (ed.), *Landowska on music* (London, 1965), p. 383.

23 George Woodhouse, 'How Leschetizky taught', *ML*, 35 (1954), p. 224.

24 Frederick Niecks, 'Tempo rubato from the aesthetic point of view', *Monthly Musical Record*, 43 (1913), p. 29.

25 For example, Jean-Jacques Eigeldinger, *Chopin vu par ses élèves* (Neuchâtel, 1970), ed. and tr. by Roy Howat as *Chopin: pianist and teacher* (Cambridge, 1986), p. 49; and Richard Hudson, *Stolen time: the history of tempo rubato* (Oxford, 1994), p. 236.

6 The acoustics of the piano

1 Further details of the acoustics of the piano and references to contemporary scientific work on pianos can be found in Neville H. Fletcher and Thomas D. Rossing, *The physics of musical*

instruments (New York, 1991) and Anders Askenfelt (ed.), *Five lectures on the acoustics of the piano* (Stockholm, 1990).

2 The pitch range quoted here is labelled according to the Helmholtz system. In modern scientific literature, the reader is more likely to encounter the rather more rational USA Standard which designates the pitch range as A_0 to C_8. For an explanation of these systems see John Backus, *The acoustical foundations of music* (New York, 1969), p. 133.

3 See, for example, Arthur A. Reblitz, *Piano servicing, tuning and rebuilding* (2nd edn, New York, 1993), pp. 36–61.

4 The term 'harmonic' is used in a more specialised way by scientists than musicians. Here we can take it to mean the individual frequency components created by an ideal string.

5 For further details of the physiology and psychology of hearing see Brian C. J. Moore, *Introduction to the psychology of hearing* (New York, 1977).

6 See the chapter by Hall in Askenfelt, *Acoustics*, pp. 59–72.

7 Voicing is discussed in detail by Reblitz, *Piano servicing*, pp. 196–201.

8 The physics involved in these coupled strings is rather complex. A good introduction is given by Weinreich in Askenfelt, *Acoustics*, pp. 73–81.

9 See Fletcher and Rossing, *Physics*, pp. 340–2.

10 Various temperaments and scales and their mathematical background and musical significance are discussed in more detail by Backus, *Acoustical foundations*, ch. 8, pp. 115–40.

11 The difficult role played by the tuner is admirably expressed by Jennifer Zarek, 'Don't shoot the piano tuner', *Physics Education*, 25 (1990), pp. 19–21.

12 See, for example, Diana Deutsch (ed.), *The psychology of music* (New York, 1982) or John A. Sloboda (ed.), *Generative processes in music: the psychology of performance, improvisation and composition* (Oxford, 1988).

13 See Askenfelt, *Acoustics*, pp. 39–57.

7 Repertory and canon

1 Glenn Gould, 'Glenn Gould interviews himself about Beethoven' and 'Glenn Gould in conversation with Tim Page', in Tim Page (ed.), *The Glenn Gould reader* (London, 1987), pp. 43, 47, 453.

2 Charles Rosen, in *The romantic generation* (Cambridge, MA, 1995), p. 285, calls Chopin 'the greatest master of counterpoint since Mozart', whose chief model for both composition and keyboard playing was J. S. Bach. Rosen's views on counterpoint in

nineteenth-century piano music are generally antithetical to Gould's pronouncement. For discussion of the formation of the canon generally and a survey of the literature on the subject see Marcia J. Citron, *Gender and the musical canon* (Cambridge, 1993), pp. 15–43.

3 Hans von Bülow, *Briefe und Schrifte* (Leipzig, 1896), vol. 5, pp. 106–9; translated as 'Mendelssohn' by Susan Gillespie in R. Larry Todd (ed.), *Mendelssohn and his world* (Princeton, 1991) pp. 390–3.

4 For a history of the étude as a genre before Chopin, see Simon Finlow, 'The twenty-seven études and their antecedents', in Jim Samson (ed.), *The Cambridge companion to Chopin* (Cambridge, 1994), pp. 50–77. Schumann's article on the études of his contemporaries is also useful, in *Neue Zeitschrift für Musik*, 1 (1836), pp. 16–18.

5 See notes to the Henle *Urtext* edition, 1974.

6 Details of the programmes given at the Gewandhaus are in Alfred Dörffel, *Geschichte der Gewandhausconcerte zu Leipzig, 1781–1881* (Leipzig, 1884). Hummel's B minor Concerto was performed eight times between 1822 and 1870; Moscheles's G minor Concerto received nine performances between 1824 and 1842.

7 For details of concertos played at the Royal Philharmonic Concerts, see Cyril Ehrlich, *First Philharmonic: a history of the Royal Philharmonic Society* (Oxford, 1995), Appendix 1.

8 Leon Plantinga, *Clementi: his life and music* (London, 1977), p. 167.

9 Fétis's review appeared in the *Revue et gazette musicale*, 33 (1865), p. 90. The review was hardly impartial, as Fétis had backed the publication of *Le trésor*. Fétis's 'canonic intent' with regard to the anthology is noted in Katherine Ellis, *Music criticism in nineteenth-century France* (Cambridge, 1995), p. 61.

10 For details on publication of Beethoven's piano sonatas see William S. Newman, 'A chronological checklist of collected editions of Beethoven's solo sonatas since his own day', *Notes*, 33 (1976–7), pp. 503–30.

11 For accounts of Moscheles's concerts see *Musical World*, 4 (1837), pp. 155, 184; 5 (1837), p. 28; 8 (1838), pp. 12, 71, 103, 163, 215; 11 (1839), pp. 149, 182.

12 The *OED* confirms the use of the word 'recital' with reference to Liszt, though cites an earlier use (1811) meaning a concert of works by one composer. For more on the rise of public concerts in this period, see Janet Ritterman, 'Piano music and the public concert', in Samson, *Chopin companion*, pp. 11–31 (see also chapter 4).

13 Chopin was often regarded as somewhat suspect in England. See Derek Carewe, 'Victorian attitudes to Chopin', in Samson, *Chopin companion*, pp. 222–45.

14 For more on this aspect of English musical life see Cyril Ehrlich, *The music profession in Britain since the eighteenth century* (Oxford, 1985), pp. 104–7.

15 Ehrlich, *Music profession*, p. 114. The Guildhall had 3600 pupils in 1896. British music colleges established between 1823 and 1898 are listed in Table 6, p. 238.

16 We are grateful to the Librarian of the Associated Board for access to past examination syllabuses in their collection.

17 Oscar Bie, *A history of the pianoforte and pianoforte players* (London, 1899), p. 303.

8 The music of the early pianists (to *c*.1830)

1 As announced in *The Morning Post*, 27 May 1795.

2 The letter is quoted in Gottfried Müller, *Daniel Steibelt* (Leipzig, 1933), p. 92.

3 For a detailed discussion of the sonata see William Newman, *The sonata in the classic era* (Chapel Hill, 1963).

4 Charles Burney, *A general history of music*, 4 (1789), p. 483.

5 Emily Anderson (ed. and tr.), *The letters of Mozart and his family* (3rd edn, London, 1985), p. 793.

6 For a discussion of Beethoven's indebtedness to the 'London school' see Alexander Ringer, 'Beethoven and the London Pianoforte School', *MQ*, 56 (1970), p. 754.

7 See the keyboard concertos K107, 1–3, which are arrangements of J. C. Bach's sonatas Op. 5 Nos. 2–4. Other J. C. Bach quotations may be found in Mozart's works.

8 Anderson, *The letters of Mozart*, p. 793.

9 Charlotte Papendieck, *Court and private life in the time of Queen Charlotte* (London, 1838), vol. 2, pp. 184–5.

10 Anderson, *Letters of Mozart*, p. 886.

11 Anderson, *Letters of Mozart*, p. 888.

12 For a discussion of aspects of Beethoven's continuo parts see Tibor Szász, 'Beethoven's *basso continuo*: notation and performance' in Robin Stowell (ed.), *Performing Beethoven* (Cambridge, 1994), pp. 1–22.

9 Piano music for concert hall and salon *c*.1830–1900

1 J. Barrie Jones, Open University, A214 *Understanding music: elements, techniques and styles*, Unit 28 (The romantic period) (Milton Keynes, 1994), p. 19.

2 See Amy Fay, *Music study in Germany* (London, 1886, reprinted, 1979), pp. 205–71.

3 Ernest Hutcheson, *The literature of the piano* (London, 1974), pp. 160–1.

4 Hutcheson, *Literature*, p. 163.

5 Quotations from Beethoven in particular and from other sources in general are prominent features in Schumann's music. See Alan Walker (ed.), *Robert Schumann* (London, 1972), p. 52 and elsewhere.

6 Hutcheson, *Literature*, p.190.

7 For some illuminating comments on the *Phantasie*, see Charles Rosen, *The Romantic generation* (Cambridge, MA, 1995), pp. 100–12 and elsewhere.

8 Rosen, *Romantic generation*, p. 83.

9 Carl Schachter's phrase in his discussion of 'Chopin's *Fantasy* Op. 49: the two-key scheme', in Jim Samson (ed.), *Chopin studies* (Cambridge, 1988), pp. 221–53.

10 J. Barrie Jones, Open University A314 *From baroque to romantic: studies in tonal music*, Units 25–6 (Romantic piano music) (Milton Keynes, 1984), p. 77.

11 See Alan Kendall, *Gioacchino Rossini* (London, 1992), p. 193.

12 For Liszt's 'programme', based on Lenau's *Faust* and often omitted from many editions, see Hutcheson, *Literature*, p. 290.

13 J. Barrie Jones, 'Fauré', in Justin Wintle (ed.), *Makers of nineteenth century culture 1800–1914* (London, 1982), p. 207.

14 *New Grove*, s.v. 'Piano duet', p. 680.

10 Nationalism

1 In Fryderyk Chopin, *Mazurkas*, ed. Thomas Fielden (n.d.), p. 127.

2 Ernest Hutcheson, *The literature of the piano* (London, 1974), p. 217.

3 After Op. 1, individual titles were printed in Norwegian, with German, English and French translations. For the sake of convenience, hereafter I shall use English titles.

11 New horizons in the twentieth century

1 Quoted (from a letter by Busoni to Woltersdorf written in 1898) in Derek Watson, *Chambers music quotations* (London, 1991), p. 229.

2 *MQ*, 2 (1916), pp. 271–94.

3 For Long's many fascinating reminiscences, see her book *At the piano with Debussy*, tr. Olive Senior-Ellis (London, 1972).

4 Quoted by Maurice Dumesnil: see Roger Nichols (ed.), *Debussy remembered* (London, 1992), p. 163.

5 Edward Lockspeiser, *Debussy: his life and mind* (rev. edn, Cambridge, 1978), vol. 2, pp. 34–5, 43–4.

6 Dent, 'The pianoforte and its influence', p. 288.

7 Dent, 'The pianoforte and its influence', p. 292.

8 Nichols, *Debussy remembered*, p. 156.

9 Bartók's answer to a questionnaire prepared by the *Musikblätter des Anbruch*, reproduced in Benjamin Suchoff (ed.), *Béla Bartók Essays* (London, 1976), p. 288.

10 Vyacheslav Gaurilovich Karatïgin, quoted in Rita McAllister, 'Sergey Prokofiev', in *New Grove Russian Masters, 2* (London, 1986), p. 118.

11 See Malcolm Gillies (ed.), *The Bartók companion* (London, 1993), p. 317.

12 Malcolm Gillies (ed.), *Bartók remembered* (London, 1990), p. 118.

13 Igor Stravinsky, *An autobiography* (New York, 1936), p. 93.

14 In Denis Matthews (ed.), *Keyboard music* (Harmondsworth, 1972), p. 349.

15 Quoted in Roger Nichols, *Messiaen* (Oxford, 1975), p. 37.

16 Reginald Smith Brindle, *The new music: the avant-garde since 1945* (2nd edn, Oxford, 1987), p. 161. Brindle gives (on pp. 206–7) selected examples of new notational symbols introduced in post-war piano music to represent some of the more radical techniques discussed here.

12 Ragtime, blues, jazz and popular music

1 As originally published in 2/4, the right hand's semiquavers give a pattern of (1) 2 3 4 5 6 (7) 8 | 9 10 11 12, as against the left's quavers on beats 1 3 5 7 | 9 11 13. If heard in 4/4, which is more commonly used today, the polyrhythmic pattern of quavers versus semiquavers is the same.

2 It must be emphasised that even those of self-confessed amateur status cannot hope to learn to play jazz with the aid of books, unless they also devote a considerable period of time to listening to relevant recordings of as many different performers as possible.

3 Many introductory texts explain the ternary form of three four-bar phrases making up the blues stanza, but fail to underline the fact that its repetitious nature remained equally compulsive despite the harmonic additions of later generations. The same is true of the 'blue notes' (typically the flat third, and flat seventh of the home key) which deliberately contradict the accompanying major chords. In imitation of the microtonal variations of vocalists, pianists of all generations have often articulated the contradiction by, for example, playing simultaneously the flat third and natural third, a semitone apart.

4 Although jazz gave its name to the decade, and did indeed enjoy its first classical period in the 1920s, it should be remembered that the huge majority of what is called 'jazz' by the media of the day has rather little to do with what is now perceived as the lasting jazz of the time.

5 In years to come, it may be more widely recognised that the jazz players' approach to composed material has had a more beneficial effect on the *performers* of European repertory than on composers. Glenn Gould's statement that 'The performer must be convinced that he is doing the right thing and that he can find ways of interpreting it of which not even the composer himself was fully aware' did not express a new ideal, but an ideal nurtured by every jazz player.

Contrast this with the dilettante approach to jazz by violinist Itzhak Perlman. Holding the traditional view that in composed music the composer's authority is absolute, he was heard to mock the typical popular performer who announces his next offering as 'A piece that goes "something like this:"' (*Kaleidoscope*, BBC Radio 4, May 1995). Missing the deliberate irony of such studied casualness which – if real – will have taken much training to achieve, Perlman also ignores the genuine freedom to reinterpret which is bestowed.

Select bibliography

This short bibliography contains references to books in the English language: references to journal articles and to foreign-language literature will be found in the notes to each chapter. The bibliography is divided into two parts: part 1 lists books on the history of the piano and its performers; part 2 concerns repertory. In addition to the titles in part 2, there is a short list of relevant published repertory at the end of chapter 12, 'Ragtime, blues, jazz and popular music'.

Part 1

Askenfelt, Anders (ed.), *Five lectures on the acoustics of the piano* (Stockholm, 1990)

Backus, John, *The acoustical foundations of music* (2nd edn, New York, 1977)

Badura-Skoda, Eva and Paul, *Mozart-Interpretation* (Vienna, 1957); tr. Leo Black as *Interpreting Mozart on the keyboard* (New York, R/1986)

Brown, Howard Mayer and Sadie, Stanley (eds.), *Performance practice: music after 1600* (London, 1989)

Cole, Michael, *The pianoforte in the Classical era* (Oxford, 1997)

Deutsch, Diana (ed.), *The psychology of music* (New York, 1982)

Ehrlich, Cyril, *The piano: a history* (London, 1976; 2nd edn, 1990)

Eigeldinger, Jean-Jacques, *Chopin vu par ses élèves* (Neuchâtel, 1970), ed. and tr. Roy Howat as *Chopin: pianist and teacher* (Cambridge, 1986)

Ferguson, Howard, *Keyboard interpretation from the 14th to the 19th century* (London, 1975)

Fletcher, Neville H. and Rossing, Thomas D., *The physics of musical instruments* (New York, 1991)

Friedheim, Arthur and Siloti, Alexander, *Remembering Franz Liszt* (New York, 1986)

Gelatt, Roland, *The fabulous phonograph* (2nd edn, London, 1977)

Gerig, Reginald, *Famous pianists and their technique* (Washington, 1974)

Harding, Rosamond, *The piano-forte: its history traced to the Great Exhibition of 1851* (Old Woking, 1933; 2nd edn, 1978)

Hofmann, Joseph, *Piano questions answered* (London, 1909); repr. with *Piano playing* (Philadelphia, 1920; repr. New York, 1976)

Hudson, Richard, *Stolen time: the history of tempo rubato* (Oxford, 1994)

Komlós, Katalin, *Fortepianos and their music* (Oxford, 1995)

Lachmund, Carl, *Living with Liszt*, ed. Alan Walker (Stuyvesant, NY, 1995)

Methuen-Campbell, James, *Chopin playing from the composer to the present day* (London, 1981)

Moore, Brian C. J., *An introduction to the psychology of hearing* (4th edn, San Diego, 1997)

Newman, William, *Beethoven on Beethoven: playing his piano music his way* (New York, 1988)

Philip, Robert, *Early recordings and musical style* (Cambridge, 1992)

Pollens, Stewart, *The early pianoforte* (Cambridge, 1995)

Reblitz, Arthur A., *Piano servicing, tuning and rebuilding* (2nd edn, New York, 1993)

Rosenblum, Sandra, *Performance practices in classic piano music: their principles and applications* (Bloomington, IN, 1988)

Rowland, David, *A history of pianoforte pedalling* (Cambridge, 1993)

Sadie, Stanley (ed.), *The piano* (The New Grove musical instrument series) (London, 1988)

Sloboda, John A. (ed.), *Generation processes in music: the psychology of performance, improvisation and composition* (Oxford, 1988)

Spillane, Daniel, *History of the American pianoforte* (New York, 1890; repr. 1969)

Wainwright, David, *Broadwood by appointment: a history* (London, 1982)

Williams, Adrian, *Portrait of Liszt* (Oxford, 1990)

Zimdars, Richard (ed.), *The piano master classes of Hans von Bülow. Two participants' accounts* (Bloomington, IN, 1993)

Part 2

Blesh, Rudi and Janis, Harriet. *They all played ragtime* (4th edn, London, 1971)

Brown, A. Peter, *Joseph Haydn's keyboard music: sources and style* (Bloomington, IN, 1986)

Citron, Marcia J., *Gender and the musical canon* (Cambridge, 1993)

Cooper, Barry (ed.), *The Beethoven compendium* (London, 1991)

Demuth, Norman, *French piano music* (London, 1959)

Ferguson, Howard, *Keyboard duets from the 16th to the 20th century for one and two pianos: an introduction* (Oxford, 1995)

Gillies, Malcolm (ed.), *The Bartók companion* (London, 1993)

Hinson, Maurice, *Guide to the pianist's repertoire* (Bloomington, IN, 1987)

Hinson, Maurice, *Music for more than one piano* (Bloomington, IN, 1983)

Hinson, Maurice, *The pianist's reference guide* (Los Angeles, 1987)

Hinson, Maurice, *The piano in chamber ensemble: an annotated guide* (Bloomington, IN, and London, 1978)

Hutcheson, Ernest, *The literature of the piano* (London, 1974)

Kernfeld, Barry (ed.), *The New Grove dictionary of jazz* (London, 1988)

Kirby, Frank Eugene, *A short history of keyboard music* (New York, 1966)

Komlós, Katalin, *Fortepianos and their music* (Oxford, 1995)

Landon, H. C. Robbins (ed.), *The Mozart compendium* (London, 1990)

Lyons, Len, *The great jazz pianists* (New York, R/1989)

McGraw, Cameron, *Piano duet repertoire* (Bloomington, IN, 1981)

Matthews, Denis (ed.), *Keyboard music* (Newton Abbot, 1972)

Newman, William, *The sonata in the classic era* (Chapel Hill, 1963; rev. edn, 1972)

Newman, William, *The sonata since Beethoven* (Chapel Hill, 1969; 3rd edn, 1983)

Plantinga, Leon, *Clementi: his life and music* (London, 1977)

Rosen, Charles, *The classical style* (London, 1971)

Rosen, Charles, *The romantic generation* (Cambridge, MA, 1995)

Rosen, Charles, *Sonata forms* (2nd edn, New York, 1988)

Samson, Jim (ed.), *Chopin studies* (Cambridge, 1988)

Silvester, Peter, *A left hand like God: a study of boogie woogie* (London, 1988)

Smallman, Basil, *The piano quartet and quintet: style, structure and scoring* (Oxford, 1994)

Smallman, Basil, *The piano trio: its history, technique, and repertoire* (Oxford, 1990)

Taylor, Billy, *Jazz piano: a jazz history* (Dubuque, IA, 1982)

Walker, Alan, *Liszt* (London, 1971)

Walker, Alan (ed.), *Robert Schumann* (London, 1972)

Wintle, Justin (ed.), *Makers of nineteenth century culture 1800–1914* (London, 1982)

Index